The CAYTON LEGACY

LEGACY

An African American Family

The CAYTON LEGACY

An African American Family

RICHARD S. HOBBS

WSU PRESS

Fine Quality Books from the Pacific Northwest

WASHINGTON STATE
UNIVERSITY

Washington State University Press
PO Box 645910
Pullman, Washington 99164-5910
Phone: 800-354-7360
Fax: 509-335-8568
E-mail: wsupress@wsu.edu
Web site: www.wsu.edu/wsupress

Library of Congress Cataloging-in-Publication Data

Hobbs, Richard S.
   The Cayton legacy : an African American family / Richard S. Hobbs.
      p. cm.
   Includes bibliographical references and index.
   ISBN 0-87422-251-6 (alk. paper)
      1. Cayton family. 2. African Americans—Biography. 3. African American
   families. 4. Seattle (Wash.)—Biography. 5. Chicago (Ill.)—Biography. I. Title.

E185.96 .H577 2002
929'.2'08996073—dc21   2002003118

*Front cover: Depicted clockwise from the upper left are Horace Cayton Jr., Revels Cayton,
Horace Cayton Sr., and Madge Cayton. A clock presented by former Confederate President
Jefferson Davis to Senator Hiram Revels appears in the background.*

*Back cover: U.S. Senator Hiram Revels of Mississippi and the Cayton home on Seattle's Capitol
Hill (1903–1909).*

TABLE OF CONTENTS

ACKNOWLEDGEMENTS

Following the trails of two generations of Caytons in the published and unpublished sources that document their lives allowed me the pleasure of incurring sizeable debts to many people. The few words offered here will not erase those debts, but will convey publicly my abiding gratitude for their contributions. The weight of those debts in no way mitigates my full responsibility for the book's contents and any errors of commission or omission.

This work benefitted enormously from the capable and generous assistance of numerous manuscripts curators, archivists and librarians across the country. At the Vivian G. Harsh Collection of Afro-American History and Literature, Chicago Public Library, archivist Michael Flug stands in the foremost ranks of assistants. His professionalism, friendship, steady encouragement, and wide-ranging knowledge of black Chicago are particularly appreciated. At the University of Washington's Manuscripts and Archives division of the University Libraries, Karyl Winn, Gary Lundell, and former head of the division, Rich Berner, deserve special thanks for their highly professional and personable contributions over the course of several years.

I am glad to offer my appreciation also to the following institutions and their present and former staff: Susan Cunningham, Carla Rickerson, and Gary Menges at the University of Washington Libraries Special Collections; friend and colleague Dave Hastings at the Washington State Archives, Olympia, Washington; the gracious staff at the Puget Sound Regional Office of the Washington State Archives, especially Mike Saunders, Janette Gomes and Phil Stairs; the able and efficient Deborah Kennedy at King County Archives; the thorough and friendly Diana Lachatanere at the Schomburg Center for Research in Black Culture, New York Public Library; Eleanor Toews at the Seattle School District Archives; Marie Byrne at the Bancroft Library, University of California, Berkeley; Sara Stewart and Carol Schwartz at the International Longshoremen's and Warehousemens' Union, Anne Rand Research Library, in San Francisco; Lynn Bonfield at the Labor Archives and Research Center at San Francisco State University; Gladys Hansen at the San Francisco Public Library; Patricia Howell at the Beinecke Rare Book and Manuscript Collection, Yale University; James H. Hutson at the Manuscripts Division, Library of Congress; Jack Casford at the San Francisco Human Rights Commission; Anita Moore, Head

Librarian at Rust College; and the able staffs at the Chicago Historical Society, the California Historical Society in San Francisco, the George Arents Research Library at Syracuse University, the Amistad Research Center, and the Kansas State Historical Society.

Interviewing the Caytons provided the most fascinating and richly rewarding experiences. My sincerest appreciation goes to the members of the Cayton family who cooperated with my work, especially Revels Cayton of San Francisco and Susan Cayton Woodson of Chicago, for their candid conversations and many courtesies. Special thanks go also to their spouses, Lee Cayton and Harold Woodson, both for interviews and for extra effort in assisting the interviewing process over a period of several years. Dr. Revels Cayton Jr. shared my early enthusiasm for this work at critical stages; I am indebted to him for his energy, curiosity, directness, and stimulating conversations. My deep appreciation is extended also to Irma Cayton Wertz of Detroit and Bonnie Branch Hansen of Olympia, Washington, for their invaluable and gracious assistance.

Author Lore Segal of New York provided some very helpful insights into Horace Jr.'s personality and reviewed part of this manuscript in an early draft. Two of Lillie's daughters, Madge Terriye Thompson and Sue Martin, helped to clarify parts of their mother's story, sharing letters, photographs, and other family records. This book also benefitted substantially from interviews with the following people: Donnie Hancock, Paul Robeson Jr., Brunetta Bernstein, Marguerite Jamison Isaac, Harry Branch, Mary Branch, Mrs. Virginia Gayton, Edward Pitter, Cyrus Colter, Enoch Waters, Sidney Williams, Ruth Williams, Fern Gayden, and Dr. Setsuko Nishi.

Several professional colleagues and personal friends lent advice, insights, and technical expertise that proved of immense value. Historian and writer Esther Hall Mumford deserves a long-overdue thank you for her keen interest in my work and generous sharing of historical information that improved the first two chapters. Denise Boudreau provided pharmaceutical expertise at a vital point in the Cayton story. For their thoughtful guidance and intellectual stimulation I am indebted to the following: Professors Otis Pease, Robert Burke, and Hubert Locke at the University of Washington; also Hazel Rowley, biographer of Richard Wright; and my friend Michael Pierre Johnson, for his discerning observations on the American historical-social fabric. Material support of various kinds helped complete portions of this study. I am glad to acknowledge contributions from the Graduate School Research Fund at the University of Washington, as well as Bob and Carol Dickson of Everett, Washington.

I am indebted to the Washington State University Press for undertaking the publishing of *The Cayton Legacy.* Editors Glen Lindeman and Louise Freeman-Toole deserve much credit for providing the final sculpting and refining of the book. In addition, Jean Taylor, Nancy Grunewald, and Sue Emory have been most helpful in accommodating and expediting final touches.

My family, extended family, and friends shared the progress in this effort, and to them I am deeply grateful. In ways too diverse to mention, each helped put some vital thread into the tapestry of this story. My heartfelt thanks to: May Libby Smith, Michael Hobbs, Bob and Carol Dickson, Margaret Ross Thrailkill, Mary Ross Kellar, Ross Sterling Hobbs, Mariesa K. Diebold, Rebecca Duran, Ruben Duran, and Rita Duran. To my soulmate and wife, Lynette Dickson, I offer my sincerest appreciation for her steadfast love and unflagging encouragement.

PREFACE

F ROM THE TIME I was a youngster, I took a keen interest in the past. In college, I began studying family dynamics, ethnicity, and social identity, and how they relate over time. When I came across an obscure journal article mentioning Horace Cayton (Sr.) and his newspaper, the *Seattle Republican* (1894–1913), my curiosity was piqued. I then quickly discovered that his son, Horace Cayton Jr., had written an autobiography, *Long Old Road* (1965). Thus began my long fascination with the Cayton story.

In the 1970s, I gradually collected information about the Caytons. For several years the material lay cocooned in a remote corner of my file cabinet, whispering for attention; however, I hesitated. Three factors finally coalesced to move me toward making a decision about writing a book. First, I read *American Hunger*, the autobiographical account by Richard Wright, a friend of Horace Cayton Jr.'s. Wright's intense, beautifully crafted words, his razor-sharp insights into race relations and our nation's history, and his dramatic personal struggles as a writer further motivated my interest in the Caytons. Second, when I heard Alex Haley describe his research and the writing of his popular account, *Roots*, I saw parallels with the Caytons and knew that someone, someday, would write their story. And third, I set aside a spring weekend to decide whether to write a Cayton book or take up house renovation.

The final nudge arrived at my front door that very weekend. The weather on Sunday morning was warm and sunny. I had played a long tennis game to give myself a break from brooding over the decision. As I stood in the kitchen gulping cold water, the doorbell rang—a chime that still rings in my mind. I opened the door to meet a young man about my age—handsome, of medium height and thin build, with smooth olive-brown skin, short black hair, and penetrating eyes.

"Richard Hobbs?"

"Yes," I said, wondering how he knew my name.

"I'm Revels Cayton…"

My mouth dropped—I had met a Revels Cayton in San Francisco several months earlier, and he was 65 years old, and had gray hair.

"…Junior," he finished.

I smiled, welcomed him in, and we spent the next two hours in intense conversation about his family and my research. When leaving, he paused at the door and turned to me. "I think you should write this book."

I knew it too.

The prospects were daunting. The research alone would be long, difficult, and costly, requiring extensive travel. Yet, the Cayton story was too important to remain so little known. I knew the project would take years, but the family consented to interviews and sharing letters and other personal materials. The Caytons were widespread geographically, and other research would need to be done in newspaper files, census lists, public records, and other sources located in a dozen libraries, archives, and manuscript collections in Seattle, Chicago, San Francisco, and New York. Thus began a journey, in my spare time, that took more than fifteen years to complete—working evenings, weekends, and on vacations. Part of the manuscript was prepared during the three years that I lived in the island kingdom of Bahrain in the Middle East. The final draft was completed at a secluded lake cabin (loaned by my future in-laws, Bob and Carol Dickson), during a three-month leave from my job at the Eastern Washington Regional Archives.

This is not an authorized family biography; however, I was given free access to a wealth of family letters, photographs, reminiscences, and other documents. Without the family's cooperation, this book would have been a far less complete, and less personal, historical contribution. While the main focus is on the Caytons' public careers, the essential components of family dynamics and the personal struggles of its individual members are also included.

The life of Horace Cayton (Sr.), the longtime Seattle editor, receives full coverage in *The Cayton Legacy*. The two sons, Horace Cayton Jr. and Revels Cayton (Sr.), also are extensively treated; however, they deserve even more consideration than what space allows for in this book. Both had extraordinary careers and left substantial documentary trails. Regretfully, by comparison there is considerably less source material concerning the Cayton women. Although their mother, Susie, did play a long-time role in various Seattle social and political circles, the other Cayton children—Ruth, Madge, Lillie, and Susan—led far less public lives than the males of the family. Like other African American women of the times, their career opportunities were limited by racial and gender barriers.

Nevertheless, the legacy of the Cayton parents and children is extraordinary—a human, and American, saga. Their story is a virtual mirror of the American past, showing our strengths and weaknesses, our glories and embarrassments.

Reflecting on this, I am reminded of one of the most touching moments in the course of the entire project. During a long interview session, Revels Cayton (Sr.) revealed some painful memories, which left him looking tired and vulnerable. He sat silently for a time in the lounge chair next to me. I switched off the tape recorder. Neither of us spoke.

At last, turning to look me straight in the eye, he said, "I just hope that my son doesn't think too poorly of me when this is all done."

I recalled the words of a friend of mine, Mike Johnson, and shared them with Revels:

"A friend once said to me, 'In the end, all we have to give to one another is our stories. This is the most important thing, the truth of us—and it's enough.'"

Revels nodded. "Yes. He's right. This would be a different country if we all did that, wouldn't it?"

Richard S. Hobbs
Whidbey Island, Washington
March 12, 2002

THE CAYTON FAMILY TREE

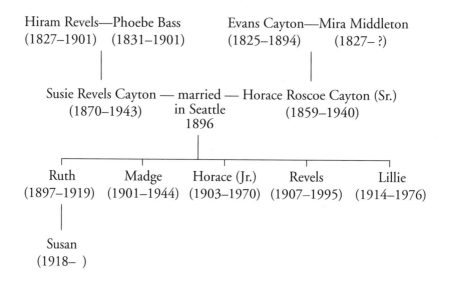

Hiram Revels—Phoebe Bass
(1827–1901)   (1831–1901)

Evans Cayton—Mira Middleton
(1825–1894)   (1827– ?)

Susie Revels Cayton — married — Horace Roscoe Cayton (Sr.)
(1870–1943)   in Seattle   (1859–1940)
                        1896

Ruth   Madge   Horace (Jr.)   Revels   Lillie
(1897–1919) (1901–1944) (1903–1970) (1907–1995) (1914–1976)

Susan
(1918–)

INTRODUCTION

The Cayton Legacy

I T WAS LATE SUMMER, August 1940. Horace Cayton, an 81-year-old ex-slave and veteran Seattle newspaperman, lay on his deathbed. He turned to his son Revels, saying, "In the life you're going to live I'll find my immortality."

This moment in the history of the Cayton family poignantly captures the drama of one generation passing its legacy to the next. It is one episode in the story of two generations of the Horace and Susie Cayton family, a remarkable and distinguished African American family conscious of their historical heritage and distinct identity. The Caytons sought to define themselves in relation to their family traditions, to other blacks, and to the white world. They valued personal identity, racial pride, and commitment to the larger society.

The responsibility of being "a Cayton" and carrying on the family legacy impelled them to a high level of achievement, education, and, sometimes, financial success. The Caytons published newspapers; served as civic leaders; authored books and articles; wielded political influence; wrote and lectured; and worked with community, church, and union leaders to improve living conditions and career opportunities for both blacks and whites. In the process, they also faced racial discrimination and duress, business and professional failures, and poverty. Some family members struggled with the personal challenges of alcoholism, depression, and drug addiction. And yet, the Cayton family endured, passing on its legacy to a modern generation.

For nearly a century and a half, the Caytons' lives have intersected with some of the major events and social movements in American history. Horace Roscoe Cayton (1859–1940) was born a slave on a Mississippi cotton plantation on the eve of the Civil War. The son of a white plantation owner's daughter and a slave, he lived his first six years in bonded servitude. He grew to manhood in the hopeful era of Reconstruction, working on his father's small farm and gaining an education, at Freedmen's Bureau schools and eventually at Alcorn University. He left Mississippi at the end of Reconstruction, migrating westward in search of freedom and opportunity, and eventually settled in the bustling frontier town of Seattle in 1890.

The young man molded by these experiences possessed a profound belief in his own self worth, a driving will to succeed, and a deep resentment of any obstacles to social justice and equal opportunity. In Seattle, the feisty, outspoken Horace rose to social prominence and financial success as owner and editor of the *Seattle Republican*, published from 1894 to 1913. The newspaper was unique in the Northwest; it was political and biracial, aimed at black and white readers alike. In this period, Horace also exerted some degree of influence in the state's Republican Party.

In 1896 Horace married Susie Revels Cayton (1870–1943), whom he had known years before in Mississippi when she was still a child. Susie was a daughter of Hiram Rhoades Revels, the nation's first black U.S. Senator and the president of Alcorn University. Susie, a graduate of Rust College in Mississippi, possessed a keen intellect and lively personality. By the late 1890s, the Cayton couple were among the most prominent, affluent, and respected African American families in Seattle. For a number of years, it seemed they and their children were living the "American Dream." But the dream did not last.

After two decades, the *Seattle Republican* failed, and the family suffered severe financial losses. Horace lost influence among white politicians, but he remained a major figure in the African American community, establishing other (although less successful) newspapers and serving as a leader in various organizations, including the Seattle chapter of the NAACP. Horace remained an eloquent voice for the rights of all oppressed people, and spoke out forcefully against the rising prejudice and discrimination of the times. Today, the Cayton newspaper files are an invaluable source for regional African American history.

Susie assisted Horace as an associate editor and in writing articles. In addition to raising the Cayton children, she took leadership roles in the black community, and, during the Great Depression, was active in the unemployed league movement in Seattle. She also initiated the family's long friendships with the nationally known singer-activist Paul Robeson and the author Langston Hughes. An insatiably curious intellectual, Susie pursued the study of theology and philosophical ideas throughout her life. While remaining a Christian, Susie in her final years joined the Communist Party.

Together, Horace and Susie established a family that would make important contributions in the struggle for personal freedom and racial equality. Out of this milieu—a mixed legacy of servitude and freedom, obscurity and social prominence, poverty and affluence, and black and white cultural influences—grew a generation of children with a distinct sense of being "a Cayton." Each gave this legacy unique expression.

Horace Cayton Jr. (1903–70), the oldest of two sons, became a nationally known sociologist, author, and lecturer. Educated at the University of Washington and the University of Chicago's renowned School of Sociology, Horace led a massive New Deal study of black Chicago. In the 1940s, he achieved prominence as the director of Chicago's Parkway Community House, shaping it into the world's largest service center for African Americans. Horace also co-authored a landmark study of Chicago, *Black Metropolis*, with St. Clair Drake, released in 1945. In these roles, he became a leading light in the flowering African American cultural scene of the 1930s and 1940s—the "Chicago Renaissance." Chicago's South Side attracted important artists and intellectuals, and Horace counted many of them as friends, including authors Richard Wright, Arna Bontemps, and Langston Hughes.

Despite success as a student of urban problems and a crusader for civil rights, Horace was emotionally shattered by discrimination and struggled with personal understanding and psychological problems, as well as alcoholism and drug addiction. His three marriages failed. In later years, he gradually overcame some of his addiction and mental problems and made an effort to improve relationships with family members, whom he had alienated. Horace remained an articulate analyst of race relations up to the end of his life. In January 1970 he died at age 66 in Paris, where he had gone to complete a biography of writer Richard Wright. (Whenever necessary in *The Cayton Legacy* to clarify the distinction between the father and son with the same name, I have used "Horace Sr." and "Horace Jr.," though it appears that neither ever used "Sr." or "Jr." with their names.)

Revels Cayton (1907–95), the younger son, was a member of the Communist Party from his young adult years. During the 1930s San Francisco maritime labor strikes, he rose to leadership positions in the Marine Cooks and Stewards Union and, later, the CIO. After World War II, Revels moved to New York to head the left-wing National Negro Congress, and became one of the founders of the black trade union council movement. He also developed a close friendship with singer Paul Robeson, who shared his interest in socialism and political issues, including African American empowerment. In the mid 1950s, Revels was one of the earliest activists to use the term "black power." Returning to San Francisco, he became the manager of a model integrated housing project, and in the late 1960s was appointed to Mayor Joseph Alioto's cabinet. Afterward, he remained active in civic service and politics until shortly before his death at age 88 in 1995.

The Cayton daughters led lives more narrowly channeled, yet expressive of the Cayton legacy. Ruth Cayton (1897–1919), the oldest daughter, was independent and a rebel. She tragically died at age 22, leaving an infant daughter, Susan (b. 1918), who was raised in the Cayton home as one of the children. As a young adult in Chicago, Susan met and married Harold Woodson, a chemist. Living in the Hyde Park area, she devoted herself to family life, community service, church work, and preserving Afro-American history and art.

Madge Cayton (1901–44), one of the first African American women to graduate from the University of Washington, was devoted to the Cayton family. After moving to Chicago and receiving additional training, she became a social worker. In Chicago, Madge served as a hostess for Horace Jr.'s business and social gatherings. She also filled a mother's role for her niece, Susan. Madge suffered an untimely death from rheumatic fever at age 43.

Lillie (1914–76), the youngest daughter, felt that living up to the achievements of her older siblings was an overwhelming burden. Married five times and an alcoholic for many years, she was on the verge of losing her four children when she turned to Alcoholics Anonymous. Lillie became a highly effective speaker for the AA circuit along the entire West Coast. Although overshadowed in earlier years by her brothers and sisters, Lillie eventually came to represent the best of the family tradition.

+≒═≒+

Not surprisingly, the Caytons have sparked public and academic interest over the decades. Horace and Susie, as leading Seattle pioneers, appear prominently in Esther Hall Mumford's *Seattle's Black Victorians, 1852–1901* (1981), and they are mentioned in other recent studies on Seattle and Washington State history. They have been included briefly in a few television productions, too. Social scientist Horace Jr.—a key player in the "Chicago Renaissance," co-author of *Black Workers and the New Unions* (1939) and *Black Metropolis* (1945), and a long-time *Pittsburgh Courier* columnist—often is cited in works focusing on black sociology and psychology, Chicago history, and African American authors (especially Wright, Bontemps, and Hughes). From time to time, a mention of Horace Jr. still appears in Chicago newspapers. Revels Cayton is briefly noted in studies of the maritime labor movement, the National Negro Congress, and blacks in unions and the Communist Party. In 1982, he was honored at a large banquet featuring San Francisco Mayor Diane Feinstein as keynote speaker.

Despite wide acknowledgment of the Caytons' contributions, the literary and scholarly attention they have so far received has been cursory, and tends to focus on the Seattle years. Horace Jr.'s contributions to Chicago history from the mid-1930s to the late 1940s, for example, have received only sketchy notice. The Cayton women, except for Susie in Seattle, have been virtually ignored. The family's contributions, regrettably, were distorted by Horace Jr.'s autobiographical *Long Old Road*, which was written as "therapy" and contains serious errors, distortions, and omissions.

The Cayton story is important for its affirmation of African American family values and lifestyles. As was typical for black families in the United States during those times, their survival was largely dependent on extended family and kinship support systems. Living was a constant struggle, a relentless striving with injustice and discrimination—against its destructiveness and wastefulness. However, the life stories of both the Cayton brothers and the sisters serve as examples of how to retain self-respect, to struggle, to achieve, and to help others.

Clearly, the Cayton story shows how African American history and white history are inextricably intertwined. Horace Jr. emphasized this theme repeatedly to whites and others when quoting Richard Wright (*12 Million Black Voices*): "[T]he ties that bind us are deeper than those that separate us... Look at us and know us, and you will know yourselves, for we are you looking back at you from the dark mirror of our lives."

Horace Jr. believed that by better understanding the differences, as well as the commonalities, between all of us, Americans could begin overcoming prejudice and ethnocentrism. Throughout their lives, Horace Sr. and Susie Cayton worked and struggled for human understanding—it lay at the heart of the Cayton legacy passed on to their children. They, in turn, have passed it on, through the stories of their own struggles, to the next generation.

Poet Maya Angelou, speaking at the January 1993 U.S. Presidential Inauguration, said, "History, despite its wrenching pain, cannot be unlived, and if faced with courage, need not be lived again."

We can all take courage to face our history by understanding the Cayton legacy.

CHAPTER 1

Of a Senator and Slaves

The Hiram Revels and Evans Cayton Families, c. 1825–1896

W HEN HORACE ROSCOE CAYTON SR. married Susie Sumner Revels in Seattle on July 12, 1896, the ceremony was more than the ritual union of two individuals in holy matrimony. Two streams of black family experience in America were joined as well. Susie, from a long-established free black family, was marrying into the Caytons, a family of ex-slaves with a markedly different heritage. Together, Horace Sr. and Susie raised a generation of Caytons who inherited a unique legacy that they in turn eventually would pass down to their own children and grandchildren.[1]

Horace Sr. was born a slave of mixed black and white parentage. He knew poverty and the rural farming life of the South. Yet, he had received an education, learned various trades, and in the six years after his arrival in Seattle in 1890, had established his own newspaper business. Susie, also of African American and white lineage, was born into a family that traced its free heritage to before the American Revolution. As the daughter of the first black U.S. Senator, Hiram Rhoades Revels, Susie had grown up in a socially prominent and relatively affluent family. College educated and with a gift for writing, she became a valued contributor to the Cayton family newspaper.

✛═══✛

Horace Sr. was raised by Evans Cayton, a slave born around 1825. The family's oral tradition indicates that Evans took the Cayton name from his former owner. Revels Cayton, Horace Sr.'s younger son, later told this story he had often heard about his paternal grandfather:

> He was said to be worth three thousand dollars, was very skilled and intelligent, and he was a leader and a rebel. He ran away down the river, three times. My Dad used to tell stories about when his father would be in the swamp, and people would be looking for runaway slaves, and the terror that took place. He was hiding in this tree and had been there for quite a time and had not moved. The dogs came almost right by him,

but the scent was completely dead by then. If he'd jumped and got on the ground the dogs would have been on him. When they finally found him, they whipped him within an inch of his life and cut off one of his feet. But, they kept him alive, because he was valuable; he was a black-smith.[2]

Whether the stories Horace Sr. told are true is less important than the fact that they became a vital and influential part of the Caytons' family history and were passed from one generation to the next. And, they help in part to explain Horace Sr.'s own unrelenting drive for a life of his own choosing, free from the fetters of servitude and race discrimination. Horace Jr., the oldest Cayton son, later described his grandfather as "proud and courageous, refusing to be held down by caste or class proscriptions."[3]

Evans, his wife Mira, and their family lived on a Mississippi cotton plantation several miles outside of Port Gibson, one of the best inland cotton markets in the South in the pre-Civil War era.[4] The town lies along the south fork of the Pierre Bayou River, some ten miles east of the Missis-sippi River and thirty miles south of Vicksburg. When the Civil War came, battles raged all around the Caytons. In May 1863, Confederate and Union troops clashed just four miles west of Port Gibson in one of the major battles that preceded the capture of Vicksburg.

The end of the Civil War brought freedom to the slaves, expanding virtually overnight the horizon of possibilities for black people. Revels Cayton's account of this dramatic event is simply stated, just as he heard it from his father: "The white woman who was running the plantation called all the slaves up to the big house. She stood there on the front porch and told them they had been declared free. That was it." Evans Cayton and his family gained more than their freedom. Evans was one of the fortunate few who also gained ownership of a piece of land—some of the same rich cottonland he had worked as a slave. Evans prospered as an independent farmer. Family tradition has it that some of his "white kin" (his former masters) worked for him as hired help.

To many freedmen, owning a few acres to farm independently was the highest symbol of being one's own master. But in post-war Mississippi, black land ownership was the exception, not the rule. The Freedmen's Bu-reau Act of 1865 recognized the need for former slaves to own their own land, but whites still viewed blacks as a labor force (albeit now as low-paid workers rather than slaves), and they refused to give up control of the land. The Mississippi legislature enacted Black Codes that forbade selling or leasing farmland to freedmen. Reconstruction legislation soon invalidated the codes, but significant land reform did not take place. Many blacks tried leaving the fields for the cities, but most of them could not find work and returned to labor under harsh wage or sharecropping systems.

Horace Sr.'s children recalled that he referred to Evans Cayton as his "father," that his stories were told with great admiration, respect, and affection, and that he always spoke with warmth of his sister Jane. It is not clear, however, whether the man Horace Sr. called "father" was indeed his real father. Like most African Americans born into slavery, few facts of Horace Sr.'s birth or parentage can be verified. Family records indicate he was born February 3, 1859, on a cotton plantation near Port Gibson, Mississippi. The "slave schedules" of the 1860 U.S. Census listed slave owners by name, but slaves were listed only as property, relegating their individual histories to oblivion. To white society of the time, Horace Cayton was merely a "black male, age 1."[5]

Revels Cayton believed that his father, Horace Sr., had been raised by a black "foster father" (Evans Cayton), while his true father was a white plantation owner who had come from England to settle in Mississippi. Horace Sr.'s foster father had loved him deeply. "My dad," Revels said, "became the apple of his eye." However, Horace Jr. remembers being told that his father was the child of a white slave owner's daughter and a slave. This story is the most probable and credible version, as it is strongly affirmed by Horace Jr.'s first wife, Bonnie Branch Hansen, who heard it from Horace Sr. himself in the late 1920s. Horace Sr. also told his children stories about being rejected by his white grandmother, and by both whites and slaves on the plantation.[6]

No matter his parentage, there is no doubt that Horace Sr. lived his first six years as a slave on the plantation. One of his earliest memories was walking with a hoe over his shoulder alongside other slaves to the cotton fields at sunrise. Noted author Arna Bontemps, who became acquainted with the Caytons in the 1940s, wrote, "As a small child [Horace] saw Pemberton surrender to Grant at Vicksburg. He saw the former slave holders of the section leave their plantation and 'go somewheres.'" There were tremendous changes in Mississippi in the fateful years of Reconstruction. The heady atmosphere of hope for the fulfillment of true democracy in America was indelibly stamped on young Cayton's impressionable mind. In November 1867, eight-year-old Horace watched African American men vote for the very first time, casting ballots to decide the date for a convention to draft a new state constitution for Mississippi. Revels Cayton said, "Many times I heard the story from my father about how he remembered walking down the road as just a boy with his father, when Reconstruction was beginning, and his father first went to get a ballot."[7]

U.S. Census data provides a snapshot of the Cayton family in 1870. Evans, age forty-five (born ca. 1825), was listed as a "mulatto" farmer born in Missouri. He owned a farm valued at seven hundred and fifty dollars and personal property valued at one hundred and fifty dollars, both common holdings for that vicinity. His wife Mira, age forty-three, was a "black" woman born in Kentucky about 1827. The family included Jane, age fifteen, Caroline, age eleven, and Horace, age nine (actually eleven). The census states that all three children had been born in Mississippi and were currently attending school.[8]

Evans and Mira had great ambitions for their children and worked hard to provide them with a good education. Horace Sr. first attended an elementary level Freedmen's school, and then in 1872 he left home for the town of Alcorn, fifteen miles away, to take classes at Alcorn University. The school, named in honor of Governor Alcorn, was founded in 1871 as the first publicly supported college for blacks in Mississippi. At the time Horace Sr. entered the institution, Alcorn University was headed by one of the most illustrious black leaders in the nation, Hiram Rhoades Revels, the first African American to sit in the U.S. Senate.[9]

+‡════‡+

Hiram Rhoades Revels was born on September 27, 1827, in Fayetteville, North Carolina, to a family of mixed ethnic heritage. In his veins flowed the blood of free blacks, whites, and Lumbee (Croatan) Indians. The name "Revels" is said to come from the Lumbee word meaning "outspoken one." Hiram's great-uncle, Aaron Revels of North Carolina, was a free African American who fought and was wounded as a patriot soldier in the Revolution. He later voted for the ratification of the Constitution in 1787 and received a military pension from the federal government.[10]

Little is known about young Hiram's family, although we know that he had at least one brother, Willis R. Revels, who became a respected physician and minister. Hiram's schooling began at the age of eight or nine at a school for African American children in Fayetteville. Hiram later described himself as "early imbued with a love of knowledge," and determined to get an education and "become a professional man, and religious teacher." By 1844, the desire for more learning had taken him to Ohio, where he attended a Quaker seminary. The following year Revels enrolled in what he called a "colored seminary" in Drake County, Ohio. Driven to achieve,

Revels became an ordained minister in the African Methodist Episcopal Church before he was twenty-five. [11]

During the years 1847-55, while the national debate raged over the slavery issue, Revels traveled widely, preaching in Illinois, Kansas, Kentucky, Tennessee, and Missouri. He met considerable opposition and in 1854 was arrested in Missouri for preaching to slaves. Hiram Revels, like most free blacks, identified closely with his enslaved brothers. He shared their hope in the promises of the Declaration of Independence, as well as the burden of America's hypocritical practices. Hiram Revels' work among slaves on plantations throughout the South is described in his autobiography: "I sedulously refrained from doing any thing that would incite slaves to run away from their masters. It being understood that my object was to preach the gospel to them, and improve their moral and spiritual condition, even slave holders were tolerant toward me. But when in free states I always assisted the fugitive slave to make his escape." [12]

Hiram settled in Galesburg, Illinois, for two years (1855–57) to attend Knox College. He married Phoebe Rebecca Bass, a student at the Old School Presbyterian Church in Galesburg. A free black woman from a Quaker background, Phoebe was born about 1837 in the town of Zanesville in Drake County, Ohio. The Revels' first child, Emma, was born in 1856. They left Galesburg the following year, and two more daughters, Lillie and Dora, were born as the family moved from the Midwest to the East Coast and back to the South over the next decade. [13]

Hiram Revels next served as minister in an A.M.E. church and principal of an all-black high school in Baltimore, Maryland. With the outbreak of the Civil War, Revels lent his energies to the Union cause by aiding in the formation of two African American regiments. In 1863 Hiram and Phoebe moved their family eight hundred miles west to St. Louis, Missouri. Here, Hiram founded a school for freed slaves and organized another black regiment. The following year he went south to Vicksburg in southwestern Mississippi and entered active Union service as a chaplain in a black military regiment. When the war ended, Hiram's long interest in education led to his appointment as chairman of a Freedmen's Bureau committee on education.

In 1866 Hiram, Phoebe, and their three daughters moved again, to Natchez, some seventy miles north of Vicksburg. The town perches on a promontory two hundred feet above the Mississippi River. The port city had experienced its heyday before the war, when its waterfront teemed with steamboats loaded with cotton for export. Here, Revels served again as pastor of an A.M.E. church, but soon politics superseded his other interests.

During the years in Natchez, Phoebe bore three more girls: Susie, Ida, and Maggie. Susie, born in 1870, was given the middle name Sumner after Senator Charles Sumner of Massachusetts, the revered veteran of the abolition movement. Susie was eleven days old when Hiram delivered a prayer that was to change his life and the lives of generations of his family to come. Hiram Revels' political career had begun two years before with his election to the board of aldermen from Adams County. He had made the acquaintance of the mayor of Natchez, John R. Lynch, who the following year urged Hiram to run for the Mississippi State Senate. He entered the race and was elected along with the rest of the Republican ticket.

When the Mississippi legislature convened on January 11, 1870, Hiram Revels opened the joint session with a prayer. Among the urgent issues pending legislative action was the selection of two U.S. senators. Hiram delivered the opening prayer with such force that he suddenly emerged as a possible compromise candidate in a contentious field of nominees. On the third ballot, when one candidate withdrew, Revels was nominated. On the fifth ballot, held on January 20, the strength of the black voting bloc swung behind him, and Hiram was elected to the U.S. Senate by an 81-to-38 vote.

Hiram Revels was the first African American elected to the U.S. Senate in the nation's history. His term of office lasted a little over one year, from February 1870 until March 1871. Despite the brevity of his Senate service, Hiram stood as a dramatic symbol of the new and important way blacks were participating in American politics. Hiram Revels had been elected to fill the unexpired term of Jefferson Davis, who resigned in 1861 to become president of the Confederacy. When it came time to seat Revels, however, Davis' seat was occupied by another senator, who refused to release it to a black man. Instead, Revels took the chair previously held by Albert Gallatin Brown. Several years later, in a surprising gesture recognizing Revels' service to the state of Mississippi, Jefferson Davis himself presented a handsome mantle clock to Hiram. (The clock became the Caytons' most cherished family heirloom after Susie Revels married into the Cayton family.)

In the Senate, Hiram served on the Senate Education Committee and the Labor Committee. He presented numerous petitions and bills, many for removing political stumbling blocks for citizens—both black and white, including former Confederates—in Mississippi and other southern states.

In his first act before Congress, Revels presented a petition for Philadelphia's African American community in favor of legislation that guaranteed equal protection under the law for all citizens. He also strongly supported legislation to enforce the Fifteenth Amendment, earning him the accolade, "The Fifteenth Amendment in flesh and blood," from the fiery Republican orator Wendell Phillips.

Senator Revels considered himself "a representative of the state, irrespective of color," speaking on behalf of both whites and blacks. The junior senator helped defeat a bill to establish a segregated school system in Washington, D.C. On February 8, 1871, before the Senate Committee of the District of Columbia, Revels spoke forcefully against segregation and described race discrimination in the United States as strong and gaining momentum. He earned wide respect for this and his other few, but memorable, speeches in Congress. Senator Revels became known for his formidable oratorical skills, honed during years in the pulpit. In the spring of 1870, Hiram embarked on a lecture tour. He spoke to mixed audiences throughout the eastern states, and only occasionally encountered difficulty acquiring the use of a lecture hall. In Boston, Revels delivered his most famous speech, "The Tendency of the Age," describing the success of democratic ideologies over aristocracy. One admiring listener likened Hiram's skill to that of the great orator Henry Clay.[14]

Contemporary accounts of Revels described him as "tall, portly, dignified." A well educated man of unimpeachable character, he was respected both in his home state and in Washington, D.C. for being intelligent and highly principled. A man of refined manners and great politeness, Hiram "would bow and tip his hat every time he passed anyone on the street." Some historians in recent years (imposing the peculiar telescope of hindsight) have criticized Revels as a political "conservative." As an advocate of amnesty toward ex-Confederates, favoring restoration of their rights to vote and to hold public office, Hiram drew criticism from more radical Republicans as well as from some of the African American press. His voting record in Congress, however, reflected strong support for the Republican Party and the Grant Administration. Such labels as "timid," "extremely cautious," and "more scholar than administrator" that some commentators of Hiram's time and historians of our own time have attached to him are not necessarily inaccurate, but they miss the essence of his character.[15]

Hiram Revels held a profound respect for all people. A man of gentle spirit, he believed deeply in harmony between the races and worked toward that goal all of his life. In speeches at churches and temperance meetings, while expounding on his favorite themes of black education, equal justice, and the evils of liquor, he urged listeners to pursue the "Christian way of life." Above all, he was a profoundly religious man, devout and forgiving, more concerned with the souls and hearts of black people and white people than with their political behavior. Although he achieved a prominence in national politics never before experienced by an African American, Hiram's calling lay in the ministry, not in political wheeling and dealing. He remained true to this calling when, at the end of his term in the Senate, Hiram declined several high-paying positions offered to him by President Grant in favor of returning home to work among his people.

Upon his return to Mississippi, Hiram Revels became the first president of Alcorn University. The former senator placed great faith in education, believing it the best means of self-improvement for African Americans. For him, education and religion were inextricably bound. Hiram said of himself, "I accomplished my greatest aims under the influence of well directed prayer." Susie emphasized that her father's "heart's desire was to teach and preach to his people where it was most needed." Hiram served two terms as president (1871–74 and 1876–82). In 1874, Mississippi Governor Adelbert Ames removed Revels from the post because Hiram leaned toward the Democratic Party. In 1876, the new governor—a Democrat whom Hiram supported—reappointed him to the presidency of Alcorn. After serving as school president until 1882, Hiram Revels retired at the age of fifty-five because of failing health.[16]

During most of the 1870s, the Revels family lived in the president's house on the Alcorn University campus. It was here that Susie spent her childhood. The Revels girls became active in campus life from an early age and were all influenced by the rich intellectual atmosphere of the university. They attended church on campus, and one of them usually played the organ or led the choir. Susie's two oldest sisters were married in the campus chapel, one to an Alcorn instructor.

Hiram returned to the ministry after his retirement from Alcorn, becoming associate pastor of Asbury Church in Holly Springs in north-central Mississippi. Holly Springs was home to Rust College, established in 1866 and named for Richard Rust, a white antislavery advocate who actively supported the Freedman's Aid Society of the Methodist Episcopal Church. The Revels family enjoyed a close association with the college: Hiram taught several courses as professor of theology; three of the Revels girls—Susie, Ida, and Maggie—attended the school in the 1890s; and Susie taught there for three years after her graduation. [17]

Phoebe and Hiram Revels found the quiet, pastoral setting around Holly Springs well suited to raising their large family. Old cotton plantation homes built in the 1850s, with colonial-style architecture featuring verandas and tall columns, dotted the landscape of lakes and rolling hills. Lush forests of oak, pine, and dogwood were filled with quail, pheasant, and deer. It was during this time that the Revels family expanded to include a homeless boy. Susie later told the story of how her "brother" came to be a part of the family. Her granddaughter, Susan Cayton Woodson, repeated the story as she heard it from Susie:

> Senator Revels was riding along on horseback and came across a little black boy on the road. He told the little boy to go on home. The boy replied, "I ain't got no home." Senator Revels asked him where his parents were. The boy replied, "I ain't got no parents." So, Revels reached down, and taking the boy by the arm, pulled him up behind himself on the horse, and took him home. He stayed with the family, and he slept behind the pot-bellied stove… He grew up with the family…[and] was known as a part of the family.[18]

The relationship between Susie's parents and their children was warm and affectionate, though by today's standards it would be considered reserved. Hiram's letters to Phoebe in 1870, while his Senate duties took him to the East, typically closed with the request that she pray for him and "Kiss the children." Son-in-law Perry Howard described Hiram and Phoebe as "very happily married," and pictured their home in glowing terms: "She was called 'saint' by all who knew her. I spent many happy hours in their home in Holly Springs. It was a nine-room house on a hillside, with lovely gardens and beautiful surroundings."[19]

Phoebe was thirty-three years old at the time of Susie's birth. An educated woman and a Quaker, she was a positive role model for her six daughters and exerted a strong influence on their upbringing and education. In the late nineteenth century, Hiram and Phoebe Revels, like most middle-class African Americans, adopted the dominant society's Victorian values. Most were devoted Christians and as parents attended church with their children and emphasized Christian morality, the virtues of hard work, piety, and the "uplift" of the race through education.[20]

From an early age Susie had a natural inclination toward writing. She penned several short stories, but unfortunately, only two survive: "Licker" and "The Storm," both written when Susie was only ten or twelve years old. Writing about what she knew, Susie set both stories in a small southern town; they feature Tobias Anthony, a church deacon and town gravedigger, and his wife in familiar domestic scenes. Susie often had long, "wonderful" talks with her father as they drove the horse and buggy to town. Half a century later, Susie looked back and concluded, "Even today I can trace some of my mental attitudes and appreciation of the beautiful in nature and in the realm of spiritual values, and a recognition of human dignity, to the conditioning of that environment in its entirety." Susie became a teacher at the age of sixteen. For the next ten years she followed the profession, teaching reading and writing in one-room cabins in the backwoods of Marshall County, as well as in larger schools in town, including the State Normal School in Holly Springs. She then continued her education at Rust College, starting in 1889. Susie and her sister, Maggie, graduated with honors in May 1893. Maggie completed the "Normal" (teaching) curriculum, and Susie, who read an essay titled "Surgical Nursing" at commencement, graduated in nurse training. Susie stayed on to teach nursing at Rust until she left the South three years later.[21]

In the years leading up to the turn of the century, Hiram and Phoebe lost three of their daughters. Emma had died in an 1879 yellow fever epidemic that hit Holly Springs just two months after her marriage to Benjamin Garrett, a teacher at Alcorn. (Of the town's thirty-five hundred residents, some two thousand fled, and over three hundred lost their lives.) Maggie married Perry Howard not long after graduating from college; she also died just a few months after her own wedding. Lillie died in 1900 and was survived by her husband Mr. Houston and daughter Emma, who had been named after her aunt.[22]

Susie and her sisters Ida and Dora survived. (Ironically, Susie had always been considered the sickly one of the Revels girls, yet she lived to the age of seventy-three.) After graduating from Rust College in 1892, Ida taught for two years before marrying. Her husband, Dr. Sidney Redmond, became a widely respected surgeon in Mississippi; they had two children, Sidney Jr. and Esther. Dora married a Mr. Leonard and bore three daughters: Phoebe, Lillie B., and Marguerite. At age twenty-six, Susie was the last of the daughters to marry. Like her sister Emma, Susie wed an Alcorn man—one of her father's students, Horace Cayton.[23]

CHAPTER 2

Way Out West

Horace Cayton Sr. and Susie Revels, 1872–1896

WHEN HORACE SR. ARRIVED as a freshman in 1872, Alcorn University had seven regular teachers, including Hiram Revels, the school president. In addition to his duties as president, Hiram Revels held the post of professor of moral and intellectual philosophy. When Horace Sr. first met Hiram Revels, the school president was in his mid-forties, an imposing figure standing about five-feet-nine inches tall and weighing over two hundred pounds, with a medium-brown complexion and kindly, sensitive hazel eyes.[1]

Alcorn provided a traditional nineteenth century Latin grammar school education, offering beginning and advanced courses in Latin, Greek, French, math, history, reading, writing, and grammar. Horace Sr. was one of one hundred and seventy students, the majority of whom were receiving instruction in basic reading, writing, and arithmetic. By 1874 most students at Alcorn were studying the college preparatory curriculum. Horace Sr. may have been supported in part by one of the one-hundred-dollar state scholarships awarded to the best students in each county. And, interestingly, family stories suggest he received money to attend Alcorn from his white plantation-owner grandfather.[2]

Already by his teens Horace displayed the energy and industry that characterized his entire working life. In addition to working on his father's farm and intermittently attending school, he played in a brass band that often went out to serenade friends. When he was just fifteen, Horace worked elections, in his words, "doing stunts to pep up campaigns." In his later teens, he served as secretary for a quarterly conference of the African Methodist Episcopal Church. Like most students who attended Alcorn and similar black institutions, Horace planned to become a teacher; at the time, teaching and preaching were practically the only professional occupations open to African Americans in the South. By the age of nineteen Cayton had passed the examination required to obtain a teaching certificate, and he began teaching to help defray his expenses at Alcorn.[3]

A family story from Horace Sr.'s college years illuminates a different aspect of his "education" in the South. One year a school friend invited him to spend the summer with his family in Natchez. Many of the African American "society folks" in Natchez had such light complexions, Horace noted, that it would have kept a white "Southerner guessing to separate the white folks from the colored folks." Upon arriving at the student's home, Cayton was delighted to learn that he was just in time to attend a special dance that evening. Horace later described the event:

> With a beautiful damsel on each arm I strutted off to the ball that evening... My lady friends and I strolled in and I was being introduced, when suddenly a clear voice was heard to say, "Well, I wonder what the nigger wants here." Although I was a mulatto I was the darkest person in the house, and as I saw the color come and go in the faces of the girls as well as my chum, I think I was even more embarrassed than they. Some months later I was tickled to death at an opportunity to humiliate the girl who made the dirty remark... Revenge is a very sweet morsel.[4]

Life at Alcorn held few diversions aside from card games, cigars, and liquor. The closest town, Rodney, was eight miles away and had only six hundred residents. Larger towns such as Vicksburg (population nine thousand) and Natchez (population twelve thousand) were approximately forty miles away by horseback, wagon, or steamboat. Cayton described the relations between blacks and whites in the rural county as "always strained." Racism remained an everyday fact of life in Mississippi. During his college years, Horace rarely came into close contact with white women.

> Not being of the servant class, I probably did not speak to a white woman once in five years, yea, if that often. Few, if any of them, knew me and I knew none of them. There were frequent reports of colored men being lynched for having been too familiar with white women... If I had met a white woman on the public highway and she had stopped me and endeavored to engage me in conversation... I would have run from her as fast as my feet would have carried me.[5]

In 1880 and 1881 Horace Sr. again attended Alcorn, which had become Alcorn Agriculture and Mining College, the first land grant institution in the Unites Stated established for the education of blacks. The state legislature had reorganized Alcorn's program in 1878, using Tuskegee and Hampton as models; standard courses included agriculture, horticulture, and mechanical arts. Besides attending college, teaching school, and working on his father's farm, Horace Sr. gained experience as an editor and bookkeeper for a local newspaper, and also as what he later called "a court-house parasite."[6]

During this time, Horace began to court one of his classmates at Alcorn, Lillie Revels—the daughter of the school president. She was the second eldest of Hiram Revels' six daughters. Lillie was the same age as Horace Sr., but it was her younger sister, Susie—then just eleven—who eventually was to marry him.

⊹━━⊹

The year 1875 brought the end of Reconstruction in Mississippi. With the state's so-called "redemption" by reactionary whites, Republicans suffered such a resounding defeat at the hands of the white Democrats that many blacks started to consider migrating. Shortly, the 1878 campaign and elections proved to be so violent that many blacks believed the time had come to leave the South. Some leaders, among them Hiram Revels and Frederick Douglass, opposed migration, and they urged fellow blacks to stay and fight for their rights. But a tide of racism was rising with the Ku Klux Klan at the crest. Near Horace Cayton's hometown of Port Gibson, the old plantation of former slave owner and ex-governor, B.G. Humphries, became the first headquarters for the KKK in Claiborne County.[7]

By the early 1880s, Horace Cayton Sr., now in his twenties, possessed a good education at a time when few African Americans had little if any schooling. He was sharp witted and articulate, with a stubborn streak and a strong sense of justice and ethics. Mississippi offered little hospitality for a man of color with such attributes. Unlike many African Americans who followed the lure of freedom and factory jobs to the North, Horace Sr. believed the sign that read "opportunity" pointed west. News of a mass exodus of African Americans (dubbed "Exodusters") who were establishing thriving settlements in Kansas had been circulating throughout Mississippi since 1878.[8]

Horace Sr. may also have been inspired by his father, Evans Cayton, who had provided him "with an education and the desire to escape the southland," according to Horace Jr. One Cayton family story suggests another reason Horace Sr. decided to leave the South. Revels Cayton said that after his father graduated from Alcorn University, he returned to the plantation and "apparently he was a big mouth to his 'white kin.' They really got upset and told him to git. I guess they meant it, because he had to be put in a coffin and sneaked out of the state." Many years later, Horace Sr. wrote of an incident from this period, in which he narrowly avoided being lynched for tipping his hat to a white woman. He hid beneath the seat of a buggy to make his escape by train in "the dead of night."[9]

+≡≡≡+

In late 1884 or early 1885, Horace Sr. left Mississippi. His trail west followed the Exodusters to Kansas. For many blacks, Kansas was an easy choice for a new home, and a more logical one than Nebraska or the Dakotas. As the homeland of John Brown, it was, in the minds of many, "the quintessential Free State," where African Americans could live and prosper in freedom and peace. Promotional efforts directed by railroad companies, land agents, and local governments found an audience in the South that was receptive to talk of freedom, political participation, land ownership, education, and other opportunities available in Kansas. Horace Sr.'s path to Nicodemus may have been more than happenstance. He may have known and used connections with one of the small family groups from Mississippi that earlier had joined the colonists in Nicodemus. Whatever his motives, Horace Cayton Sr. joined the westward thrust, carrying with him the weighty heritage of slavery and Reconstruction.[10]

In Kansas, Horace Sr. lived for a time in Wyandotte (later to become Kansas City) and Hill City before settling in Nicodemus. The town had been established in 1877 by thirty African American colonists; just three years later, in 1880, the town had over seven hundred residents. When Horace Sr. arrived in mid-decade, Nicodemus was a robust and thriving community. He opened up a real estate and loan business and advertised in the local newspaper: "H.R. Cayton, land and loan agent, will put mort [mortgage] money on your farm, and get your loan through, sooner than any agent in the county; good rates; business attended to for Rook and Graham counties." His ambitious style quickly earned him remarks in the town press as "a promising young man…[who] has got 'get up and git' to him and will undoubtedly make his mark."[11]

Horace Sr. was filling in as assistant editor at the *Western Cyclone* when the anniversary of Emancipation Day was celebrated in Nicodemus. The celebration was marred by a shooting and a fistfight, prompting editor W.L. Chambers of the Stockton *Rooks County Record* to write: "If this is a sample of the high state of civilization the emancipated Negroes of Graham County have reached, their anniversaries will cease to attract the attention of respectable people."[12]

Outraged, Horace Sr. penned a letter in response, which he published in the *Western Cyclone*. Displaying a flair for colorful name-calling that would land him in trouble later in his career, Horace Sr. called Chambers a "Bobtail erudite" and a "dirty gas-bag" who was totally ignorant of the facts and had no other purpose than to defame the town of Nicodemus. He pointed to the equally unruly behavior of a group of whites at the celebration:

> Only thirteen empty beer bottles were found and filth too horrible to mention. Sir, is this that high state of civilization that the *Record* holds up as an example?... In conclusion I will say that Negroes are advancing as rapidly as could be expected. The dark clouds of ignorance are rapidly passing away and they are gradually forming a nucleus around which they will gather the elements of their race now repelling each other and thus move on to a most glorious success.[13]

The Stockton editor responded the following week, referring to Horace Sr. as "Our woolly-headed Ethiopian friend." While claiming "a warm place in our heart for the Negro," Chambers emphasized, "we have no sympathy for the ruffians of this race and their abettors, like this man Cayton, who condone their crimes."[14]

Horace Sr. fired back in the next issue of the *Western Cyclone*:

> You say personally you have a warm place in your heart for the Negro; now we are informed by those who know that Nicodemus and its people never did receive a favorable mention in your sheet; you always speak of them with contempt or derision. But... it is known that you once edited a dirty vulgar sheet abetting the killing of Negroes in the South... Like the *Record* I have no respect for the ruffians of any race or their abettors; but I do claim it unjust, unprincipled and narrow minded to censure the entire race for what a few folk do, like this turn-coat, lying editor of the *Record*... If you have not the ability to answer, keep quiet, and don't make such an ass of yourself again.[15]

Horace Cayton Sr. got the last word, for here the bitter exchange ended.

In Kansas, Cayton also taught school for a short time and worked as a clerk. In the autumn of 1888 he became embroiled in a scheme that would come to haunt him years later. In November, some businessmen for whom Cayton was bookkeeping in Hill City were taken to court for failure to deliver goods to creditors. Cayton became involved when his employers' attorney advised him to testify that he had purchased the goods and was the actual owner. It was a trick. The attorney quickly filed a complaint against Cayton and he was charged with perjury. Cayton pleaded not guilty, but on November 24 was convicted and sentenced to serve one year in the Kansas State Penitentiary. He arrived at the prison in Lansing, Kansas, on

November 29, 1888. Meanwhile, outraged citizens of Nicodemus and Hill City took up Cayton's cause, and eventually gained the attention of the governor, who granted a full pardon to the unfortunate young Cayton. Upon his release a couple months later, Cayton returned to Hill City, where he was "kindly received," as he later said. He was soon at work again as bookkeeper for a "druggist firm" and then became editor of the *Graham County Times*. Cayton remained in Hill City for about a year before deciding it was time to head west and leave Kansas for good.[16]

The opportunity came when Cayton spotted an advertisement in the *Rocky Mountain News* for a bookkeeper position in a bank in Ogden, Utah. Always quick and accurate with figures, Horace Sr. had experience as a bookkeeper, so he applied for the job by return mail. The bank responded, sending a set of questions, which Horace Sr. completed and returned. Finally, the bank cashier notified him by letter that he had been selected for the job from among eighty-six applicants.

Horace Sr. immediately set off for Ogden, delighted with the opportunity to get a good position, as he later wrote, "way out west." Upon arrival, Horace Sr. presented himself to the bank cashier, the letter of acceptance in his hand. The cashier eyed the letter suspiciously and then, with mouth open, stared at the young black man for several long moments. As Horace Sr. later wrote, the cashier finally spoke:

> "I did not know you were a colored man and I will not give you the place. Under no circumstances would I put a colored man to work in a bank with white men. I have no apologies to make." I left the bank, but how I got out I do not know. Within my life I may have had more embarrassing moments, but if so I do not now recall them. Ten years later that cashier was convicted of embezzlement, and I went to the depot to see him start to the pen, and I fear mine was a look of triumph rather than sympathy, which should have been my Christian duty.[17]

For the next several months, Horace Cayton Sr.'s search for opportunity took him to Colorado. He worked at odd jobs, including a stint as a purchasing agent for a Denver cattle company. At times he found himself with little money, so he took whatever work was to be had, although he "abhorred" hotel work, or, as he said, "any kind of employment that made of me a 'coon' to be whistled for by the passing throng." He remembered one particular job with some amusement, introducing his story with the adage, "a little education is a dangerous thing." He met a young black man hurrying down the street and asked him if he knew where he could find a job. "My boss wants a man," was the reply, so Horace Sr. ate a quick breakfast and set off to find the boss, who turned out to be a construction crew supervisor. Horace Sr.—short, slightly built, and wearing glasses—did not appear to be up to heavy masonry construction work. But, after some persuasion, the boss told Horace to join the hod carriers. Horace later described the incident in one of his Seattle newspapers, *Cayton's Weekly*:

> Among the ten colored men employed there one of them had seen me at a rooming house and had gotten the idea that I had "a little education," and he no sooner saw me carrying a hod of brick to the third floor, when he shouted to the gang, "College graduate carrying the hod, set him on fire." Believe me, that was an embarrassing moment such as you read about... My first impulse was to sneak away and this the boss advised me to do, but I braced up and with clinched teeth and dogged determination fell in and never lost a trip.[18]

Horace Sr. often told this story to his children. Younger son Revels recalled it years later almost exactly as his father told it, although he had never read the newspaper account. He added a vital piece of information— the culmination of the episode for his father: "He got a lot of rest and good food, and finally the day came when those other guys were pleading with him, 'slow down, Cayton, slow down, Cayton!' But he wouldn't, he just kept on, leaving them behind."

It seemed to Horace Sr. that better opportunities lay farther west. He decided to head for Portland, Oregon, but getting there proved not so easy. At the train depot he slipped five dollars to a porter, who let him climb aboard the train for Salt Lake City. But a "spotter" for the railroad threw him off the train in Cheyenne, Wyoming. Mustering his courage, young Horace approached the regional superintendent of the Union Pacific Railway for assistance. Cayton told the superintendent that he had only one dollar to his name and that he was trying to get to Salt Lake City. "I am not a tramp," he declared, displaying his twenty letters of recommendation from county officials and business colleagues in Kansas. The railroad man looked Cayton over, then without a word rang for the porter and told him to put the young man on the next train to Salt Lake City. When it was time to board, Horace Sr. later recalled, "I went in to thank [the superintendent] for his kindness and before I could speak great lumps came up in my throat and I stood speechless. He reached out his hand and shook mine good-bye and neither of us spoke."[19]

An incident on the train as he traveled to Portland provides some insight into race relations at the time and Cayton's perspective on them. When the train stopped briefly for breakfast, Horace Sr. moved to the dining car, where he sat at an empty table "lest I run up against a color prejudice snag." He had just begun his meal when two well-dressed Native Americans entered the car. Immediately, he became nervous that they would be given a seat at his table. If that happened, Horace Sr. later said, "I intended to show my American blood and either have the table myself or insist that they be seated at some other table." To his surprise the proprietor rushed to the two men, greeted them warmly, and seated them at the best table in the room. Then, said Horace Sr.,

> [the proprietor] entertained them while three or four waiters fell all over themselves in their endeavor to show them [the Indians] in what high esteem they were held in that house. As they passed me [after the meal] they gave a second look to be thoroughly convinced of my identity and then a look of disgust beclouded their faces. If you think that was not a most embarrassing moment for me, then…you are off your trolly.[20]

By early 1890 Horace Cayton's search for opportunity took him briefly to Portland, then finally to Seattle. The thirty-year-old adventurer was one of the many flocking to the growing frontier town. He was, though, one of the few African Americans; just three hundred blacks lived in Seattle at the time. Horace Sr. arrived with only ten dollars in his pocket, but he was undaunted. He firmly believed that a man like himself—educated, hardworking, honest—might live the "American Dream" if he could find a place where he would be respected for his abilities. The "Queen City" bustled with energy and optimism as the community rebuilt itself after a devastating fire in 1889. Seattle, Horace Sr. thought, might be the place. He felt a sense of freedom in the West that he had not experienced in Mississippi. While he found race prejudice as common as in the South, instances of overt discrimination occurred less frequently and were less severe than those he had experienced back home. In later years he would look back and say, "I had spent many years in the West and my color had given me no trouble in getting the same accommodations in public places as were accorded to white citizens."[21]

Soon Horace Sr. landed a job with a struggling Populist newspaper, the *People's Call*. The paper's masthead proclaimed "devoted to the emancipation of industrial slaves." The publisher and managing editor, Judge Richard Winsor, once had been associated with the Underground Railroad in Michigan, helping escaped slaves to find safe passage to Canada.

Impressed with Horace Sr., he dismissed his white city editor and hired the young black man in his place. When the twelve white men working in the composing and press rooms heard of the change, they confronted Winsor and Cayton, insisting, "we will not take copy from a colored man." Horace Sr. expected to hear that he had lost the job before he had even started. To his surprise, Winsor told the crew to "get your belongings, go to the office and get your money and then leave my place of business at once. You run my work room, but you will not run my editorial room." Horace Sr. later reported that Winsor's outburst was "interspersed with forcible ejaculations that would not be proper for a Sunday school." The men stayed on the job and eventually accepted the hardworking newcomer. Horace Sr. was still able to call some of these co-workers friends almost thirty years later.[22]

Horace Sr. quickly became active in Republican Party politics in Seattle, and he made many valuable contacts. When the *People's Call* closed its doors less than a year after he was hired, fellow Republican Will H. Parry (then editor of the *Seattle Post-Intelligencer*) helped Horace Sr. get a job as a reporter on a new daily Republican newspaper. Again, he faced racial prejudice in his new workplace. When Cayton reported to his job on the first day, the managing editor said there was no work for him. Parry heard of the incident and told Horace Sr. to report to work again. The next day the managing editor handed out assignments to the nine other reporters, but spoke not a word to Cayton. Horace Sr. looked at each of the men, "but did not meet a sympathetic eye." After the others had left on their assignments, the editor abruptly handed his new reporter a pile of miscellaneous items and told him to "write something." Horace Sr. produced a political story that made the editor's hair "stand up like the quills of a porcupine." The story was published verbatim, and by the end of the week the editor was assigning him to cover the hotels and to get interviews from "big politicians visiting the city."[23]

Horace Sr. loved the blend of politics and journalism. The fortuitous combination brought more than a means of earning a living; it opened the door to what he had sought for so long—real opportunity. Soon, Horace Sr. took a job on a small weekly published by a friend named Britain Oxendine. The *Seattle Standard*, established in 1891, was the first newspaper for African Americans in Seattle. The two-page weekly solidly backed Republican politics and advocated racial justice, political recognition for blacks, and the general "uplift of the race." Despite support from African American community figures such as George Grose and Israel I. Walker,

Oxendine struggled with severe financial problems. Finally, in the fall of 1892 he leased the *Seattle Standard* to Horace Sr.[24]

As the *Seattle Standard*'s new editor, Horace Cayton Sr. continued the paper's focus on racial justice; but again, his outspoken views soon plunged him into controversy. In the spring of 1893 he published a series of articles attacking white community stalwarts Arthur A. Denny, Governor John McGraw, and Seattle's chief of police. Upset members of the city's black community held a meeting, chaired by William Grose, and passed a resolution publicly denouncing Cayton and his editorial policies as "scurrilous" and "unjust." They exclaimed, "the paper fell into unscrupulous hands, and recently it has done all in its power to incite race prejudice and to antagonize the good will of white citizens." The signers, who included former publisher Oxendine and the paper's major subscribers, demanded that Cayton "properly apologize" or they would withdraw their support until the paper was under new management.[25]

Horace Sr., of course, was not cowed. Asked to soften his stance on corruption to avoid offending a white readership, the idealistic new editor refused to yield. When the lease expired, Oxendine demanded that Cayton return the printing equipment, but he refused. Oxendine took matters into his own hands: that night he and four friends stole back the presses, moving them to north Seattle. Oxendine resumed publication of the *Seattle Standard*, but it folded not long afterward in the 1893 financial downturn.[26]

Despite his stormy time at the ill-fated *Seattle Standard*, within a year Horace Sr. was able to position himself to launch his own newspaper. On May 19, 1894, he issued the first edition of the *Seattle Republican* from an office in the Burke building on Third Avenue. The *Post-Intelligencer* marked the founding of Cayton's paper with the pronouncement, "The tone is manly, and its politics Republican, based upon an intelligent appreciation of party principles. Mr. Cayton, who addresses himself to the better element of his own race, says that 'the only plausible and certain manner of forever settling race or national issues is by full and free discussion of them.'"

The *Helena Colored Citizen* hailed the publication as "one of the brightest, best edited…colored papers published." Horace Cayton Sr. felt like a man on his way. The *Seattle Republican* became the second of seven black weekly newspapers started in Seattle between 1891 and 1901, but it was the only one to survive. The paper would last, in fact, nearly two decades.[27]

In the years following the Great Fire of 1889, Seattle had seen important growth. An expanding railroad network brought new people and increased trade. The city surged with the activity of a frontier town being transformed into a modern metropolis. By 1896 Cayton had established himself as part of the growing business community. He had a thriving newspaper business and strong ties to the powerful white Republicans who dominated city politics. Horace's New Year's editorial on January 4, 1896, reflected his characteristic optimism and high idealism:

> We live in the present and in the future, and not the past; let bygones be bygones, and today let all men, irrespective of race, color, creed, or nationality, meet on one common ground, smoke the pipe of everlasting peace, and bow without murmur or complaint to the inevitable. Let there be one flag and one country for all manner of man that swears allegiance thereto. Let America be for Americans, without either color or race distinction cutting any figure in the contest. Let the race be for all, and the prize to the winner.[28]

The same issue of the *Seattle Republican* included an article about the Atlanta Exposition and Booker T. Washington, written by Miss Susie Sumner Revels. Editor Cayton told his readers, "For the past few months Miss Revels has furnished the *Republican* with some very meritorious stories. She gives every evidence of becoming a very forcible and effective writer and seems especially adapted to fiction and verse." Much had changed since Susie and Horace Sr.'s first acquaintance fifteen years earlier in Mississippi. They recalled warm summer evenings when young "Mr. Cayton" came to the college president's home on the Alcorn campus to court Susie's older sister, Lillie. The two would sit on the front porch, while eleven-year-old Susie played in the yard, running to and fro and waving long sulfur matches that blazed like sparklers.[29]

Horace Sr. had kept in contact with the Revels family in the intervening years. He sent copies of his Seattle newspaper to Susie's father. Hiram Revels wrote back by dictating letters to Susie, who would add her own "P.S." telling of other family news. As time passed, the postscripts grew longer, and soon Mr. Cayton and Miss Susie became regular correspondents. Horace Sr., now in his early thirties, felt ready to settle down. In one of his letters, Horace Sr. asked for Susie's hand in marriage. Susie made the long trip west by stagecoach and train. When she arrived in Seattle, her betrothed—a proper Victorian gentleman—arranged separate lodgings until they could be married.[30]

In a letter to Susie shortly after her wedding, the Revels family expressed longing for her company but also great hopes for her future:

> We could but feel sad, for we will miss our dear daughter and sister; as we believe that she will be happy, that alone will bring comfort to us... Mama...wishes you a long and happy life. [She] says tell Mr. Cayton he must take good care of you, as she knows he will do.[31]

Despite some obvious contrasts in their backgrounds, the couple shared several things that were to form the core of the Cayton family legacy: a heritage of mixed black and white ancestry and belief in an integrated society; a progressive, optimistic spirit (attributable in part to growing up in Reconstruction Mississippi); and an acceptance of nineteenth-century Victorian manners and morals. Furthermore, they were both college-educated teachers, writers, and intellectuals. The products of strong family environments, Horace Sr. and Susie carried with them the strengths common to many African American families. For centuries, church and family had been the major institutions providing a buttress against slavery, racism, segregation, violence, and other injustices blacks experienced in America. Christian beliefs were combined with traditions brought from Africa, where communal ties and extended kinship were highly valued. The constant adaptation and cooperation necessary to ensure their survival in both the pre- and post-Civil War eras created a sense of individual pride and community identity among many African Americans, including Susie Sumner Revels and Horace Cayton Sr.

Finally, the Revels and the Caytons were families that espoused peace between all peoples, believed in education as the best means to "uplift" African Americans, and expressed a profound faith in the equality of blacks and whites. Horace Sr. and Susie emerged as adults with an unswerving devotion to fighting injustice, which was to carry them through four decades of life and work in Seattle.

CHAPTER 3

The Queen City

Susie and Horace Sr., 1894–1913

W ITHIN A FEW YEARS AFTER MARRYING, Horace Sr. and Susie would achieve substantial success in the newspaper business. At the height of their prosperity in the first decade of the twentieth century, the Cayton family lived in a large, beautiful, two-story home with eight rooms, carriage house, and horse carriage situated on Capitol Hill, one of Seattle's most affluent neighborhoods. Horace Sr. also attained status of some significance in the state's Republican Party, while Susie was a respected community leader on issues affecting Seattle's African Americans, particularly the women and children. The Caytons worked hard to make the weekly *Seattle Republican* successful and to support their family and community. Together they had launched careers that would merit them a place among Seattle's most respected and prominent African American pioneers.

And yet, despite all of their achievements for one and a half decades, the Caytons were living in an era of increasing racial unrest and they would suffer as a result. Racial prejudice eventually would oust them from their lovely Capitol Hill home in 1909. Over the next few years, their American dream unraveled. Horace Sr. was embroiled in a civil rights lawsuit, and he lost money on real estate investments. The political climate changed, too, and suddenly, Horace's political career faltered. Subscriptions to the *Seattle Republican* newspaper fell off, and in 1913, after nearly two decades in print, the newspaper failed. The family had lost their privileged position in Seattle society and drifted to the edge of poverty.

It was not until the next generation of Caytons left Seattle that the family extricated themselves from this financial and social limbo. The story of this rise to success, followed by the reversal in fortune and how the Cayton family responded to it, provides one measure for understanding race relations and the black experience in the fast-changing Pacific Northwest of the early twentieth century.

Several aspects of Seattle's turn-of-the-century business and social environment contributed to the Caytons' initial successes. The city's heritage as a frontier town, where individualism, ability, and respect for the self-made man were sometimes more important than skin color, provided a climate of opportunity favorable to the ambitious. Seattle differed significantly from the older, more industrialized cities of the Midwest and East Coast, where there were large unassimilated ethnic groups and clear class divisions. Seattle's history, geographic location on the far northwest frontier, economic base, and social dynamics created a young city fundamentally different from the cities Horace Sr. knew in the South.

Seattle was yet in the "frontier city stage," and it seemed to Horace and many other observers to be a place of unlimited opportunity. The "Queen City" had come into its own and embarked on an era of substantial financial growth as it emerged from the depression that had beset the nation after the Panic of 1893. The Caytons benefited, too, from Seattle's overall rising prosperity that followed in the wake of the 1897-98 Alaska Gold Rush. In fact, Horace Sr. shared "directly" in profits from the gold excitement. In 1897 he had grubstaked Klondike-bound Israel I. Walker with five hundred dollars. After eight years of barbering miners, Walker returned in 1906 with enough money to buy a rooming house and mercantile business after splitting his earnings fifty-fifty with Horace Sr.[1]

Seattle developers poured tens of millions of dollars into the construction of pretentious buildings, radically altering the city's skyline. Seattle's population experienced equally spectacular growth. From less than forty-three thousand residents in 1890, the number nearly doubled over the next ten years, reaching approximately eighty-three thousand at the turn of the century. The strong economic upsurge and influx of newcomers created substantial opportunities for people at almost all levels of society. However, with most industrial operations and the unskilled and semiskilled workers located outside of the city proper, the bulk of Seattle's resident population was composed of skilled and white collar workers, who were overwhelmingly white (95 percent) and native-born (73 percent). Seattle's homogeneity contributed to a lack of sharp class divisions, or at least the appearance of such.

A related and probably more significant reason for the Caytons' success was the fact that African Americans were few in number at the turn of the century. In 1890, when Horace Sr. arrived, there were around three hundred in the city. Ten years later, the number had grown to only about four hundred, comprising just 0.5 percent of the population, whereas the largest minority, Asians, numbered around three thousand, or 3.7 percent of the overall population.

In Seattle, as in many places outside of the South, as long as African Americans remained relatively few in number, they were more accepted by the white majority. Well before Horace Sr. arrived, the editor of the Seattle *Daily Intelligencer* articulated the ground rules for amicable white-black relations in the city:

> There is room only for a limited number of colored people here. Overstep that limit and there comes a clash in which the colored man must suffer… The few that are here do vastly better than they would do if their numbers increased a hundred fold.[2]

Nevertheless, from the very founding of the *Seattle Republican*, Horace Sr. consistently advocated that blacks migrate to the Northwest—to the "Queen City," a place of opportunity where they could take advantage of the better conditions and more easily prove themselves. At one time, Cayton Sr. cooperated with Dr. Samuel Burdette and Paul Schultze to recruit blacks from southern states to establish homesteads in the Yakima Valley and create a Horse Heaven Hills colony. In 1906 Horace Sr. proclaimed "Negro Help Wanted," urging blacks to come west "and take advantage of the golden opportunities" in Seattle, where African Americans had three churches, an investment company, and two fraternal lodges (Masons and Elks). Horace Sr. was aware that opportunities were limited, and that prejudice increasingly was circumscribing the lives of Seattle blacks. Nevertheless, to him the Northwest was a great improvement over the South. In 1907, Horace Sr. issued a special edition of the *Seattle Republican*, "with the hope of inducing Afro-Americans from the South to come to the Northwest." His editorial beckoned, "Come West, Black Man."[3]

Horace Jr. later described his father's strong feelings about the need for African American migration:

> My father…was impatient with Negroes who stayed in the South, and his hatred of things southern was deep and profound… [He said,] "There is no hope for them down there… The colored people of this country should make a bold strike for freedom… Here in the Northwest we are striking out in every direction… Here the race is to the swiftest, and here the American dream is being won… I believe in democracy. And here democracy is being worked out. We are the new frontier, and thousands of Negroes come to this part of the country and stand up like men and compete with their white brothers.[4]

In Horace Sr.'s eyes, Seattle differed strikingly from the South, where whites waged a "war of extermination" on African Americans. In the West, he believed, blacks had no need to form clubs and associations separate from whites. He considered unnecessary a call made in 1898 for black newspapermen in the West to meet in Omaha and form a Negro Press Association. "If the Negro editor is not made as welcome in the press associations where the majority of the members are Caucasians," declared Horace Sr., "it is because he will not permit himself to be made welcome." African Americans, he said, were all too fond of secluding themselves and complaining about not being wanted because of their race. "Show that you have ability and it will be recognized by the whites in any kind of an association or convention, and this is especially true of the West." His own experience seemed proof enough.[5]

Equally important to Horace Sr.'s successes were his substantial personal attributes. His sharp wit and gift for articulation, his great capacity for hard work, his strong mind and independent spirit, combined with a firm belief in his own abilities, all gave him a drive and ambition to "make it." While his often-brusque manner, flashes of temper, and bristling pride convinced some that he was haughty and arrogant, friends and enemies alike typically saw Horace Cayton as a man to be reckoned with. And, being married to a daughter of Hiram Revels was prestigious. Susie's gentle, refined bearing, her sharp wit and informed, intelligent conversation also helped give them status, or at least credibility, with a large segment of both the black and white communities.

Skin color—more accurately, whites' attitudes about skin color—clearly played a role in the Caytons' early acceptance in Seattle. Both Horace Sr. and Susie were relatively light-skinned. Horace Sr.'s eyes were steel gray. His son, Revels, said, "I once surprised him in the bathroom, when he had just finished bathing. His skin and body were near white, except for his hands, neck and head. When I remarked on this, he smiled and said he got that way from the sun and wind on the Midwest plains." Since ante-bellum days, mulattos—the light-skinned men and women of mixed racial heritage—had received preferential treatment from whites. Mulattos were viewed as more intelligent, more competent, more educated and cultured, as well as more physically attractive than other blacks. They usually had better access to education and a wider range of occupations. Laws and customs often worked to their advantage.

As part of a small African American professional "elite" in the city, the Caytons counted among their close acquaintances the John Gaytons,

J.P. and Laura Ball (photographers), attorney J. Edward Hawkins and his wife Etta (who worked with Susie on charitable causes), Dr. Charles Maxwell, Israel I. Walker, and others. Most were political and/or business associates, many of whom advertised in the Cayton paper. Others, such as the Gaytons, were frequently mentioned in the "Personals" column of the *Seattle Republican*. On one particular mid-summer evening, the Caytons entertained a number of friends in high Victorian style at their home, which was "tastefully decorated with the national colors." The soiree offered polite conversation and featured a musical program that included an instrumental solo by Susie's niece, Emma Houston. The guest register listed some of the most prominent names in black Seattle society, including Samuel DeBow, Mr. and Mrs. Booker, and Mr. and Mrs. Walter Washington.[6]

Some of the Caytons' successes also can be attributed to the connections they made with Seattle's elite white society. Horace Sr.'s generosity and willingness to reach out to others had attracted attention even before he achieved recognition as a publisher. Horace Sr. established one such early friendship with James D. Hoge Jr. The two men had arrived in Seattle at about the same time—both near broke—and Horace had befriended the eighteen-year-old white youth, occasionally giving him money for a meal. By 1894, when Horace Sr. started the *Seattle Republican,* Hoge also was deeply involved in Republican politics and had secured a controlling interest in the *Seattle Post-Intelligencer.* A few years later Hoge became president of the First National Bank of Seattle. Hoge, in fact, may have been the prime supporter of Horace Sr.'s paper in the early years. In 1895, the editor of the *Seattle News* criticized Horace Sr. for running a "subsidized" paper, and Cayton later admitted that between 1896 and 1901 (at least) the *Seattle Republican* had been set up and printed by the *Post-Intelligencer's* presses.[7]

In early 1896, Hoge and Cayton were involved in a political intrigue that allowed the *Seattle Republican,* in Cayton's words, to "bloom into a daily paper overnight." The city charter, which had been revised to meet the needs of the growing town, was required to be published in two daily papers. Hoge's *Post-Intelligencer* already had landed one of the contracts. The editors of the Seattle *Daily Times* and the *Seattle Evening News* teamed up to obtain the other contract. As Seattle Mayor Byron Phelps later recounted, he and a few members of the city council decided to thwart their efforts.

[W]ith the assistance of James D. Hoge, then chief owner of the *P-I,* [we] decided to make the *Seattle Republican* a daily paper and in less than two hours thereafter, it being Friday morning, "it was did"…and thus did those fellows get beat at their own game.[8]

The *Daily Republican,* however, lasted only for the month required to publish the charter. The city saved over four thousand dollars because Horace Sr. had agreed to do the work for much less than the competition. The editor of the Seattle *Argus* sniped that what bothered the editor of the *Seattle News* the most was "that the contract had been given to a 'nagger.'" Cayton's paper had been a pawn in more powerful hands, but it proved important for Horace Sr.'s political career. Later that year the Washington State Republican Editorial Association elected Hoge as president and Cayton as secretary.[9] Horace Sr. remained a member of the association, and also the King County Weekly Publishers Association, until the demise of the *Seattle Republican* in 1913.

+≡≡+

Horace published the weekly *Seattle Republican* for over nineteen years, from 1894 to 1913. He devoted its pages primarily to national, state, and local political news and opinion. As a newspaper of intense political spirit, it typified most journalism of the day. Two features of the Cayton paper, however, made it unique in the Northwest: it was a political newspaper owned and operated by an African American; and it was biracial, directed at both white and black readers. Editor Horace Sr. proclaimed:

> The *Republican* lays no claim of being the official organ of any race, class or clan of citizens… It stands for right, and champions the cause of the oppressed as it sees it, whether that oppressed be black or white. The success of the Republican Party is one of its highest ambitions. We have no desire to be classed.[10]

A regular and prominent feature of the *Seattle Republican* was Horace Sr.'s weekly column "Political Pot-Pie." As the "Pie-Maker," he recounted the latest political gossip in the state, while peppering his reports with staunchly Republican opinions. His discussion of the issues of the day always included the impacts on both blacks and whites. Sketches and photographs of prominent white Republicans frequently appeared next to similar presentations of blacks. Weekly columns were often titled "Brother in Black" or "Afro-American." In the same fashion, even much of the general interest or filler material in the *Seattle Republican* commented on inter-racial issues, and it usually carried Horace Sr.'s sardonic touch: "The colored citizens in Nanse County, Virginia have made more increase in actual wealth…and own more property than the whites. What shall be done with the non-progressive whites will yet be a puzzling question."[11]

Most of that time, the *Seattle Republican* ranged in length from four to eight pages, with three columns per page, and sold for five cents a copy, and two to three dollars a year for subscriptions. In addition to political news, the weekly included topics of general interest, legal notices, and a variety of advertisements by local businesses. Advertisers included many white-owned businesses whose names are still familiar to modern-day Seattle residents: Rainier Brewing Company, G.O. Guy Drugs, Ernst Brothers Hardware, National Bank of Commerce, Northern Pacific Railroad, and Seattle Gas & Electric Company. Black businesses advertised in the paper, too, including restaurants, law offices (J. Edward Hawkins), realtors (B.F. Tutt's Afro-American Land & Investment Company), barber shops, and many others.[12]

From the beginning, the Caytons' paper had reflected, and also channeled, their involvement with the area's small African American community. In 1898, for example, a disaster struck the coal mining town of Franklin, located south of Seattle. The miners, most of whom were black, had been brought into the region in the late 1880s and early 1890s as strikebreakers. Horace Sr., along with Attorney J. Edward Hawkins and others, set up a relief fund to aid the victims and their families, using the Cayton newspaper to rally Seattle blacks to the aid effort.[13]

Horace was highly principled and not one to mince words. As his son Revels later noted, "He was a real stand-up guy." This pronounced trait led to the widely held perception that he was self-righteous. Horace Sr. realized this and made no apologies. He stated his editorial philosophy bluntly: "When an editor attempts to please everybody…then he pleases nobody, and as a result of his foolish attempt a paper is forced on the public that is not worth the ink it takes to make the letters on the paper."[14]

Horace did not just voice his opinion in the newspaper, he readily acted on his beliefs. Sometimes he appeared to provoke events to call attention to issues he considered important. One illustrative incident occurred in January 1895 between Horace Sr. and a black barber, John F. Cragwell. Early one evening, the young editor walked into Cragwell's shop, which catered exclusively to whites. He sat down in the first chair and ordered a shave. The shop-owner and the feisty editor got into a fight and Horace Sr. was thrown out into the street. As the two scuffled on the sidewalk,

Horace Sr. gave "a sudden twitch" that sent the barber flying into the shop's large plate glass window. When Cragwell told his story to a *Post-Intelligencer* reporter the next day, he charged that Cayton had entered the shop as a pretext to bring a civil suit against Cragwell for refusing to shave him. In an editorial a few years later, Horace Sr. referred to a certain prejudiced black barber as "puke of the lowest ilk."[15]

+≡≡+

Cayton's savvy combination of running a successful newspaper business and delving in politics provided him with a powerful impetus to redirect the paper. In the late 1890s, what had started as a weekly publication for African Americans in the Puget Sound region evolved into a weekly Republican political sheet aimed at garnering a statewide readership of both blacks and whites. The turning point for the paper and for Cayton came at the 1894 state Republican Party convention, held in Spokane. Horace Cayton Sr. was one of seven blacks in the eighty-three-member King County delegation dominated by U.S. Senator Watson Squire and his followers. Squire's "ring" favored the nomination of Thomas Humes as state supreme court judge and sought to impose the unit rule, binding the entire delegation to vote on the convention floor for the nominee favored by the majority. Horace Sr. and seven white delegates, however, defied the old guard and refused to endorse their candidate. Horace Sr. delivered a "fiery challenge" to the party regulars. His faction loudly applauded, their opponents hissed, and the stormy session erupted in a fistfight with Horace Cayton Sr. in its very midst. The turbulent caucus finally ended after midnight, and the next day the fifteen-hundred convention delegates nominated J. J. Gordon for State Supreme Court Judge. Horace Sr. had made some good political allies: Gordon was the candidate favored by Governor John McGraw. He had made some powerful enemies too. The "ring" bluntly informed Mr. Cayton that he would never again attend a Republican convention.[16]

Horace Sr. continued to back Gordon, and the *Seattle Republican* proved a forceful means to do so. Cayton succeeded in gaining the support of his ward for the forthcoming caucus to elect delegates to the county convention in 1896. Many years later, Horace related the events of the caucus day:

> [A] colonel of the great Civil War was stationed at the polls to curse me during the entire voting period and shame white voters for bowing down to a nigger leader. Be it remembered there was not another Negro

voter in the entire ward. My followers pleaded with me to have my adversary arrested, but I pleaded with them to leave him alone, knowing full well it was a well-laid plan to bring about the defeat of my faction. I won, and from then on I was always taken into consideration. My paper became state wide in circulation and many took it without knowing my racial identity. If perchance I was introduced at some public function the other fellow was usually greatly surprised.[17]

Horace Sr.'s handling of the Gordon affair had shown true backbone, and both his visibility and reputation were raised substantially. Throughout the next several years, the *Seattle Republican* saw spectacular growth. Most copies of the newspaper were distributed in the Seattle-King County area, but with the regular inclusion of news from Tacoma and from eastern Washington communities, such as Spokane, the paper began to develop a statewide readership, which it maintained for most of the years it was published. In 1896, Seattle-area subscriptions numbered between one hundred and four hundred; by 1898 it reached a peak of around thirty-four hundred. The paper was able to sustain this subscription level until 1902; including statewide single-copy sales, readership may have been as high as ten thousand.

The Caytons' newspaper also grew in prestige and influence along the West Coast. In the 1890s, the *Seattle Republican* was the only paper on the Pacific Coast receiving cable and telegraphic news reports directly from the *New York World* and the *New York Sun*. Other Washington State newspapers often quoted the *Seattle Republican,* and at least three turn-of-the-century newspapers in the state patterned themselves on it: the *Snohomish County Tribune,* the Spokane *Citizen,* and the Tacoma *Forum.* Several other African Americans started newspapers in Seattle in the early twentieth century, but only two of the weeklies survived. (One of them, the Seattle *Searchlight,* 1902-27, gradually became the *Seattle Republican*'s main competitor and eventually outlasted it.) Horace Sr. took pride in the paper's long-term survival. In 1909, he derived additional satisfaction for its inclusion, along with one hundred and eighty-five other black-owned newspapers, in *Efforts for Social Betterment among Negro Americans,* edited by W.E.B. Du Bois.[18]

In Seattle in the 1890s, African Americans attempted to advance the "interests of the race" through political recognition and patronage, mainly by continuing their long-standing support of the Republican Party. They focused on jobs, since overt violence and voting rights were not major issues as they were in the South. The party's record for placing few blacks in appointive offices, however, remained a problem, and Cayton repeatedly drew attention to the issue. Despite his party loyalty, Cayton never let his newspaper become a mouthpiece of the Republican Party. Only token numbers of blacks had been appointed as delegates to county and state party conventions, while most job appointments of blacks were to far less prestigious posts. In an early issue of the *Seattle Republican* the editor chided his fellow Republicans for their unwillingness to support African Americans for public office. "Let any other nationality under the sun have as many votes as the colored people in this county and state," he prodded, "and they would be willingly granted ten times the recognition that is now given the negroes." The *Post-Intelligencer* printed the excerpt from the *Republican* under the title, "A Well-Founded Complaint." In 1894 when Republicans swept the Democrats out of office in Seattle, the *Seattle Republican* lamented that despite strong black support for the Republican city ticket, their only reward was the appointment of a dogcatcher. The new black "bull catcher" was paid sixty dollars a month and had the additional duty of serving as poundmaster, although the previous dog catcher, who was white, had but one job and was paid one hundred and fifteen dollars a month.[19]

Disillusionment over their exploitation led some black Republicans to change parties or to drop out of politics altogether, but most African Americans simply swallowed their pride and remained loyal to the Republican Party. Horace Sr. used the *Seattle Republican* to voice his unflagging support of the party that had given him citizenship. The Republicans remained the lesser of political evils for the newspaperman. "It is much better," Horace Sr. concluded, "to stay with a party with a few bad men than go to a bad party with all bad men and still worse principles." He seldom missed an opportunity to throw barbs at Democrats and Populists. Following the 1894 Republican State Convention in Spokane, the *Spokesman-Review* interviewed Horace Sr. about black politics in Washington State. Cayton estimated that there were thirty-five hundred African American voters in the state, and added, "Of that number I believe there are about five pronounced Democrats and probably about ten Populists. The colored people are pretty good Republicans."[20]

Horace Sr. frequently attacked bastions of white supremacy, such as the Fraternal Order of Eagles, for excluding African Americans. Of course, not all blacks appreciated his efforts. The prominent Democrat, Dr. Samuel Burdette, regularly complained about Horace Sr. in letters to the *Post-Intelligencer,* claiming that Cayton did not express the sentiments of most blacks in Seattle. Despite occasional conflicts, usually over political issues, most blacks respected Horace Sr.'s efforts. Over the years, Horace Sr. received many tributes. In 1897, for example, a small group of businessmen gave him a silver urn as a token of their respect and gratitude for his service and contributions to the community.[21]

+⊨═⊨+

Susie and Horace Sr., although busy running a newspaper business, continued to correspond regularly with their families in Mississippi. Horace Sr. sent copies of the *Seattle Republican* to his father-in-law in Holly Springs. In January 1897, Hiram Revels wrote to Susie, "My dear darling daughter, I received your very kind and daughterly Christian letter, and must confess that it filled my heart with joy." He praised the hard work and study that had allowed her to make her mark in literary and other directions. "God," he wrote, "gave you wings of prosperity which have borne you to a higher plane—a plane of bright prospects, a plane of mental and spiritual ease and comfort."[22]

After their marriage, the Caytons lived for a few months downtown at 5th and Seneca streets, then from 1896 to 1903 rented a wood frame house at 1223 7th Avenue. On October 8, 1897, Susie gave birth to the Caytons' first child, Ruth. In 1899 Susie again gave birth; the baby boy, named Hiram after his grandfather, did not live long. Susie now combined the duties of motherhood with the typical household activities of urban middle class women of the time. Simple maintenance of the home required many hours of hard physical work; Susie, indeed, enjoyed having a few modern appliances. In 1936, looking back on the early days of marriage, she said, "Seattle was a decidedly up-to-date city forty years ago. I cooked on a glass plate two years after I married." While meeting her responsibilities as mother and maintainer of the household, Susie continued to write short stories, essays, and articles. She was one of the best-educated women of her time, yet she empathized with the great mass of black women who still lived under the shadow of the plantation—poorly educated, economically exploited, socially restricted, and politically deprived of even the vote. In June 1900 the *Post-Intelligencer* published one of her short stories, "Sallie the Egg-Woman," which reflected these views.[23]

Susie's opinions also appeared in the *Seattle Republican,* for by now she was making regular and substantial contributions to the weekly publication. In January 1900 she became associate editor and was officially listed on the paper's masthead. When Horace Sr.'s professional activities took him out of town, she ensured that the weekly edition appeared on time. On one occasion when the office was left in her hands, Susie cautioned readers, "If the paper does not come up to its usual excellence while he [Horace Sr.] is absent, the cause is apparent."[24]

The first year of the twentieth century brought a loss to the Revels family in Mississippi. Susie's older sister, Lillie, died on June 22, 1900, leaving a husband and a teenage daughter, Emma. Both Susie and Horace Sr. took the news hard. Horace Sr. tersely reported the information in the *Seattle Republican:* "The editor of this paper, who was a classmate of Miss Lillie Revels, before she was married, also sorrowfully regrets to learn of her death. She had given her entire mature life to the betterment of the colored race, and she will be greatly missed in that line."[25]

A few months after Lillie's death, Susie became pregnant again. Her sister, Dora Revels Leonard, came to help out, accompanied by her daughter, Lillie (Lillie B. Leonard). While they were staying with the Caytons, a letter arrived from Susie's father, who still grieved and felt burdened by the loneliness of the almost-empty Revels house in Holly Springs. Hiram wrote that Susie, "Mr. Cayton," and Dora were constantly in his thoughts. "My heart is roomy and filled with affection for you and them," he continued. With three of his six daughters now dead he lamented, "O Susie, how greatly we are reduced as a family... This place does not seem the cheerful home it once did." He reported that Susie's mother, though permanently enfeebled, was in better health than when Dora had left for Seattle. Hiram discussed his plan to bring the entire remaining household—Phoebe, the grandchildren Emma and Little Phoebe, plus himself—to Seattle to live with the Caytons. He intended their presence to be beneficial. "I desire to go as a helper and not as a burden," he stressed. He and Phoebe hoped to reach Seattle by November, with Emma and Little Phoebe to follow a few months later.[26]

Hiram's plan to reunite the family never reached fruition. On January 16, 1901, Hiram Revels collapsed and died while attending the annual Upper Mississippi Conference of the Methodist Episcopal Church North, held in Aberdeen, some ninety miles south of his home. Hiram's funeral during the following week in Holly Springs included Masonic honors, followed by burial in Hill Crest Cemetery. On his passing, the town newspaper observed, "He was one of the wisest, best, and noblest men of his race; dignified and gentlemanly in manner and deportment, and enjoying to the full the esteem of all classes." Horace Sr. published a half-page article in the *Seattle Republican* that highlighted his father-in-law's distinguished career as minister, college president, and U.S. Senator.[27]

Only days later, on January 25, 1901, Susie gave birth to the Caytons' second daughter, Madge. The next week Horace left for Holly Springs to help Phoebe and the rest of the family settle Hiram's estate. The seventy-four-year-old former Senator had died leaving a rather meager estate of $593.30. While Horace Sr. was in Holly Springs, his mother-in-law Phoebe died of a long-term illness. Horace Sr. cabled Susie with news of her mother's passing on February 18, hardly more than a month after her father's death. Horace Sr. returned to Seattle in early March, bringing Susie's motherless niece, Emma Houston (Lillie's daughter), to live with them. Thanks to Hiram, the Caytons were able to send Emma to a women's seminary in Portland later that year; before his death, Hiram had made arrangements to provide for his granddaughter's education. Horace Sr. also carried back the clock that Jefferson Davis had given to Senator Revels, which would remain in the Cayton home for the next four decades.[28]

Almost immediately upon his return to Seattle, Horace Sr.'s aggressive journalism thrust him into the public spotlight, and he became the focal point of a major controversy. On Friday, March 23, 1901, the *Seattle Republican* published an article that off-handedly accused the police chief of graft. "Chief Meredith proposes to run quack doctors out of business, which, perhaps is not a bad idea, but we suggest…that he likewise run grafting policemen out of business; then, perhaps, the city of Seattle would be rid of Meredith himself." W.L. Meredith was furious. Meredith arrested Horace Sr. the same night that the paper appeared and charged him with criminal libel. It was not the first time that Horace Sr. had been jailed for libel. Six years earlier, he had printed an unconfirmed story about the Sheriff of Lewis County, E.R. Carpenter, which stated that Carpenter had problems with "wine and women" and had been jailed for embezzlement. Horace Sr. soon found himself arrested and jailed in Chehalis. Released the next day, the chastised editor had a full retraction printed in the *Post-Intelligencer*.[29]

This time events turned in Horace Sr.'s favor. Sheriff Meredith's ill-considered action and high-handed methods proved his undoing. The following Monday morning edition of the *Seattle Post-Intelligencer* headlined the story:

POLICE POWER USED TO OPPRESS
Disgraceful Details of the Arrest and Incarceration of Editor Cayton

The dramatic article filled half of the front page. Meredith's deposition was printed, followed by Horace Sr.'s account of the arrest. It began, "I was all alone in my sitting room holding in my arms my 3-months-old baby, my wife and the other two children having gone down town." About nine o'clock, Cayton said, he responded to a knock at the door, letting in two police detectives. They announced that they had come to arrest him. Horace Sr. asked them to wait until his wife returned so he could leave the baby with her, but they refused. Horace Sr.'s frustration mounted. "At least take your muddy feet off my chair, and your hat off your head, and act like a gentleman," he demanded. The detective threatened, "I'll do you up in five seconds. Come on or I'll bust your head." Horace Sr. left baby Madge with a neighbor and went with the two detectives.[30]

At the jail, they locked Horace Sr. in a drafty basement cell along with a vagrant. He was not allowed to place any phone calls. Meanwhile, Susie had contacted his attorney, Judge Milo Root, and his friend and banker, James D. Hoge Jr. Bail was set at five hundred dollars. Hoge, the president of Seattle's First National Bank, offered a personal check, but the police officers were under orders from Meredith to only accept the full amount in cash. Hoge and Root were finally able to raise the cash, and at three o'clock in the morning, Horace Sr. was released. The front page of the next edition of the *Seattle Republican* carried a lengthy article on crime in the city with a large artist's drawing titled "Seattle Police Outrages."[31]

On the day of Horace Cayton Sr.'s court appearance for a preliminary hearing, the courtroom was crowded with people, both blacks and whites, of "all professions and all walks of life" declared the newspapers. One observer described the hearing as, "one of the most sensational events of its kind that ever took place in the city." Horace Sr. pleaded not guilty, and the trial was set for late May.[32]

In the two months between Horace Sr.'s arrest and trial, a storm of public outrage brewed against Meredith's tactics and the city police in general. "No occurrence in recent years in Seattle has aroused the indignation of the people so much as the treatment of Cayton," declared the *Seattle Post-Intelligencer*. The incident had occurred at a time of growing public concern over blatant gambling, prostitution, and the political corruption that allowed social vices to continue in Seattle. Progressive and reformist elements in the city took up the editor's cause. Letters expressing broad community and press support poured into the newspaper offices. The *San Juan Islander*'s reaction was typical: "It happens that Mr. Cayton belongs to the African race…but that fact furnishes no warrant for persecution." Some writers called Meredith "a disgrace to Seattle" and "unfit." While the *Post-Intelligencer* and the *Seattle Star* dramatically publicized "The Cayton

Case," other local newspapers downplayed it. *Seattle Times* editor Alden Blethen dismissed the affair as a "Republican Row," but he grudgingly concluded that the police department's treatment of Horace Cayton was "indefensible from any standpoint, and if it is permitted to go unrebuked is sure to be followed by other arbitrary abuses of power."[33]

By the time "The Cayton Case" came to trial on May 21, the public virtually had forgotten about the original incident that precipitated the trial. Now the issue was whether the city would tolerate corruption in government and wide-open vice in the streets. On the eve of the trial, the *Post-Intelligencer* declared: "Interest in what will be the testimony of... [the] witnesses and the public sentiment on the police and social evil problems of this city have made the Cayton case of such importance that its progress will be witnessed by one of the largest crowds that ever gathered in a local court room."[34]

Three days of high courtroom drama ensued. Jury selection took half of the first day. Horace Sr.'s attorneys—Judge Richard Winsor and Judge Milo Root—carefully questioned each prospective juror, asking whether the fact that Horace Cayton was black might influence their verdict. Though all of them denied having any racial prejudices, Winsor and Root challenged and had excused all those who were born south of the Mason-Dixon Line. The defense then opened, declaring flatly, "we expect to prove that the police force of this city is corrupt." The star witness for the defense was John Considine, proprietor of the People's Theater and part owner of a saloon and gambling house. Considine delivered sensational testimony against Meredith, stating that the sheriff had "levied tribute" and taken bribes from bunko men, giving them in return immunity from arrest. The prosecution tried to discredit Considine and suggested that Horace Cayton for a long time had been attacking the police department and personally bore malice against Meredith. On the final day of the trial, May 23, Horace Sr. took the witness stand in his own defense. The press noted that the defendant "had nearly been lost sight of in the fierce battle that was being waged over Meredith." Horace Sr. offered his matter-of-fact testimony: "My object was in my own feeble way to purify the moral atmosphere of the city. I had heard of all kinds of crime being rampant in the city and I deemed it my duty to show the criminals up." The defense called several more witnesses, then final arguments concluded the last court session at five o'clock. The twelve-man jury deliberated for thirteen hours but could not reach a verdict. There the case ended, and the judge discharged Horace Sr.[35]

The editor's supporters proclaimed that the lack of a verdict was a complete vindication. The prosecution had failed to prove that Horace Sr.'s charge that Meredith was a "grafter" had been false or that it had been published with malicious motives. The *Seattle Post-Intelligencer,* Cayton's champion throughout the ordeal, sought to draw the significance of the affair on a larger canvas:

> This remarkable case has brought out more facts than the *Post-Intelligencer* could ever have established; has presented public conditions to the public mind in such a way that they cannot be misunderstood. Again the question comes to the people of Seattle, what are they going to do about it [?][36]

On a different side of the issue stood those like the editor of the *Argus,* who called Cayton "gullible," but "not vicious." The unfortunate Republican editor, he condescendingly stated, had "fallen completely under the influence of John L. Wilson & Co., who have been making of him a catspaw to pull their chestnuts out of the fire." Cayton downplayed the political dimension of the whole matter. "The *Republican,*" he editorialized, "does not believe that the affair is so much of a political mix-up as a moral mix-up, and so...whatever it has done...has been done from a moral standpoint and with a view of at least strengthening what is commonly known as the church element in this city."[37]

Three days after the end of the Cayton trial, the Seattle City Council established a special committee to investigate allegations of police corruption. Chief Meredith and one of his detectives were declared "unfit" and were dismissed. At this point the episode suddenly came to a dramatic and bizarre end. Meredith went into a rage, intent on revenge. He grabbed two revolvers, a knife, and a shotgun, and went looking for the two men he deemed responsible for his ruin—witness John Considine first, and Horace Cayton Sr. next. Meredith found Considine at G.O. Guy's drugstore. They exchanged shots and seconds later Meredith lay dead on the floor. The next issue of the *Seattle Star* headlined the story as "Seattle's Horror," and editor Cayton expressed his shock at the violent events—and his relief.[38]

The year 1901, laden with so many changes for the Caytons, was pivotal. Throughout the late 1890s, the Caytons had worked to establish themselves in Seattle. By the turn of the century, they had built a firm political and financial base. The death of both of Susie's parents and Horace Sr.'s father loosened their emotional ties to Mississippi, and the young couple began to focus on building a family and business in Seattle. In the decade to come the Caytons would reach the pinnacle of their success in their adopted city.

+⪼⪻+

After 1901 Horace Sr. increasingly avoided the limelight, preferring to work behind the scenes as what he called "a quasi-public personage." The *Seattle Republican*'s editor once described this political tactic, saying, "If a Negro feels that he can hold his own among white campaigners and wants to play the game, though without a Negro constituency, he should 'back his ears and pitch in.' If he gets knocked down, never admit it was on account of his color and never sulk in his tent." Though reluctant to admit color as the reason for "getting knocked down," Horace conceded that because of white prejudice—in the party and the electorate at large—he knew very well that he "would not be the recipient of any of the fat jobs in the state." Under the circumstances, Horace Sr.'s achievements were remarkable, even though they fell short of both his abilities and expectations. As he observed, the "nigger objection" remained for his opponents a convenient and powerful weapon.[39]

The newspaper and publishing business brought financial success to the Caytons. At the peak of the *Seattle Republican*'s circulation, Horace Sr.'s monthly income reached a high of six hundred dollars a month—a significant amount for the times. When the paper was in what Horace Sr. called, "a flourishing state and making considerable money," he employed a white female stenographer. Horace Sr.'s commercial printing shop, which ran in conjunction with the *Seattle Republican,* contracted for business cards and various other jobs, including campaign literature. In 1905, the shop became the official printer for the Republican-dominated Ninth Legislature. The result was proudly presented to the public as *Cayton's Legislative Manual of Washington, 1905*. The fifty-six-page volume contained sketches of the state legislative, executive, and judicial membership, plus brief descriptions of the counties and the state's industry and population.

In 1908 he published another booklet, *Cayton's Campaign Compendium*. This purely partisan volume contained biographical sketches, with full-page pictures of Republicans seeking nomination for the major state offices and the national presidency. It also included the state's Primary Election Law. Horace Sr. sent a copy to President Theodore Roosevelt, who replied with a letter expressing his thanks and congratulations.[40]

Cayton's print shop also produced special issues of the *Seattle Republican* in a slick magazine format. These "special editions," which appeared periodically from 1903 to 1909, featured short biographical descriptions and photographs of prominent Seattle businessmen, bankers, lawyers, and government officials. The first special edition focused on white community leaders. But in 1907, Horace Sr. shifted recognition to black leaders with an edition titled "Northwest Negro Prosperity Number." John and Ella Ryan, publishers of the Tacoma *Forum,* congratulated Cayton on the impressive work, which, they said, "will serve as a reminder to those who have treated the progress of the Negro lightly." Two years later, the even larger "Northwest Negro Progress Number of 1909," mirrored his own success and that of other Seattle blacks. The seventy-eight-page issue featured extensive sketches and photos of Seattle's leading African Americans and included pictures of four of the Cayton children, born between 1897 and 1907.[41]

+≒≑≓+

In 1903 the Caytons bought a beautiful two-story home with a carriage house on Capitol Hill where they lived for the next six years. The home, located in one of the city's most affluent residential areas with white neighbors such as the Denny family, was among the finest owned by any blacks or most whites in Seattle. The house and lot, valued at ten thousand dollars in 1906, was one of only eleven homes in the five-thousand to thirty-thousand dollar range of properties owned by African Americans.

On April 12, 1903, Susie gave birth to a son, Horace Jr. Four years later, on June 5, 1907, she bore another son, Hiram Revels Cayton, named for her father. (In first or second grade, young Hiram dropped his first name and began using his middle name.) Susie's niece, Emma Houston (Lillie's daughter) lived with them during this period. The household also included a Japanese servant named Nish and, at one time, a Swedish maid.[42]

The Caytons belonged to the small black middle class in the better-paid service trades and the professions. Most black businesses at the time, like the Caytons', were family or individual enterprises operating on a small scale and attaining modest success. Not until the turn of the century had businesses emerged that could be supported almost wholly by the modestly growing African American community. Earlier, local enterprises such as the Caytons' newspaper or Cragwell's two hotel barbershops were dependent upon white clientele.[43]

One of the civic activities to which Horace Sr. and Susie devoted themselves was the "Sunday Forum." Though Horace Sr. earlier had opposed the formation of separate all-black business organizations, by 1906 times were changing and his thinking shifted. He became a strong proponent of the Sunday Forum, reporting to his readers that it had been formed because of "a sad lack of unanimity among the Negroes in this city, in the struggle for the goal of success." Employment discrimination was a prime concern. One company, Sunset Telephone and Telegraph, to which African Americans paid some five thousand dollars a year for phone rentals, had "never given a single colored man or woman a day's employment." But, a group like the Sunday Forum could demand that the company provide some jobs, "or their patronage will be withdrawn." The forum received Susie's enthusiastic support. How "exceedingly pleasant" it was, she wrote, "to see the leading men of the city coming into this hall to consult together for the good of the race."[44]

The forum met twice a month from 1906 through 1910, fulfilling its goals of providing a place for exchanging ideas and developing "united thought and prayer" on topics of concern to the African American community. At the meeting on March 11, 1906, I.F. Norris, George W. Turner, T.C. Collins, J. Edward Hawkins, and Susie Revels Cayton addressed the question, "Does the Negro better his condition by coming West?" Other Sunday Forum topics included whether blacks should enter the U.S. Army and serve under white officers, and how to organize a boycott against Frederick and Nelson's department store in response to their refusal to serve a black woman in the store's café.[45]

Susie contributed frequently to the Sunday Forum. One afternoon she spoke on "Our Heroic Women," and another time on "The Negro's Handicap: An Excuse or a Spur." In the latter talk, Susie, ever with a positive emphasis, argued that a "handicap" was a spur that brought out the "real good" in blacks, who were rapidly developing in their citizenship, property accumulation, and business acumen. She also participated in literary and musical programs at the St. Paul Methodist Episcopal Church on Madison Street, which Horace Sr. praised for its inclusion of all races. In addition, Susie became a founding member of the Dorcas Charity Club, serving on the executive committee and in 1908 as president, and occasionally entertaining the club in her home.[46]

Horace Sr. and Susie played prominent roles in other African American civic activities. Horace Sr. often took a leading role in the forum-sponsored annual celebrations on January 1 in honor of the Emancipation Proclamation, sometimes as chairman of the Arrangements Committee and other times as a speaker. In 1907 when he was president of the Sunday Forum, his opening speech at the celebration described the present status of the black race and paid tribute to Abraham Lincoln and the Union Army. At the 1908 celebration, held at the Afro-American Citizens Hall, he delivered the final address of the evening on "The Negro as a Citizen." In the next issue of the *Seattle Republican* he proudly reported that the program, which included various vocal and musical selections, upon closing "was voted one of the best ever held in the city under the auspices of Afro-Americans." The anniversary festivities in 1909 were held at the YMCA auditorium, and Horace Sr. spoke on the progress of blacks since slavery days.[47]

Susie continued as associate editor of the *Seattle Republican,* making a significant contribution that often went recognized. In July 1909, however, the *Seattle Times* paid a modest but notable tribute to the Caytons, emphasizing that not a single edition had been missed in the fifteen years since the *Seattle Republican* appeared, to fill "a long felt want," and that its success was partially due to Susie's contribution. In the next issue of the *Seattle Republican,* the editor commented on the piece in a front page article titled "Good Woman's Helping Hand," accompanied by Susie's photo. The newspaper's success, Horace Sr. said, was sometimes "wholly due" to her efforts. In a rare moment of public sentiment about his personal life, he continued in glowing terms:

> [B]less her heart, she has for all these years stood like a stone wall by our side and some times when the battle for existence was so severe that to live through it seemed more than human, she never wavered. [The] woman, the associate hereof and likewise life partner of the editor, has more than borne her part. The woman who works on and on amid privations not only for herself but for her little ones and yet always sees victory ahead is the woman that not only makes husbands men in the true sense of the word, but who makes the men and women of tomorrow. The woman who can jot down a note or an article while the baby is soothed to sleep or while the dinner cooks and thereby hold up her end, and at the same time always having a stock of love and tenderness for the discouraged man is the woman that rules the world. All honor is due to such women.[48]

Horace Sr. distributed the 1909 special edition of the *Seattle Republican* free to blacks visiting the Alaska-Yukon-Pacific Exposition. From June 1 to October 16, 1909, this grand promotional fair sponsored by Seattle developers attracted 3.7 million visitors to a lavish site on what later became the University of Washington campus. Horace Sr. and Susie in early June opened "The Cayton House," at 2107 E. James Street, to accommodate fair visitors, "thinking that a majority of Afro-Americans would prefer to stop with people of their own class…and spend a week or so in Seattle, and yet not pay exorbitant prices."[49]

For much of his publishing career, Horace Sr. had admired Booker T. Washington, whose moderate approach to race relations appealed to many white political and civic leaders. Cayton once called Washington "the world's educator." He was not uncritical of the man from Tuskegee, however, admitting that Washington too often "truckled to white sentiment." Yet, when most black editors criticized Washington, Horace Sr. would shake his head, saying, "What strange freaks come over an oppressed people." The important thing to Horace Sr. was that Washington's "every act and every move seems to have been done with no other purpose than the gaining of a new foothold for the black man." Horace Sr. concluded that African Americans could choose one of only two paths to success: either they could "pick up bag and baggage and go to some other country," or they could stay and follow the Washington course, "use diplomacy—that is, make haste slowly." Horace Sr. had, in some fashion, done both: he had picked up and left the inhospitable state of Mississippi; and in Seattle he had worked diligently to improve conditions for blacks. Though he gradually grew more radical as race relations deteriorated, diplomacy seemed to him to provide the best leverage in Seattle business and political circles.[50]

Part of the difficulty between the races, to Horace Sr.'s way of thinking, lay in the fact that many whites simply had no exposure to the "new Negro" and assumed that blacks were under-educated and ignorant. However, if blacks would avail themselves of every opportunity to show whites that they were equally educated and competitive, then whites would form different opinions. Horace Sr. counseled African Americans to ignore the all-too-frequent snubs of ignorant whites, and to remember that only the "ill-bred brute" shows himself thus; simply "take no notice of such would-be insults." The glorious reward of this approach would benefit all blacks: "To succeed among persons who think you without capacity to succeed…is a laurel won that will be of a hundred fold more benefit to the Negro race."[51]

Subscriptions and advertising for the *Seattle Republican* dwindled after 1908, and Horace Sr. and Susie Cayton's financial status and social position began to slip. In 1909 they lost their home on Capitol Hill. Finally, subscriptions fell so low that Horace Sr. could no longer support the paper. In 1913 the *Seattle Republican* closed its doors forever.

What caused the reversal in the Caytons' fortune? The economic, political, and social forces that had aided Horace Sr. and Susie's rise in Seattle had changed and now contributed to their decline. First, the panic of 1907 and the business depression that followed dealt a severe blow to the Northwest economy and adversely affected Horace Sr.'s finances. He had made risky investments in suburban property, expecting a real estate boom that never materialized. Subscriptions for the newspaper had leveled off at twenty-five hundred between 1903 and 1908. But in 1909, they fell by one-third to seventeen-hundred and fifty. The figure dropped steadily by one hundred or more each year thereafter.[52]

Political forces also undermined the *Seattle Republican* and its outspoken editor. Rumors had surfaced, back in 1901, that Horace Cayton had received special treatment. The *Seattle Standard* claimed that the Cayton paper was "getting right under the plum tree and the land and county offices and shaking the fruit right into its hat." The editor of the *Northwest Republican,* published in Blaine, sniped, "This rascal, in exchange for the patronage of the federal land office and such prerequisites as could be thrown to him by 'the gang,' has slandered every man in public life in this state not in good odor with...John L. Wilson."[53]

Even Horace Sr.'s political connections worked to his disadvantage during this period. Horace Sr., indeed, had been one of Wilson's close allies since 1897. Wilson was one of the Republican Party's leading personalities, serving in the U.S. House of Representatives,1889-95, and in the U.S. Senate, 1895-99. To a large degree, Horace Sr.'s fortunes were tied to Wilson and other white friends in the Republican Party. In 1899 Wilson had purchased the *Post-Intelligencer* and used the paper to continue to align himself with large business interests and control Republican state conventions. By the time he sold his interest in 1910, Wilson's influence had declined; he had not won an election since 1900, and would fail again in his last bid for office in 1910. Wilson was one of many political bosses who lost much of their old manipulative power over the party as a result of reform measures—including the direct election of senators and direct primaries—enacted in 1907.

An indication of the changing times for Horace Sr. surfaced in June 1906, when he attempted to secure a printing contract for proposed city charter changes, as he had done in 1896. The effort failed, and Horace Sr. drew public ridicule. The *Seattle Star*'s headline gloated, "Mayor to Spoil Cayton's Graft." In 1908 Cayton had been appointed to the Republican

State Central Committee, but by December 1909 publicly admitted that he now was "barred out of the political game." Nevertheless, in the following year he entered a race for the state senate but withdrew before the primary. The year 1910 also marked the last time that Horace Cayton Sr. sat on the Republican State Central Committee. He never again served in a county or state Republican convention as a delegate.[54]

The fate of the *Seattle Republican* also was tied in part to the fate of the Republican Party in general. In 1912, the year before the newspaper failed, the Republican State Convention in Aberdeen ruptured over the selection of delegates to choose a presidential nominee. The bitter fight between pro-Roosevelt and pro-Taft forces left the Republicans thoroughly demoralized, and in the general elections that followed they took a beating as the Democrats captured the state governorship, in addition to the national presidency. Another element in the adverse political situation confronting Horace Sr. was the rising influence locally of the lily-white faction of the Republican party during President Theodore Roosevelt's term (1905-1909) and especially under President Howard Taft (1909-1913). Complications had arisen earlier, too, when Horace Sr. attacked the Seattle Police Department for their refusal to put even one African American on the force.[55]

One of the most important factors in the Caytons' fall was a general deterioration of white-black relations in the United States in the early years of the twentieth century. As the migration of blacks to the North and West increased, hostility toward them grew. Signs of this deterioration in race relations appeared in the pages of the *Seattle Republican*. Horace Sr. promoted Dr. Samuel Burdette's 1900 anti-lynching booklet that included a list of lynching victims in the United States over the previous twenty years. Race riots became frequent and widespread in many parts of the country. A 1908 riot in Springfield, Illinois, was especially violent, and it sent shock waves across the nation. It began when a white woman accused a black man of raping her, and soon a white mob went on a rampage. Several nights of violence resulted in the lynching of two black men, the death of four whites, the burning of several buildings, and injury to some seventy people before five thousand state militia restored order to the city. The currents of unrest across the nation started to affect Seattle, which was not as insulated from racial conflict as it had been several decades earlier.

By 1910 Seattle was the fastest-growing city in the Northwest, with a population soaring to two hundred and thirty-five thousand. The city was strikingly different from the frontier town it had been in 1894 when the *Seattle Republican* was founded. Between 1900 and 1910, Seattle had become less homogeneous. The number of African Americans in the city rose from just over four hundred to twenty-three hundred—a dramatic five-fold increase.

As more African Americans moved to Seattle and white hostility grew, the *Seattle Republican* appealed less and less to each group. It offered too little news about blacks to attract subscriptions from their growing numbers. Moreover, after 1902, the *Searchlight,* a weekly newspaper published specifically for the city's African American community, proved a stiff competitor for subscriptions. At the same time, the *Seattle Republican* contained too much "colored" news, and less and less news about general state and local political issues, to retain the interest of its white Republican readers. In an article titled, "Stop Your Paper," Horace Sr. lamented this state of affairs and sighed, "So between the two, the financier has the devil's own time to keep things going."[56]

One of Horace Sr.'s strengths had been his ability to bridge the gap between the white and black communities by focusing on shared concerns within the Republican Party. Now the Cayton newspaper's politics were considered too Republican by some whites and "too black" for most. This, combined with Horace's outspoken style, regularly prompted racist remarks and other derogatory comments in the columns of his white counterparts.

White-owned publications like the *Argus* and *Olympia Chronicle* were reprinting more and more racist articles from Southern newspapers about lynchings of blacks for raping white women. Horace Sr. unflaggingly and bitterly denounced these reports. Although his public outrage at lynchings usually drew swift response, Horace Sr.'s defense of those accused of raping white women attracted the most emotional lightning. On one occasion he asserted that the women had been "in every instance willing subjects" and had cried rape to "shield their own crime" when their deviltry was detected. Following vicious race riots in Atlanta in 1906, Horace Sr. published a full-page article titled "What of the Poor Black Woman?" condemning the white Southerner's double standards:

> The world seldom if ever gets the black man's side of the story… [T]he white men of the South do not practice just what they preach. How many black mothers' and fathers' hearts have been made to bleed over the downfall of their daughters to satisfy the criminal lusts of white men.[57]

Much of Seattle's white press reacted angrily to Horace Sr.'s attacks on "sacred" white American womanhood. They attacked him with racial slurs, personal insults, and political innuendo. The editor of the *Argus,* one of the most racist of Horace's critics, called him "a Negro nuisance…a combination of asinine imbecility and negro stupidity," and a "nigger" who had been "led on by a crowd of white men as low and mean as himself… until he has come to think that he is something more than a cheap negro, and to believe that 'ole Uncle Abe' made him the equal of respectable people." The long-time editor of the *Seattle Times,* Colonel Alden Blethen, regularly hurled a host of insults at his counterpart at the *Seattle Republican.* And the editor of the *Sun,* a Democratic paper, suggested, "It is often said that 'the only good Indian is a dead one.' The same thing could be said of the Negro, if they were all of the Cayton stripe." Another editor called Horace Sr. "Sambo Cayton," and yet another labeled him as one of John L. Wilson's "political slaves," and "a journalistic hambone polisher."[58]

After 1905 the downward spiral of race relations accelerated, heightening anxieties in black communities across the nation. Seattle's African American community expressed its concerns at the Sunday Forums, and sometimes prompted the forum to action. Such was the case after a riot in 1906 in Brownsville, Texas, that involved three companies of a black regiment. A white investigator of the incident issued a report exonerating whites in Brownsville and putting full blame on the blacks involved. President Roosevelt issued dishonorable discharges to not only the three African American companies involved, but the full battalion. This prompted the Sunday Forum to send a strongly worded petition to Washington Congressmen, though it found no sympathetic ear.[59]

With growing frequency the *Seattle Republican* carried front-page news and commentary on lynchings and riots in the South. Headlines such as "Lynch the Lynchers," and "Tennessee Continues to Kill People" brought this slur from the *Goldendale Sentinel's* editor: "We used to think that the 'Seattle Republican' was published by some ambitious legislator, but recently we have come to the conclusion that it is conducted by some astute 'cullud' man." Horace Sr. retorted that the editor's "suspicions were aroused not because the editorial work of the *Seattle Republican* was any less clever than it had been, but because it recently defended the rights of the oppressed Negroes in the United States."[60]

+≡+

The year 1909 marked the turning point for the *Seattle Republican*. Horace Sr. was fifty years old and nearly a half-century removed from slavery. Yet, the racial prejudice that had linked his chains in childhood, and which he thought he had left behind in Mississippi, found him in Seattle. In April 1909 a white realtor went to court charging that a black family living in an "exclusive community" on Capitol Hill had caused the real estate values to depreciate. Although the defendants were not named, it is likely that the homeowners were the Caytons. By September the Caytons had lost their Capitol Hill home and moved to "The Cayton" rooming house at 2107 E. James St., in an interracial middle-class neighborhood, where they lived until early 1913.[61]

The Caytons' experience reflected a broader social pattern. In the Northwest, the status of African Americans had reached a peak around 1910. Up to then, places of residence had not been confined to segregated areas, and occupations were not strictly constrained to stereotypical "colored people's jobs." After 1910, as the color line began to be drawn ever more sharply, restrictive covenants appeared, limiting land ownership only to whites in certain neighborhoods. Attempts to pass anti-interracial marriage laws in several successive sessions of the state legislature was another indication that African Americans' rights were being eroded, as Seattle's generally tolerant attitude toward blacks changed to animosity.

In 1910 and 1911, more articles and comments on racial conflict and lynchings appeared in the Cayton newspaper. About the same time, Horace Sr. got into an altercation with a political enemy and struck the man, who happened to be white. Horace Sr. returned from downtown to find that Susie had heard about the incident. Together, they hid with the children in the basement of their locked and unlit home. Horace Sr. merely said to Susie, "You can take them out of Mississippi, but you can't take Mississippi out of them."

In August 1912, Cayton filed a fifteen-thousand-dollar lawsuit against H.L. Wilson, owner of the Epler Cafeteria, who had refused to serve Horace. From this incident came a further unpleasant turn of events. As the case unfolded over the winter of 1912 and spring of 1913, court proceedings brought out the fact that Horace Sr. had been imprisoned in Kansas. Few were impressed by the details of Horace Sr.'s eventual exoneration and pardon in Kansas. The scandalous revelation damaged Cayton's reputation in the wider black and white communities, a setback from which he never completely recovered.

Subscriptions declined and advertisers canceled their business with the Cayton newspaper and printing company. Horace Sr. cut annual subscription rates from three to two dollars, but rather than attracting new readers, it merely reduced the paper's revenues. The *Seattle Republican* now was a shell of what it had been just a few years earlier. By the end of 1912, in the midst of Horace Sr.'s highly publicized court case, the *Republican* had shrunk to four pages and carried only a few ads for such companies as the Bon Marche and Rainier Beer. Advertising virtually disappeared in the early months of 1913. (One of the few remaining ads was for "the Cayton House," where the family was then living.) In April, Horace Sr. started spreading the word that he intended to sell the newspaper and devote his energies to the boarding house. This prompted Ella Ryan of the Tacoma *Forum* to note, "If Cayton disappears from the journalistic field, the cause will have lost one of its brightest and most scintillating writers." In early May, after a short trial without jury, Judge J. Ronald ruled that Cayton had not been deprived of his civil rights and dismissed the suit against the cafeteria.[62]

For Horace Sr., as for many African Americans during this period, life seemed to have become a losing struggle. As he was to write several years later, "From a colored man's standpoint in the United States life is just one damn thing after the other." While her husband struggled to keep the newspaper afloat, Susie continued as associate editor, while balancing her efforts with maintaining the Cayton household. She had long since reduced expenses, having let go the Japanese servant, the housekeeper, and the horse and carriage when the family moved from Capitol Hill in 1909. Gradually, the vestiges of middle class Victorian life slipped away. The Caytons managed to keep, for now, the baby grand piano on which the children were beginning to take lessons. Susie watched over the children's growth and education. In 1913 Ruth was a sixteen-year old student in her second year at Garfield High School. Madge, age twelve, was in the sixth grade, ten-year-old Horace Jr. was in the fourth grade, and the youngest, Revels, was in the first grade.[63]

Horace Sr. had reached his fifty-fourth year and his newspaper its nineteenth. In early March, the middle-aged editor, sensing coming changes and the imminent passing of the paper, reflected:

"God bless our home," sighs him on whose head the weight of fifty odd seasons press heavily and whose tingling fingers vainly search the recesses of an empty pocket for a penny for bread. He thoughtfully runs over the past and thinks, what might have been, and from the past and the present he madly plunges into the future and exclaims, what will it be? The man fifty past with neither a present nor a future is like unto a ship in mid ocean without sail or rudder, it may drift to land, but the odds are decidedly against it... [W]e encourage you not to lose hope, for with hope gone all is lost... Oh for a peace of mind in the sunset of life that will gently lead us from the scenes of life's fitful fevers, through the valley and shadow of death to the fields of everlasting life.[64]

Amid the public embarrassment of his court battles and the changing social relations in Seattle that left no middle ground for a biracial newspaper, the end of the *Seattle Republican* was at hand. Horace Sr. and Susie issued the last edition on May 13, 1913. An era ended, not only for the Cayton family, but for Seattle.

CHAPTER 4

Life on the Horns

The Parents—Work and Family, 1914–1932

AFTER 1913, HORACE CAYTON devoted great energy to earning a living, reviving his newspaper business, and participating in various political and business activities in the community. As disappointments in the outside world mounted, the focus of his life turned increasingly toward home. Horace and Susie held fast to their old dreams, while facing the hardships of financial difficulties and political frustration. It was a formative and occasionally turbulent time. These were hard years for raising children. The hostile racial climate made a distinct and long-lasting impact. Still, it's important not to over-emphasize the Caytons' abilities to adapt and endure. In the words of Ralph Ellison, "Men have made a way of life in caves and upon cliffs, why cannot Negroes have made a life upon the horns of the white man's dilemma?"[1]

Following the failure of the *Seattle Republican* in 1913, Horace Sr. found himself struggling to provide for his wife and the six children in the household. He opened a restaurant at the foot of Yesler Way, but, his son Revels later recalled, "it proved a real flop." For a brief time, Horace Sr. earned a little money writing articles for the *Searchlight*. The family was then living at The Laurel, an apartment house they owned at 303 22nd Avenue South. When they could no longer afford a janitor, Horace Sr. himself took to tending the furnace and doing the maintenance work on the twenty-three room apartment house.[2]

In 1918, Horace Sr. would look back on the dramatic changes he had experienced, musing, "[O]n the whole he thought himself some man among men, and there were others of a like mind. The sun, however, does not shine on one man's door all the day, and he suffered heavy financial reverses and to such an extent that even the necessities of life were quite a problem for him to solve."[3]

Loss of the respect and prestige that the Caytons once enjoyed in the white community accompanied their financial losses. Horace Sr. later

recounted how he appealed for a position to the state auditor, an old political friend with whom he had worked for years building the Republican
political machine:

> This public official…very deliberately replied: "I know of no man in
> the state that I would favor more readily than yourself, but I have noth-
> ing to give you except a position I will not offer you…" Despite hun-
> dreds of places at his and his friends' disposal a janitor's job was by
> innuendo offered, and if it worked all was well; if not, then the other
> places were all taken. Yes, it's discouraging, if one will be discouraged,
> but Horace Roscoe Cayton is made of sterner stuff and will die fighting.[4]

Indeed, Horace Sr. was a fighter, and gradually he recovered from the
1913 setback. Three years after the closing of the *Seattle Republican,* Horace
Sr. had achieved enough financial stability to start another paper. *Cayton's
Weekly* reflected Cayton's changed circumstances and differed in two major respects from the *Seattle Republican*: first, it was a publication of general information; second, it was directed solely toward Seattle's African
American community. Otherwise, Cayton attempted to maintain much
the same style and emphasis. He was publishing the paper, he declared, "In
the interest of equal rights and equal justice to all men and for 'all men
up.'" Although he touted the newspaper as being "Regular, Reliable, Republican, Readable," it lacked the energy and verve of its predecessor.[5]

Horace Sr. used *Cayton's Weekly* to publicize black accomplishments
and heroes. The weekly contained general news items and events of interest about blacks from across the country, and, of course, Cayton's own
pithy observations on national and local politics. Even more so than its
predecessor, *Cayton's Weekly* presented the editor's personal expressions with
more commentary and opinions, and less hard news. During World War I,
for example, instead of chronicling details of the war's military progress,
Horace Sr. offered his perspectives on the broader significance of events.
He bitterly noted the irony of America claiming to be fighting a war "to
make the world safe for democracy," yet perpetuating such undemocratic
practices as segregation and discrimination against blacks in the United
States. "Charity begins at home," Cayton reminded whites: "The black
man will fight, and fight like hell to make the world safe for democracy if
the 'Huns' of the southern states will stop shooting, lynching and burning
at the stake almost daily for petty offenses colored men and boys, and stop
the daily 'outrages' made against the black women of the southland." Our
highly touted civilization, Cayton concluded, "is but savagery veneered."[6]

The political spirit in *Cayton's Weekly*, however, seemed muted. Naturally, Horace Sr.'s political humor remained anti-Democratic: "An ex-Union soldier once drew an enormous pension for total mental and physical disability and was subsequently elected to Congress on the Democratic ticket." But to a community fixated on the World War, Cayton's Civil War frame of reference must have seemed far removed, if not irrelevant. Although editor Cayton would never admit to any sympathy for the Democratic Party, especially its southern wing, he more often expressed disenchantment with failings in the Republican Party. [7]

Horace Sr. focused his political activities in the King County Colored Republican Club, which he helped lead for over fifteen years. Cayton and a handful of others established the club in 1915 (absorbing in the process the Negro Betterment League), and he served as the club's first president. As advocates for black Republicans in particular, and the African American community in general, club representatives regularly attended Republican Party gatherings and sought to raise the political standing of blacks in the county. Two years after the club's founding, Horace Sr. proudly proclaimed in *Cayton's Weekly*, "The Club has created a better understanding with certain persons in office who were apparently hostile to the Negroes and is now working harmoniously with them. It took a prominent part in defeating a discriminatory bill introduced in the last legislature, and has been instrumental in securing positions for Negroes in the state."[8]

Over the next few years, Horace Sr. and other Republican club members doggedly tried to increase the black community's political influence. In 1923, when Cayton was serving as president as well as publicist for the group, he counted the club's membership at five hundred, and noted that the organization had succeeded in increasing black employment in the county government by "one deputy assessor, one extra helper in the treasurer's office, and five janitors…with the promise of others in 1923." Cayton viewed such accomplishments with pride, but it fell far short of the group's original aspirations.[9]

Horace Sr. also hoped to promote the African American community financially by helping to form a business self-help organization. Around the time that the King County Colored Republican Club was established, a core group of businessmen, including Cayton, launched a Seattle Chapter of the National Negro Business Men's League, which Booker T. Washington had founded in Boston in 1900 to stimulate black business enterprises. "Trying to get our share by individual efforts is completely out of the question," Horace Sr. told *Weekly* readers. But a strong, organized group such as the league, he felt, could encourage "the enterprising colored man" to get involved in business instead of labor.[10]

Thereafter, promoting the business interests of the African American community occupied much of Horace Sr.'s time. In August 1917 he released a special "Northwest Prosperity Number" of *Cayton's Weekly* that presented the accomplishments and profiles of the region's black population, as he had done earlier in special *Seattle Republican* editions. He still touted opportunity in Seattle. "No city in all the U.S. has a more flattering future," he proclaimed. The front page showed a sketch of downtown Seattle, with the Smith Tower dominating the skyline and a ship, identified as "Prosperity," steaming into Elliot Bay. The *Portland Advocate* praised the special edition, of which "every man, woman, and child in the state of Washington should be proud." A political ally, Senator Wesley Jones, sent congratulations from Washington, D.C., applauding Cayton's "ability" and "enterprise." One of the editor's political cronies from the early days, former mayor Byron Phelps, took the occasion to tell Cayton, "In spite of your general cussedness you have done the community a little bit of good."[11]

Cayton used the occasion of publishing the "Northwest Prosperity Number" to promote the National Negro Business Men's League. In September, at the organization's first public meeting, Horace Sr. spoke on "The Benefits Derived from the Combination of Labor and Capital." He sounded a familiar note, telling the gathering, "It is the duty of each and every one of us to see to it that our brethren in the South be made acquainted with the conditions out here, with the view of inducing many of them to come West and enjoy the prosperity that prevails in this section." Despite the positive message, Horace Sr. experienced little prosperity himself. At two dollars for a yearly subscription, the *Weekly* provided only a meager income for the Caytons. Just two months earlier, the hard-pressed editor had told readers, "No, the editor of *Cayton's Weekly* is not earning $300 a month just now, and that amount would look very much like the side of a mountain peak to him."[12]

+═══+

In the late 1910s, Seattle's African American community remained small and restricted to the periphery of the city's political, economic, and social life. In 1917 Seattle's total population reached an estimated 280,000, yet census figures in 1920 showed only 2,894 blacks living in the city (an increase of just 600 over the previous decade). Although the number of African Americans would increase to 3,303 in 1930, and 3,789 in 1940, they remained about 1 percent of the city's population. A significant increase in the black population would not come until World War II.[13]

After the failure of the *Seattle Republican* in 1913, Horace Sr. turned away from the philosophy of Booker T. Washington. Increasingly, he adopted the approach of W.E.B. Du Bois, stressing political action and agitation in the community. This he combined with consistent efforts to promote civic self-improvement organizations and middle-class virtues. In the face of systematic discrimination, and his own economic and political frustrations, he raised a strident voice of protest.

With such diminutive numbers of African Americans in the city's population, it is remarkable that Seattle's branch of the National Association for the Advancement of Colored People (NAACP) reported three hundred and fifty members by 1920. Horace Sr. had been involved with the Seattle NAACP from its inception, only four months after the *Seattle Republican* had closed its doors. The Seattle branch had been organized in 1913 as a response to the increasingly hostile racial climate. A mass meeting was held September 5, 1913, to protest segregation in U.S. government agencies, and, within two months, the protestors had organized a local branch of the NAACP. The first official activity for the Seattle chapter was to sponsor an Emancipation Proclamation anniversary celebration. Horace Sr. was elected chairman of the NAACP press committee, and in later years he served on the executive committee.

As community-based activist groups across the country, the local NAACP branches worked to implement a national program that included the abolition of forced segregation, enforcement of the Fourteenth and Fifteenth Amendments to the Constitution, equal educational opportunities for black and white children, and broadened economic opportunities. Under W.E.B. Du Bois, the head of national publicity and research, the NAACP launched the magazine *Crisis,* which also led the campaign against mob rule and lynching.[14]

Violence against African Americans continued to increase across the nation after 1915, the year that a new Ku Klux Klan organized in Georgia. *Cayton's Weekly* monitored the gradual deterioration of race relations in the United States. Horace Sr. soberly reported the count of "Lynchings for 1919," and regularly editorialized on atrocities suffered at the hands of white mobs. He also reported on racist incidents closer to home. In August 1918, NAACP Seattle branch president Samuel H. Stone and executive committee member Horace Sr. led a protest against the commander of Camp Lewis (now Fort Lewis), who had issued an order for segregated housing quarters for black soldiers. The storm of outrage from the small but vocal African American community proved sufficient to change the commander's mind. The very next week, Cayton reported with restrained satisfaction that the order had been rescinded.[15]

Such incidents were becoming all too common in Seattle. During and following World War I, segregation lines were drawn more and more sharply. Restrictive covenants limited home ownership in certain areas to whites, which contributed to a concentration of African American families and a few businesses in the Madison Hill area. Job opportunities, always limited, further diminished and became almost strictly confined to personal and domestic services. Many hotels, movie theaters, and restaurants that previously had served blacks now often refused to do so. In December 1917, editor Cayton was refused service in a cafe that had formerly accommodated him. He promptly filed suit against the owner, but the judge dismissed the case. Horace Sr. told readers that the court had in effect "ruled that a colored man had no rights that the restaurant keeper need respect." Thereafter, it was impossible for blacks, he reported, "to get a meal in any of the uptown restaurants and cafes, owing to the prejudice to color."[16]

In the *Weekly,* Cayton spoke more often of his disenchantment with the Republican Party. At the opening of the 1918 election year, he warned Republicans that unless the party gave greater recognition to its African American constituency, he would urge voters to support "that man or men who will agree to recognize them the same as they do all other classes of voters…whether the nominee is allied with the Republican, Democratic, or Damphool party."[17]

Horace Sr. decided to become a candidate for political office, filing as one of six Republicans seeking the party's nomination for state representative from the 43rd District. He announced his candidacy in the *Weekly* prior to the primary:

> No one who has filed for the legislature in King County is more thoroughly conversant with the workings of legislative bodies than is Horace R. Cayton, who has filed for the nomination of representative from the 43rd legislative district, he having attended every session of the Washington legislature since 1893 and was at all times in close touch with the party machinery. If Mr. Cayton is nominated and elected he will be able to begin work the first day of the session and continue to the very last. Mr. Cayton has published a paper in Seattle since 1892 and has a wide acquaintance with the leading political spirits of the state. Though always an ardent Republican yet in the primaries he has always been very independent and only supported men who seem to him best fitted

for the positions. He is a heavy taxpayer and owns an apartment house located at 303 22nd South where he and his family reside. He is in full sympathy with the President's war aims.[18]

One of Horace Sr.'s prominent political supporters was Senator Wesley Jones, a Republican who served in the U.S. Senate from 1909 to 1932. At Horace's invitation, Jones was the featured speaker at Seattle's Emancipation Celebration in 1914. When *Cayton's Weekly* first began rolling off the presses, Jones wrote to Cayton and wished him "the greatest of success." The senator, however, had a paternalistic attitude toward African Americans. While he considered Horace Sr. "one of the leading colored men" in Seattle and "a fine man," Jones wrote to one associate that Horace Sr. was "making something out of himself."[19]

Cayton's candidacy was short-lived. The vote tally in the primary election revealed Cayton trailing the other five candidates. With only partial results in, the *Seattle Times* reported that Horace Sr. had received 111 out of 1,899 votes cast.[20]

+≈≈+

The year 1919 brought another series of difficult and dramatic changes for the Caytons. It began with Horace Sr., now facing his sixtieth birthday, publicly taking a long, nostalgic look back at his life. The first three issues of *Cayton's Weekly* in January carried lengthy "Embarrassing Moments" reminiscences about his early years in Mississippi and Seattle. In May, he penned an even more personal piece. It is one of the most remarkable articles Horace Cayton Sr.—usually a reserved man—ever published. It is both a public statement of despair and a loving tribute to his wife, Susie.

WAS IT A DREAM

In a state of utter despair, I, Horace R. Cayton, stood on the banks of Lake Washington and gazed into the deep, dark water below, which never gives up its dead, and just as I had reached the conclusion that life was not worth living and that I would bury my sorrows with my body in the silent waters below, a woman, comely in form, but fearful in frown, appeared on the scene and administered unto me a tongue lashing that made even the cold still waters of the lake sit up and take notice. I pulled myself together and forgot my determination to find that peace that passeth all understanding and I said to myself, I will not die, but I will strive to live and capture the affections of that woman because the woman single-handed and alone that will beard the lion in his den and tell him things as she sees them is some woman and under proper guidance will be the means of both man and woman reaching the eureka of life, which will end in happiness forever beyond this vale of tears.[21]

In that summer, the Caytons' money troubles were noticeably worse. Horace Sr. and Susie decided to sell a small house that they were living in at the time, just up the street from the Laurel Apartments. The *Weekly* carried Horace's short advertisement offering a six-room house in "A-1 condition" and available for immediate occupation.

Within the next two months, however, other critical events surpassed the Caytons' financial concerns. On the night of October 30, the Cayton family received devastating news, as recalled by Revels:

> Snow was on the ground; it was bitter cold; and a taxicab came up. You could hear this auto stop, and someone came to the door and started pounding on the door. And she said, "Mr. Cayton, Mr. Cayton!" And my Dad said, "Yeah?"...She said, "Ruth died in Portland at a hospital." There was a real cold silence in the house. Dad got up and started shaking up the wood stove.

Ruth had just turned twenty-two. She and her husband, Floyd, had separated three months earlier, when Floyd left for Portland. Ruth had been working nights as a waitress and wrote to her mother saying she was "getting along good without Floyd." Then in October Ruth traveled to Portland to see Floyd. She ended up in the Good Samaritan Hospital with a mysterious illness. Just before her death, Ruth was converted and received the sacrament of holy baptism from the hospital chaplain. Her body was brought to Seattle for services held at a small funeral parlor. Susie and Horace Sr. grieved for their oldest daughter, and the children for their elder sister. Revels recalled, "I remember putting my hands on her head in grief, and holding her, and trying to hold her forehead."[22]

The Caytons learned that Ruth was pregnant and had tried to abort herself with medicine given to her by someone named "Joe." Without stating the cause of death, Horace Sr. aired his sorrow in the *Weekly,* printing a brief death notice on November 1, and a longer article in the week following the funeral. "I am sixty past," Horace Sr. wrote, "and have been a more or less quasi-public personage...called upon to attend the funerals of the leading public functionaries of this commonwealth, and as important as they were, they paled into insignificance in comparison to my Ruth." He spoke of "her loving memory," of the "intense anguish" of the whole family, and of "the stinging pangs of the heart."

Susie said with remorse, "It's such a shame Ruth had to die. She was just maturing so well. She was going to be a great woman." Ruth left a young daughter, Susan, then only twelve months old. Susie and Horace Sr. took the baby in and raised her as one of their children.[23]

Just a few weeks before Ruth's death, news of racial violence elsewhere in the country had reached Seattle. In the first week of October, three bloody incidents rocked the nation: a man was lynched in Omaha; three others were shot in cold blood by an Alabama mob; and twenty-five blacks—men, women, and children—were massacred in Phillips County, Arkansas. On Saturday morning, October 11, 1919, *Cayton's Weekly* proclaimed in a large, bold headline "FAKE NEGRO UPRISING." Below it ran a one-column article in broad italic type, decrying the bloody killings in Arkansas by whites fearful of an "uprising." Articles with titles such as "Negro Extermination" filled the four-page paper, describing the horrors of the week's events. One article held Omaha's mayor responsible for the lynching there. The last page contained only advertisements.

The October 11 edition produced local shock waves; it was not that Cayton was reporting the bloody horrors in the South, but that he devoted an entire issue of the newspaper to the topic. Equally striking was the paper's format and appearance. With single column articles throughout, it more closely resembled a political broadside than a newspaper. Horace Jr. in *Long Old Road* recalled that family members were "shocked" and that Susie disapproved of the edition. If true, perhaps the adverse financial implications that might result from the public arousal were her main concern. The African American community's reaction to the October 11 issue is unknown, but today, many decades later, more copies of this edition of *Cayton's Weekly* have been saved in private Seattle homes than any other.

The response from Cayton's white readership can be gauged more easily. His assessment of the situation in Arkansas in particular, and black-white relations in general, was not geared to the genteel, liberal paternalism of white subscribers. Cayton cited the twenty-five years he himself had lived in Mississippi, and declared that the alleged "uprising" differed "in no way from the thousand and one that have been nipped in the bud 'down South' by the ever vigilant white man for the protection of white womanhood and for the continuance of the absolute purity of the white race." This incident was clearly another case where one or two slaves "refused to be whipped" and were "murderously regulated." Then, "after having killed the 'smart niggers,' the whites would return home and praise the Lord with one accord." In fact, said Cayton, human slavery in this manner had been perpetuated in the South and was "almost as bad today as it was prior to Lincoln's Emancipation Proclamation."

Cayton appeared to aim his sermon at white readers and the white daily press. He held nothing back. He thought it absurd of the white press to allege an "uprising," when a few blacks were merely "refusing to be bulldozed to death." He continued, "could more be expected than a Negro uprising when Negro men are brutalized to keep them in subjection and Negro women are beastialized to satisfy the animal lusts of white Christian men?" Under the circumstances, he repeated, we should expect not one bloody revolt but many. Next, he assailed the daily press for telling only one side of the situation—"the biased white man's side."

More provocative was Cayton's closing paragraph:

> This reign of terror that is running riot all over this Christian land and country at present is a well directed propaganda with no higher aim and object than to intimidate the colored soldier, returning from "over there," back into his former crouching condition, and while it may result in the murdering of multiplied thousands of them and their friends, yet, be it understood, the remaining ones will continue to lift high their heads and shout aloud, "and yet we are men for a' that. And if the officials of the law refuse to protect us, because we are black, then we will endeavor to protect ourselves as long as we can, and when we fail we will fall with our faces to the enemy and die like men."

In January 1920, when the NAACP issued a report of its investigation into the causes of the Arkansas riots, Cayton reprinted the "Fake Negro Uprising" article—this time in the paper's regular three-column format. He noted, "Many of the white readers of this paper took exceptions to the article and openly declared the facts did not justify such a view to be taken." In the three months since the Arkansas tragedy, most of the public and the press had quite forgotten about the Arkansas incident, until the NAACP report appeared. Cayton reprinted an editorial from the *Seattle Post-Intelligencer* commenting on the sharp contrast between the NAACP account and the original Associated Press reports about the riots. Cayton pointed out that the NAACP investigation and the *Post-Intelligencer* editorial validated his own reporting in October. But three months after the riots, the fire had gone out of the issue. Harm to *Cayton's Weekly*, however, already had been done.

The damage was reflected in Cayton's political career, which ebbed to a low point later that year. Two white colleagues had promised Cayton he would be seated as a delegate at the King County Republican Convention, but the promise went unkept. Perhaps, they had concluded that Cayton no longer could be counted upon to deliver a certain number of voters for the Republican Party. Horace did attend the convention, but as a mere spectator. In general, black Republicans fared dismally in the 1920 election. At the end of November, Dr. Felix B. Cooper, the president of the King County Colored Republican Club, reported that the strenuous effort to get voters registered in the community had failed.[24]

+≓+

When Horace Sr. turned sixty-one in February 1920, he told his readers, "[M]y struggle for a mere existence is just as great and my concern for the necessities of life for the future is just as acute as it was forty years ago." He tried to be optimistic, however, adding "We live on hope." The coming end of *Cayton's Weekly* was apparent to the aging editor. His energies were ebbing and advertising income had fallen steadily. Samuel DeBow's *Searchlight*, and then the *Northwest Enterprise*, began drawing away advertisers and readers. With a reported four hundred subscribers and a maximum circulation of fifteen hundred, *Cayton's Weekly* never approached the success of the *Seattle Republican*. It did not grow beyond four pages (except for special editions), and it carried few ads, and those mostly placed by small local businesses such as Tutt's Barber Shop, the Afro-American Hotel, and the Alhambra Cash Grocery. Despite Horace Sr.'s initial optimism about the future of *Cayton's Weekly*, the paper survived only five years. In the final month of 1920, Horace Cayton Jr. would publish the last edition.[25]

"From a colored man's standpoint in the United States life is just one damn thing after the other," Horace Sr. wrote in the *Weekly* in June 1920. The previous winter, Madge, at the time a University of Washington freshman, had been stricken by inflammatory rheumatism. During the summer of 1920, Susie and the Cayton children went to nearby Puyallup to earn money picking raspberries. The entire extended household also was with them, including Susie's nieces Emma and Marguerite and their children (Emma's sons, Donnie and Farnsworth; and Marguerite's twin girls, Verna and Violet). The children would remember this as a time of being very poor. There was only a hand pump for water where they stayed, and they walked along the railroad tracks picking up coal for "free heat." Horace Sr. stayed in the now mostly empty apartment house in Seattle. Occasionally he brought corn meal, lard, and a five-gallon can of peanut butter to the family before returning to the city.

Despite reduced circumstances, Cayton did what he could to further community causes. In the spring of 1920, he released a special "Souvenir Number" of *Cayton's Weekly*, with all proceeds going to help a friend, Reverend Carter, build a new Mt. Zion Baptist Church. It was the last "special" he would publish for two years. Simply putting food on the table became a major effort.[26]

Horace Sr. thought a monthly publication, with its lower costs, might succeed where the *Weekly* had failed. In February 1921 he came out with *Cayton's Monthly*. Page one headlined "Our Requiem," referring to the bygone *Cayton's Weekly*, which had ceased publication just two months earlier. Unintentionally, and prophetically, it applied equally to the *Monthly*. The inaugural issue was the first of only two. "The shadows of my final night are slowly gathering 'bout my sight," wrote Cayton somberly. He ended the piece on an up-beat note: "*Cayton's Weekly* is in the grave, but *Cayton's Monthly* is on the wave." Notably, the February edition of *Cayton's Monthly* included an article by Madge R. Cayton on "The Origin of Jazz." Cayton devoted the March issue almost exclusively to news about Seattle's African American community, giving considerable space to the new Mt. Zion Baptist Church. Both issues of the *Monthly* reflected the fact that the Cayton family had moved temporarily some fifteen miles south to the Kent Valley.

An easing of the Caytons' financial problems, however, allowed them to return to Seattle in 1923. Madge's health had improved, and she resumed her schedule of alternating work with attending classes at the University of Washington, where she served as secretary of a "colored students club" that she helped organize. Horace Sr. embarked on another publishing project, *Cayton's Yearbook; Seattle's Colored Citizens, 1923*. Its stated object, wrote the editor, was "to give to the world facts about the Colored Citizens in and around Seattle...especially those making headway in the business and professional world." Like similar special editions of the *Seattle Republican* and *Cayton's Weekly*, the thirty-three-page bound volume included photographs and brief sketches of community leaders and activists. This time, however, a person's inclusion in the volume depended on the individual's willingness to help defray costs, thus somewhat marring the *Yearbook*'s objectivity.

One factor in Cayton's lack of success at this point was the community's ambivalent attitude toward him. A loner, Cayton was viewed by some in the black community as "snobbish" and "uppity." He remained proud, too, of his former connections to influential whites, such as James D. Hoge, to whom he paid tribute in the 1923 yearbook. To others his worst sin was not that he had been too dependent on whites and their patronage, but that the Caytons actually retained a servant and housemaid when they lived on Capitol Hill. Meanwhile, others in the community began to play more active and important civic roles—people such as the Gaytons, Felix B. Cooper, and Samuel P. DeBow. The Caytons and the Gaytons, though long-time acquaintances, did not get on well. Revels relates a conversation he overheard between his father and John Gayton. Gayton prodded Horace Sr., saying, "Well, there was *Cayton's Weekly*, then *Cayton's Monthly*, and then *Cayton's Yearbook*—what's it going to be next?" Such jibes may not have affected an old-timer like Horace Sr., but his teenage son would still remember the comment's sting many years later.[27]

In the mid-1920s Horace Cayton's publishing career moved into its twilight. Following the 1923 *Yearbook,* two years passed before his next venture, a community celebration organized with other local business and professional men. In October 1925 they launched a weeklong promotion called the "First Annual Lincoln Industrial Fair," coinciding with the 60th anniversary of Emancipation. Horace headed the publicity committee, writing and publishing a 28-page pamphlet, *Lincoln Industrial Fair Association.* President of the association was the Reverend J. Sterling Moore, pastor of Mt. Zion Baptist Church, where the fair was held. The six evenings of the fair that began October 18 featured dramatic performances, speeches by Dr. Felix B. Cooper and *Northwest Enterprise* editor W.H. Wilson, patriotic songs and other musical entertainment, a "Tacoma Night and Fashion Show," and finally, "Joy Night." The promoters hoped the event would stimulate business and foster community spirit. Cayton's pamphlet declared the Lincoln Industrial Fair would "enable the colored citizens of the state to better know themselves," would highlight the business and social activities of Seattle African Americans, and would provide an opportunity for "white citizens getting acquainted with his brother in black." Cayton and the other promoters aimed to make the fair an annual event to be joined by similar celebrations in other communities in the state. They managed to stage the fairs in Seattle only the following two years. Both the 1926 and 1927 celebrations featured similar programs, and in the 1927 fair on October 27 Cayton presided over "Abraham Lincoln Night." But, community enthusiasm for the weeklong celebrations faded, and the pamphlets Cayton published for the fairs grimly reflect the waning energy behind the efforts. The 1925 first-year issue counted 28 pages; the second year 20 pages; and the 1927 issue only 12 pages.[28]

Horace Cayton Sr.'s next publishing effort was the *Cayton Yearbook, 1930.* It closely followed the pattern of the *1923 Yearbook,* with sketches of prominent Seattle African Americans of the past and present. The thirty-five-page booklet contained essays by Horace Sr. on Lincoln's birthday and "Washington's Colored Citizens." The bits of personal, family information added a poignant tone to the *Yearbook.* Among the individuals featured with a photo and sketch was Susie Revels Cayton. In the short biography of his wife, Horace Sr. named their children and noted, "Her husband, as may be observed, is something of a fifth wheel to the whole." He also included a photograph and a sketch of himself. He wrote, "Horace R. Cayton, Sr., too, has seen Seattle grow and if he did not leave his footprints on the sands of time as the years went by he certainly tried to, but two sons and two daughters, all well known, are some of his Seattle achievements." Later in 1930 came Cayton's last known publishing effort, an eight-by-ten-inch artist's drawing in Currier and Ives style, titled "Colored Men Who Have Served as United States Congressmen." Of course, Susie's father was featured prominently in the middle of the group. The simple purpose of this publication too, was to make money—a goal it failed to meet.[29]

Horace Sr.'s interest in the past and his desire to create a link to the future reflected his deep interest in history. It was a personal, family matter, as well as a civic activity, for him. As his family grew, Cayton's journalism had taken on a more personal tone. Perhaps he knew that his remarks and tributes to family members would last beyond his lifetime. Notably, the 1923 yearbook was published by "Horace Cayton and Son," indicating the elder Cayton hoped that there would be a new generation of publishers in the family to carry on his work.

Horace's legacy of publications provided the raw material from which later generations of Seattle's African American community would discover a rich cultural heritage. Today, Cayton's journalistic efforts are valued for their documentation of a period and a group of people for which there is little other evidence. In retrospect, he can be called a forerunner of what historian John Hope Franklin later termed "the new Negro history." Cayton consistently articulated his resentment of the dominant society's efforts to misrepresent black people's true role in U.S. history. Like many of his fellow journalists, he never ceased prodding the American conscience, demanding recognition of African Americans and the fact that their historical role was inextricably bound with the destiny of the nation. As his pen probed the confusion and contradictions in American values with one hand, the other was extended in conciliation and friendship. Full citizenship for African Americans, Cayton believed, must never be contingent on their losing a sense of racial identity and pride. His lifelong struggle against racism at times had made him bitter, other times angry, and sometimes merely wistful, as when he observed, "We are yet children in our attitude toward the world-old problem of race toleration, and…our thoughts about it are crude and elementary."[30]

During the Caytons' financial difficulties in the 1920s, Susie spent more time outside the home working, "in service." More and more often when not at work, she kept to her bed; there she spent long hours reading, writing, and cutting out articles for her scrapbooks. Horace Sr. helped with the cooking, without marked success. Madge continued waitressing and working as a cashier, while at home she shouldered an increasing share of the household chores. Horace Sr. began to rely on her to handle the family's financial matters. Madge also became a substitute mother to the younger children, making dresses for Lillie and Susan and taking them (along with their cousins Verna and Violet) to Grace Presbyterian Church, where she helped run the Sunday school. Madge even took responsibility for organizing the family's holiday celebrations.

Toward the end of 1930, Horace Sr. and Susie decided to make one final trip to Mississippi to visit Alcorn University and see old friends and relatives. While they were gone, Madge and Revels went over the family's finances, but they were unable to find a solution to their parents' longstanding monetary problems. Ultimately, Horace Sr. and Susie were forced to turn over the Laurel Apartments to the bank. In 1931 the family moved to a run-down, two-story, wood frame house on 21st Avenue. The loss of the Laurel Apartments was one of many hard blows that the Caytons suffered. Proud and independent, Horace Sr. found much to be disappointed and bitter about. Now over seventy years old, he had no chance of securing a job. Still, he would say he was "going to the office" and head downtown to City Hall to visit with one or two of his cronies from the old days.[31]

The Caytons, too, struggled in the Great Depression, which brought havoc to so many people's lives. In the Northwest, as elsewhere, the Depression hit African Americans and other minorities hardest. In Seattle and other cities, the unemployment rate for blacks was approximately twice that of whites. In 1929, about one in five black industrial workers joined the ranks of the unemployed. African Americans already had been excluded from most white-collar, skilled, and semi-skilled jobs, of course, but as the Depression deepened, even the menial, undesirable positions traditionally reserved for blacks were being taken over by whites at "Negro wages" or lower. Once again, black workers became victims of "last hired, first fired" practices.

The election triumph of Franklin D. Roosevelt over President Herbert Hoover in 1932 signaled the beginning of a new political era for the country. Although politics always had been of great interest in the Cayton household, Revels and his father now seldom had enough in common politically to hold a discussion. One day that changed—the day that Horace Cayton Sr., like many life-long Republicans, voted for Roosevelt, a Democrat. The occasion prompted a brief interchange that many years later Revels recalled as one of the most touching memories of his father:

> I came home and found my father sitting on the front stoop of our house. "Hey, Dad, what's wrong?" I asked, seeing him looking thoughtfully at the ground.
>
> He looked up and answered, "I just voted for a Democrat, son."
>
> "Well, what's so bad about that, the Democrats are gonna feed ya?" I snapped back.
>
> "Yes, that's true," he said, "but the Republican Party *freed* me."[32]

CHAPTER 5

Go Out and Achieve

The Family Crucible, 1914–1931

THE YEARS OF CIVIC ACTIVITY and publishing were also the prime family years for the Caytons. The children grew from childhood through adolescence and began to shape their own lives outside the home. In the dynamic crucible of the family, the children watched this process and learned, adapting their parents' visions of the family legacy to the harsh realities of growing up black.

Each day as the Cayton children left for school, Horace Sr. and Susie directed the youngsters to "go out and achieve." Both parents felt strongly that their children should understand they were part of a special family. The "Caytons" were educated, and they came from the top echelons of black society, both in Mississippi (on Senator Revels' side), and in Seattle due to their father's business and political activities and their mother's social and charity efforts. Very early on, the children knew this. It was bound up in their cultural activities and social aspirations, even under the circumstances of living in integrated neighborhoods. Often, the children heard their father say, "Colored society starts with us!"

For many years the Caytons lived away from the black community, physically and often in spirit, in largely white neighborhoods. The children gradually realized, however, that they stood apart from the white community surrounding them. As Ruth, Madge, Horace Jr., and Revels (and later, Lillie and Susan) progressed through the school system, their association with exclusively white teachers and mostly white classmates gave them perspectives on their mixed race parents and the balancing act that they had to perform in maintaining their social position in Seattle. As the younger generation grew, too, they came to understand the Caytons' special responsibility to the African American community. As an adult, Susan Cayton Woodson reflected on the way Horace Sr. and Susie had raised them. "They taught us that you don't just take from the community, you give back too, whatever you can."

Consciously and subconsciously, Horace Sr. and Susie passed on their values, hopes, and aspirations to their children. The parents derived much of this from their own formative years. In the Cayton household, family history substantially shaped the children's vision of who they were and where they came from. Said Revels Cayton, "Our whole family lived in the memory of Reconstruction. Reconstruction was as much a part of life in our house as if it were still going on. My mom and dad talked about it all the time."[1]

Horace Sr. and Susie's parents, though long gone, remained a significant presence in the Cayton household. Horace Jr. later wrote about the influence that the grandparents had on the family, particularly the fact that each of the grandparents had succeeded in his or her own way. This heritage profoundly affected the Cayton home:

> We, unlike most Negroes, lived in a tradition of success, achievement, and hope for Negro liberation. With such sterling examples to guide us, surrender to prejudice seemed cowardly and unnecessary. Our goals were dictated by our past; we were obliged by our family history to achievement in our fight for individual and racial equality.[2]

None of the children's grandparents loomed larger, or greater, than Senator Hiram Revels. A large oil portrait of the senator dominated the living room, and the children heard stories about the achievements of their famous and illustrious grandfather. Both Horace Sr. and Susie often told humorous tales about the senator, too—how his wife Phoebe henpecked him; how absent-minded he was; and how he sometimes took a "nip" of liquor, though he was an "ardent dry."

Susie even based one of her short stories on an anecdote Hiram once told about himself during the Civil War, when he became isolated from the regiment one night. It was dark and raining heavily. Suddenly, he heard footsteps coming. He ran like crazy, but stumbled and fell into a ditch. Then, almost paralyzed with fear as the footsteps came closer, he heard "the unmistakable 'moo' of a cow." Despite the laughs at Hiram's expense, Susie and Horace Sr. both felt fiercely proud of him, not only for what he had achieved, but also for what he had come to symbolize for all African American people.

Susie often told the children about her early life—her girlhood in Ohio, and the influence of her family's Quaker traditions; her adolescence in bucolic Holly Springs, Mississippi; the stimulating cultural atmosphere in their home when her father served as president of Alcorn University; her youthful desire to become a writer; the courtship via correspondence with "Mr. Cayton"; and traveling to the Northwest frontier to marry the young newspaper publisher. Horace Sr. told his sons and daughters about his life, too, although his stories took second place to those of the more "illustrious" Revels family. Horace Sr. related his early memories as a young plantation slave; his struggle to earn an education during Reconstruction; courting the Revels girls; his travels and adventures in the West; and how journalism, politics, and race issues coalesced to become his life's focus.

The Cayton siblings' differing personalities, gender, and even skin color determined how they responded to the challenges of finding a place for themselves within the family, and in Seattle's social order.

Ruth (b. 1897)

Ruth, the oldest of the Cayton children, was strong-willed even as a little girl. From an early age, she began to chart her own path and assert independence from the strict values and behavioral codes of her parents, especially her father. Said Revels, "Dad just was at war with her. She wouldn't take it, she was a spirited woman."

She got on well with her mother, however, and Susie became her daughter's defender against Horace Sr. Ruth was darker complexioned than her parents or the other children. Ruth accepted both whites and blacks equally, and the "tenderloin" district was a place where she could work, enjoy herself, and find a level of acceptance that she did not get at home. As Horace Jr. noted, "Ruth did what she wanted to do, and what she wanted to do was have fun; in a way, she made the most healthy adjustment of all us children... And she was the first in our family to break away and seek full membership in the Negro community with no apparent thought about our family mission or the manner in which we had been raised."

Revels fondly remembered Ruth, who had been "always good" to him and called him "Hun." Horace Jr., on the other hand, who was four years older than Revels and six years younger than Ruth, "respected," but "feared" her. To him she was "unreachable, far removed by age and temperament."[3]

Madge (b. 1901)

Madge was everyone's favorite. Her given name was "Maggie" (after her mother's sister), but at an early age she dropped it for Madge. She had the lightest complexion of the Caytons, and both brothers described her as very pretty.

"My Dad," noted Revels, "used to say Madge could pass [for white] any time that she would want." Horace Jr. claimed that one time when the family was having financial difficulty, Madge briefly took a job in San Francisco, passing as white. A quiet, shy, young woman, Madge kept most thoughts and feelings to herself and had the self-effacing habit of biting her lower lip. Bright, conscientious, and hardworking, she became a top student at Franklin High School (1915–19) and the University of Washington (1919–25).

Madge was sincerely modest, even protesting having her photograph taken when she graduated from college. She observed and analyzed her world, and tried to ameliorate emotional conflicts and racially caused disturbances in the family by rationalizing and intellectualizing problems. Only occasionally did she open up to one of her brothers or sisters, but when she did the effect was profound. To Horace Jr., she was wise and "more worldly." Revels respected "How much she knew, and how much she kept in her head!"[4]

Horace Jr. (b. 1903)

As the oldest son, Horace Jr. quickly became his father's favorite. From an early age he was energetic and intelligent, and quick to question and probe the incongruity between the racial equality preached at home and the hard realities of black-white relations in the neighborhood and at school. Unlike Madge, he readily fought back. Only two years younger than Madge, he felt a close kinship with her.

He also was Revels' protective older brother during their early school years. Later, the brothers did not get along, but Revels fondly remembered times when Horace Jr. was an ideal older brother. When Horace Jr. saved money he had earned selling the *Seattle Post-Intelligencer*, he bought his younger brother a bicycle. Horace Jr. also defended Revels from older, tougher Italian kids at the Coleman School and took a beating in the process. When Mrs. Kane, the Coleman School principal, was going to spank Revels, his older brother interceded.

Horace Jr. was lonely in the Capitol Hill neighborhood because white children would not play with him. After the family moved to Rainier Valley, he became more aggressive. In school he received poor marks for attitude, but earned good grades and occasionally made the "B" honor roll.

Despite scholastic success and active involvement on debating teams in the eighth grade and at Franklin High School, Horace Jr. felt like an outsider. Rejected by whites because he was black, and excluded by blacks because he was "stuck up," Horace Jr. turned his unhappiness and frustration outward. In his words, he "became rebellious and bitter and determined to fight back against this oppressive white world."[5]

Revels (b. 1907)

Hiram Revels Cayton, four years younger than Horace Jr. and six years younger than Madge, started school at Rainier Elementary in 1913 when the family moved to Rainier Valley. Classmates teased the youngster, "Hi, Ram," so he soon dropped the first name and became known by his middle name, "Revels" (or "Rev" to his friends). He could say more convincingly than before—if he chose to—that he was named for his illustrious grandfather, the first African American ever elected to the U.S. Senate.

Athletic and personable, Revels made friends easily. He enjoyed neighborhood street hockey, family picnics at Volunteer Park, and ardently loved baseball. Because of the family's several moves to new neighborhoods, Revels attended four different grammar schools by the eighth grade. Revels showed less interest in classwork than Madge and Horace Jr., repeating the seventh grade at Washington School.[6]

Lillie (b. 1914)

Lillie was light complexioned and plain featured, with a small raised scar in the middle of her forehead from an accident when, as a baby, she fell head-first onto the end of a pick. She was born at a change-of-life stage for her parents—Susie was forty-four years old and Horace Sr. fifty-five. Lillie came into the world in 1914, a dark period for the family, which was still reeling (both financially and emotionally) from the failure of the *Seattle Republican* the previous year. In a sense, this was a foreshadow of things to come. The Cayton parents were cold and strict toward their youngest child, apparently more so than with the other children. Lillie's path in life would bring her more hard times than those faced by her siblings.

In his autobiography, Horace Jr. described Lillie as "a tender person, generous and good." As the youngest Cayton child, she found that, even as an adult, it was difficult to bridge the gap between her much-older siblings and herself.[7]

Susan (b. 1918)

Only twelve months old when her mother Ruth died, Susan became the youngest child in the Cayton household. To her, Horace Sr. was "Dad" and Susie was "Mother."

Following the public expression of grief in *Cayton's Weekly* at the time of Ruth's death in 1919, both Horace Sr. and Susie fell silent regarding their oldest daughter. The pain of her untimely death was compounded by the social stigma attached to abortion in those times. For years, this matter simply was not discussed by the Caytons, either inside or outside of the family.

For a long time Susan thought Ruth was a sister. Every year on Mother's Day, Horace Sr. and Susie gave a red carnation to each of the children, but Susan received a white one. Susan had no idea that this was meant to honor Ruth. Susan hated the white flower, because it seemed to imply that she was different from the other children. Not until Susan was a young adult did she learn the full truth about her mother.[8]

+≡·≡+

As he experienced mounting disappointments in the outside world, Horace Sr. turned increasingly to his children and wife for support. Although Horace Sr. was a very private person, and a loner from the point of view of many, he was above all a devoted family man. According to his nephew, Donnie Hancock, "He didn't do anything without his family in mind." It became increasingly important to Horace Sr. to pass on to his children what he had learned in his decades of struggle. He began reminiscing in *Cayton's Weekly,* including in it much more family news than had appeared in the *Seattle Republican*. For example, he had briefly announced the birth of his son, Revels, in June 1907 with a one-liner, "A bouncing baby boy, Shake!" By contrast, in 1918 he wrote at length of the loving concern he and Susie felt for their children, all of whom survived the flu epidemic sweeping Seattle at the time.[9]

Horace Sr., however, was a strict parent to his children, particularly the younger ones. They saw him as a person to be reckoned with, a man of great courage and moral integrity who was devoutly dedicated to advancing social freedom and equality. He was middle class in his thinking—in terms of his belief in the value of hard work, his admiration of success, and his fervent desire to have the best in material comforts for his family. Horace Sr.'s aspirations for his children and his expectations that they should achieve and accomplish seemed virtually unbounded. However, his expectations for the children did not extend to religion—that was Susie's arena.

Horace Sr. had been raised in a Christian home and for a part of his youth attended an A.M.E. church in Mississippi. While he espoused considerable support for Seattle's African American churches, his motivation was more political, social, and financial than religious. He was agnostic, believing that a person lived a life here on earth, and when he or she died it was as though a match was extinguished or a light bulb was turned off.[10]

Susie had grown up under the religious influence of her minister father, Hiram Revels. At some point before her children grew to school age, Susie broke with the A.M.E. church. Although supportive of churches as valued institutions, she was not a regular churchgoer. Nor did she involve herself in formal church responsibilities or social activities. Following more closely her Quaker mother's approach than her minister father's, she called herself a "free thinker." Susie took an interest in various faiths, and attended numerous churches, including those of the Methodist, Baptist, Presbyterian, Catholic, Unity, and Christian Science denominations. The breadth of her intellectual curiosity and her interest in spiritual growth led her occasionally to embrace several religious doctrines at the same time. Revels remembered his mother as an avid reader of Unity Church publications, especially the *Daily Word*. In the early mornings, the children often saw her standing with her hands folded on her forehead. Revels recalled, "We would say, 'Mama, what's the thought?' and she would give us the thought for the day" that she had in mind.[11]

Susie's presence in the home, as well as in public, reflected her strong personality. Horace Jr. described his mother as a tall, attractive "Southern lady" of "stately bearing," who possessed the "cultivated grace of many southern women who have been reared in gentle homes." She had inherited a "primness" and a "hard streak" from her mother; and, from her father, a "warm earthiness" and generally kindly disposition. While both Susie and Horace Sr. shared a devotion to "principle," her personal warmth and gentility set her apart from her husband. Horace Sr. had many friends and acquaintances in political and business circles, but in personal and family matters, he maintained a strict privacy. He often carried himself with aloofness and reserve. Susie possessed a freer willingness to relate to people outside of the family.

For example, Horace Sr. believed that people such as Nish, their servant for years on Capitol Hill, and Mr. Fontello, a garbage man at the Laurel Apartments, should be "kept in their place." To Susie, Nish was someone from whom she could learn some Japanese, and Mr. Fontello a man to engage in extended intellectual discussions. When Horace Sr. challenged her about talking to Fontello, she stubbornly praised the garbage man as "one of the most intelligent men I have ever met, and I will continue to talk with him for as long as I please."[12]

The moral code that the Caytons passed on to their children was rigidly Victorian, especially regarding women. Said Revels,

> I never once heard Dad talk dirty about a woman, or tell a dirty joke about a woman. That's the kind of man he was. "We Caytons don't do that sort of thing," he often said. I can hear him saying that in my mind today, clear as a bell. He really put a monkey on my back.

In their children's eyes, formality and propriety governed Horace Sr. and Susie's relationship. Susie called Horace Sr. "Mr. Cayton" most of the time, and sometimes "Father." Rarely did she refer to him as "Dear." When he spoke to her directly it was "Susie," but to the children it was "your Mother," and to those outside the family, "Mrs. Cayton." The children saw their parents relate to each other, not with familiarity or displays of physical affection, but with a reserve appropriate to their characters and era.

As parents who maintained a certain level of formality and distance, Susie and Horace never discussed sex with their children. Not only was it a taboo, according to the church and to Victorian moral standards, but it also was offensive to them as community leaders interested in the uplift of all African Americans. To them, sexual involvement represented the exact sort of "common," low-class "Negro behavior" that whites expected of blacks. In the words of Horace Jr., "We children soon learned to identify any sort of loose sexual behavior or talk with lower-class Negroes and to look down upon it. And there were parts of the city, the sporting area, where we were not even allowed to ride through...for those people were morally corrupt and of great discredit to the race."[13]

When Ruth dropped out of high school and took a waitressing job in the tenderloin district, it was difficult for the elder Caytons to accept her actions. Horace Sr., in particular, abhorred the fact that Ruth associated with people in the seamier part of town. At age twenty, Ruth married Floyd J. Wright, a young man originally from Portland, Oregon, who worked in or around the "sporting world." Many years later, Revels remembered him warmly as "a very nice guy." After their marriage in 1917, Ruth and Floyd moved into the Laurel Apartments along with the rest of the Caytons' extended family.

Ruth's rejection of her parents' values—namely, education and Victorian morality—was painful for Horace Sr. and Susie, who had high expectations for their children. The Caytons tried hard to give their children the skills and confidence they would need to make their way in both black and white society. The Caytons taught their children to consider themselves equal to anyone—not greater, not lesser. Revels Cayton said, "We just missed a big inferiority complex about whites." As parents, Horace Sr. and Susie opened the doors to both the black and white communities by having their children associate with—and become comfortable with—people of all races and ethnicities. When Revels had a white girlfriend, such as Anna Ziloski in the sixth grade, that was fine by Horace Sr. and Susie. When Horace Jr. dated Gladys Schockley, a beautiful brown-skinned girl, both parents approved. They measured the merit of their children's friends by character not color. Thus, both parents transmitted strong messages to the children about race relations: you stand up for who you are and what you believe in, you never back down—especially to a white man ("not one iota," Horace Sr. would say)—and integration on the basis of full equality is the proper and appropriate relationship between blacks and whites.[14]

Despite Horace Sr.'s efforts to provide support and leadership in the black community, at a deep emotional level he never fully accepted his blackness. He gave the impression that he was paternalistic—that he was not *of* the black community. Susie felt emotional ties to the race much more deeply. Reflecting on this, when interviewed by a government worker and asked about her "nationality," she responded "African-American." Having fully accepted her own blackness, she had a love and democratic acceptance of black people and exhibited an ease and comfort around them that was noticeably absent in Horace Sr. The children perceived this difference between their parents. Before Susie had married Horace Sr., she almost married a young man in Mississippi whose complexion was quite dark. Horace Sr., asserted the children, almost certainly would never have considered marrying a very dark-skinned woman. "My Dad," said Revels, "really did not have in his heart, or in his guts, the thing that my mother had. He was a striver, but my mother had it."[15]

Horace Sr.'s children often heard him say, "Miscegenation, miscegenation is the answer. There's gonna come a time in this world when all colors gonna be blotted out and all the races will begin to blend into one color." At this Susie retorted, "Well, Father, there'll have to be an awful lot of miscegenation, because white folks say if you've got one drop of Negro blood in you that's enough to take over all the white blood." To Horace Sr., "solving the race problem" by race amalgamation was an article of faith.[16]

Susie continued to take a leadership role in the African American community, particularly in the Dorcas Charity Club. Susie often was asked to speak before various groups. On one occasion she delivered a presentation at the Baptist Literary Society on the subject, "Black Baby Dolls." Noting the general lack of black dolls in stores and shops, she urged others in the community to find, buy, or make them for their children, and not to settle for ubiquitous white baby dolls. Susie occasionally wrote pieces for *Cayton's Weekly*, mostly short fictional articles with strong religious overtones, such as one titled "From a Daughter of Solomon."[17]

The Cayton children grew up observing their mother prominently involved in civic and literary affairs, and their father engrossed in politics and business—these were as much a part of home life as eating and sleeping. The Cayton parents strived actively to introduce the children to these activities. When Horace Jr. was nine, his father began taking him to political meetings. Meanwhile, Susie involved the children in cultural activities. In the early days, before times became difficult, the older children—Ruth, Madge, and Horace Jr.— often were taken to concerts, plays, and the opera.

✦══✦

The age differences of the Cayton children, their strong and diverse personalities, and their parents' tendency to play favorites all contributed to create complex and often conflicted relationships. The hard times resulting from the successive failure of Horace Sr.'s newspapers exacerbated family tensions, too.

As the children grew older, cliques developed within the family and became more noticeable. Horace Jr. and Madge were their father's favorites. Susie, who had been the supporter of Ruth even during her rebellious period, became the protector and closest parent to Revels. Lillie and Susan were still too young to be much affected, although later Lillie's position would become much like what Ruth's had been. The relationship between the elder Caytons also suffered. Though Horace Sr. could write of his love for Susie and the children publicly in the newspaper, he was not a demonstrative, openly warm husband or father.

Attitudes about color and family background complicated the situation, especially between Horace Jr. and Revels. In their rivalries, pejoratives resulted when tempers rose. Horace Jr. was "lighter" and Revels was darker, but Horace Jr. envied Revels for being named after the illustrious senator.

Revels, on the other hand, resented the preference his father showed to his brother and Madge. In that color-conscious period, Horace Jr. took pride in being lighter skinned. He taunted Revels, calling him "liver lip." Furthermore, Revels "hated to be treated like a younger brother."[18]

Seattle's social environment also helped shape the children's concept of race and family. The Cayton apartments, the neighborhoods they lived in, and the schools they attended were all integrated. Many playmates at school and at home—and later their co-workers and employers—were white. When Horace Jr. took a summer job at a condensed milk plant after his freshman year of high school, he was the only African American teenager working there. On the surface, Seattle seemed a relatively liberal and progressive community, especially compared to the South where there was overt hostility toward blacks. Yet, both Horace Jr. and Revels felt that the psychological effect of prejudice in the Northwest was virtually the same. In the words of Horace Jr., "Frightened parents transmit their feelings to their children in various subtle and not so subtle ways. There were isolated incidents which I did not quite understand but would remember with curiosity and sometimes with a tension verging on fear."[19]

As the children grew older, their experiences outside of the home gradually brought into focus the nature of Seattle's social and racial environment. During and after World War I, prejudice and segregation increasingly made life difficult for non-whites in Seattle. Employment options for the Caytons' oldest daughter, Ruth, were limited to domestic service or waitressing. Being called "nigger" by white kids was a frequent occurrence. The Cayton children turned to each other for support in dealing with the prejudice they faced regularly.

When Horace Jr. asked Madge about this, she told him that she pretended to not hear the name-calling. Horace replied, that when he asked their mother about what to do, she only said, call them "niggers" back. The problem was, he told Madge, "it doesn't work."

Madge concluded, "I don't think our parents know what to tell us."

Unable to replicate their parents' tenuous balance in both African American and white society, the children's solution frequently was to move closer to the black community. Revels often played with his cousin, Donnie, and became best friends with the few black kids at school, such as Benny Beasley and Chuck Ragland. Later, when Revels began attending Garfield High School in 1924, he and Horace Jr. went to "Friday night stomps" in the Madison area with black girlfriends.[20]

The grave concerns about worsening race relations that Horace Sr. reported in *Cayton's Weekly* often were discussed at home over the dinner table, especially when new editions of the *Crisis* arrived. The lynching reports deeply disturbed twelve-year-old Revels. One day he overheard his mother saying, "Mr. Cayton, this continual talk about what's going on in the South is upsetting Revels no end. I don't know whether we can hide the magazines or what, but at least we shouldn't make it a continuous topic of discussion in the house." Horrible nightmares tormented Revels, with demonic, white-hooded Klansmen appearing in his dreams night after night.[21]

+⸬⸬+

As his father had done as a younger man, Horace Jr. began entering restaurants that refused to serve blacks, hoping to provoke confrontations. Some cafes reluctantly served him, but when others refused, he "made a scene." Horace Jr. also tested the Strand movie theater, which had begun to segregate blacks to balcony-only seats. When the manager asked Horace Jr. to leave, he refused. The police arrested the sixteen-year-old and hauled him off to jail; later he was released into his father's custody. Horace Sr. advised his son to study hard and prepare himself to carry on the fight by becoming a lawyer. He gave Horace Jr. an ultimatum: "Go to school or go to work, and stay out of this senseless trouble between the races."

But the troubled youth remained alienated and continued to struggle in school. Horace Sr. used an old political connection to get his son appointed as a mail clerk in the Washington State Legislature in Olympia, hoping that the job would change his son's ways, but with no effect. Finally, Horace Jr. decided to ship out as a bellboy and sailed for Alaska, where, among other adventures, he worked for a short time in a house of prostitution in Nome. Horace Jr. hopped from job to job for the next four years, leading a nomadic existence. He worked variously as a steward, cook, boilermaker, and ship rigger on steamships that sailed out of Seattle to ports in Alaska, California, Mexico, South America, and Hawaii. Interspersed during this time, he also worked as a coal miner, railroad crewman, and taxicab driver. When in Seattle, the well-traveled youth had little interest in middle-class morals, the Cayton family name, or the rigors of high school academics.[22]

Then one winter night in early 1920, Horace Jr., acting as the "wheel man," drove the Cayton family car during a gas station hold-up that netted just $13.70 for him and two companions. They were arrested for the crime. At the court hearing, Horace Jr. received a suspended sentence and was remanded to the custody of his parents. An account published by his father claimed that Horace Jr. was "exonerated and sent home" because he was "not aware" of his friends' intent to commit the robbery. There is no such pretense, however, in Horace Jr.'s autobiography. He described his actions as "mischievous rather than criminal." Horace Jr. continued to get into trouble. In May a judge found the juvenile had "disregarded the confidence and instructions of the court" and committed him to the State Training School in Chehalis.[23]

The incident caused a major breach within the family. According to Revels and his cousin, Donnie Hancock, Horace Sr. could have prevented his son from "doing time" in reform school, but he refused to do so, believing that the experience would be good for his son and "teach him a lesson." Horace Jr. maintained that his father agreed to his son's voluntary internment so there would be no police record of the crime, both for his son's and the family's sake. In either case, the results were the same. On May 20, the entire family drove Horace Jr. to the reform school. On the way home, Susie was extremely upset and would not speak to her husband. Everyone was silent. At last, Susie said slowly, "Mr. Cayton, I want him back in a week's time."[24]

Horace Sr. did secure his son's release within a matter of weeks. Earlier, at the time of the arrest, Horace Sr. had written in *Cayton's Weekly,* "One day this week my son went wrong and though I love him to distraction...yet he will have to reap his reward just as your son. The ones we seem to love the best are generally the ones that give us the most concern." When Horace Jr. returned home, father and son appeared to mend the relationship, but to others it never seemed quite the same—some deep bond had been irreparably broken. Horace Jr.'s first wife, Bonnie Branch Hansen, later recalled the brutality of reform school. "For Horace this was a most horrible experience—one he never forgot and of which he often told me during the years we were together...He was traumatized, and I am not sure how or if he ever resolved this agony."[25]

Horace Jr. returned to Garfield High School in 1921 to complete his junior year, which proved difficult. Having spent time in reform school, young Horace had a bad reputation, and the Gaytons and other former school friends snubbed him. Again he dropped out of school, spending the next year wandering—traveling the railroads as a hobo and getting by as a "ham and egg prize fighter." Returning to Seattle, he got a job selling political ads for the African American weekly, *Searchlight.* Finally, in 1923, tiring of blue-collar jobs, Horace Jr. at last decided to complete high school by taking a special YMCA college preparation program. His delighted father lifted up one of the carpets in their apartment house home and pulled out a small stash of money to support his son's schooling. The next few years were the happiest the family had known for some time. With young Horace Jr. finishing high school and Madge at the university, this was a brief but richly significant period of family life. Horace Sr. bought a console phonograph player and classical records. Conversations at the evening dinner table buzzed, with Horace Sr. drawing on his classical Latin education and Horace Jr. on his debating skills, while Susie or Madge interjected on a wide array of political and social topics.[26]

The two oldest children, Madge and Horace Jr., reaped the most benefit from these friendly intellectual discussions, simply because the other siblings were too young to participate much. Revels was in his teens, Lillie about seven years old, and Susan still a toddler. Revels, too, was more interested in sports than in conversation. Revels, however, had been greatly impressed by Horace Jr.'s standoff at the Strand theater and felt proud of him. Revels was beginning to understand the nature of discrimination following a series of personal "little incidents." For instance, when he was fourteen, Revels with a group of YMCA friends entered a local restaurant and was served apple pie. Later that day, Revels returned to the restaurant alone, but was told, "we don't serve colored here."

Horace Jr. later reflected on similar personal incidents and concluded that despite the many advantages of the Cayton home, and his father and mother's "apparent adjustment," there was something lacking in their parenting. "Possibly, in their frenzied efforts to surmount the color barrier," he concluded, "they somehow failed to teach me what to expect or how to act as a Negro in a white world.[27]

In 1922, just prior to his fifteenth birthday, Revels followed his older brother's example and went to sea. That summer he shipped out as a telephone operator on passenger ships plying the West Coast, first on the *Ruth Alexander,* then the *Curacao* and the *H.F. Alexander.* He was one of many blacks finding low-paying jobs as shipboard telephone operators, bellboys, and waiters. At the time, Revels was represented by "Lt. Roston's" company union, the Colored Marine Employees Benevolent Association, which had begun the integration of the West Coast maritime industry after a 1921 waterfront strike.

The conditions that young Rev Cayton found himself in would have appalled his parents if they had known about it. Revels worked sixteen or seventeen hours a day for extremely low wages and was segregated from the white seamen. Later that summer, Revels traveled as a "mascot" with Doc Hamilton's All-Stars, a local baseball team touring the Northwest. This exposure to older, experienced men from poorer, less educated backgrounds helped Revels mature, but his studies suffered. While Horace Jr. and Madge gained good educations, Revels faltered, especially in spelling, even though he was bright, personable, and better adjusted than his older brother to the racial realities of Seattle schools.

The brothers' differences soon widened. Horace Jr. described a conversation between them in San Francisco, probably in 1922 or 1923, when they were still going to sea:

> I suddenly thought of the glory hole, and its fetid air, its cursing inmates, and the inevitable all night gambling game. "I just can't go back to the ships, Revs," I said. "I hate it—it's dirty and rotten…I hate those black niggers I have to work with . . ."
>
> "You shouldn't talk like that, bubba," my brother said with some concern. "It's disloyal to our people. Do you want to be white?"
>
> "Not exactly…I just want to be free."[28]

This conversation, like many reported in later years by Horace Jr., probably never occurred—Revels said it did not. But it portrays the brothers' contrasting attitudes and personal differences. Horace Jr. soon was fired and never again worked at sea. But Revels continued shipping out, eventually spending many of his early working years aboard steamers.

Madge escaped the adolescent conflicts with her parents that her brothers experienced. She devoted herself to the family and was loved by all. "Madge was not negative about people," recalled Susan. "I never saw her angry." Madge, being older, took on many of the household chores, while pursuing her studies at the University of Washington and working outside of the home to help support the family. In June 1925, Madge received a baccalaureate degree in business administration. At the time, at least in Seattle, there were no opportunities for a black woman with training in international business. Light complexioned enough to "pass," she might have secured a civil service job with local or state government, but she refused to do so. She took cashiering and waitressing jobs at several cafes—even working for a short time at Doc Hamilton's Hickory Pit in the tenderloin district.

Horace Jr. graduated from the YMCA program in 1925. Like Madge, he was interested in business and economics and attended the University of Washington, receiving a bachelor's degree in business administration in

1929, and continuing with graduate courses in sociology until 1931. While studying at the university, Horace Jr. worked as a King County deputy sheriff. His experiences on the vice and gambling squads and in assisting at the county jail, plus his own earlier brush with the law, gave him a strong interest in criminology. It was in a criminology class at the University of Washington—taught by Dr. Norman Hayner—that Horace Jr. met a bright, quiet white girl from Olympia named Bonnie Branch. On June 5, 1929, they drove to Olympia to get a marriage license, and then, on the return trip, stopped in Tacoma to be married by a black minister. The couple honeymooned on a farm in central Washington, where they were warmly hosted by old family friends of the Caytons.

Susie, Revels, Madge, and the rest of the Caytons loved Bonnie from the beginning, but Horace Sr. found his son's marriage hard to accept at first. Although he liked Bonnie personally (and professed support for miscegenation), he considered mixed marriages typical of "sports" and a fast, disreputable lifestyle. In a short while, however, as the family came to know her, Bonnie gained their full acceptance. "Whatever they may have felt," remarked Bonnie, "they came to our rescue."

As Ruth and Floyd had done earlier, Horace Jr. and Bonnie made their home with the rest of the family in the Laurel Apartments, fixing up a two-room "love nest." Bonnie spent long hours on the front porch listening to her father-in-law's stories. Soon, she became his favorite companion. His wife's friendship with his father eventually brought Horace Jr. to a deeper understanding of the old newspaperman. "Indeed," he said, "it was through Bonnie that I first became aware of the drama and pathos of his heroic tale."[29]

The newlyweds were in for a bumpy ride from the outset. Outside of the Cayton home, the couple faced severe social pressures and racial bigotry. "How we managed to develop a caring then passionate relationship," Bonnie later wrote, "seems almost miraculous. While inter-racial relationships were not forbidden by law, social taboos were so strong that they might almost as well have been."

Even in the face of the hardships imposed by the prejudices around them, Horace Jr. and Bonnie were blissfully happy at first. Bonnie's mentor at the university, Professor Marion Hathaway, helped her get a job as a social-worker-in-training at a local service agency. When her boss learned that Bonnie was married to "a Negro," he fired her. Hathaway and other white liberals at the university then helped her find a position as an assessment counselor at the YWCA, thus averting serious financial troubles for the couple.[30]

Horace's part-time studies at the university progressed with marked success. When an eminent sociologist, Dr. Robert Park from the University of Chicago, visited Seattle and met young Horace, he took an immediate interest in him and encouraged him to pursue graduate studies at Chicago. In the summer of 1931, Horace Jr. left Seattle to begin a new chapter of his life in Chicago. Meanwhile, again through Marion Hathaway's intervention, Bonnie arranged for a new job at United Charities in Chicago. Horace Jr. returned for Bonnie in the autumn, and they bid farewell to home and family. On the day they left Seattle, Horace Jr. could not find his younger brother to say good-bye. "I just conveniently wasn't around," Revels later admitted. This small act was just one indication of the breach between the two brothers that continued to grow in the years ahead.

+≈≈+

In 1925, with Madge graduating from the University of Washington and Horace Jr. just beginning his studies there, Revels was in his second year at Garfield High School. He enjoyed football, until he broke an ankle, and baseball, although several instances of a coach's blatantly preferential treatment for white players disheartened Revels and he walked off the team. Revels began to take his studies more seriously. Chaucer and other English literature classics fascinated him. He took typing classes and thought about a career in journalism, dreaming of following in his father's footsteps. Socially, too, he was maturing and had a steady girlfriend.

Up to this point, Revels had led a life similar to that of other middle-class African American youths in Seattle. Then, without warning, an event occurred that completely recast his life. After several days of illness, suddenly one night a searing pain shot through his head, "just like a streak of jagged lightning." His parents rushed him to Swedish Hospital, where the malady was diagnosed as *encephalitis lethargis,* commonly called "sleeping sickness." It nearly proved fatal. For days Revels lay comatose. Each night the doctors punctured his spine to remove infected fluid. But, Revels was young, athletic, and strong, and after two weeks his condition improved. He remained a month in the hospital and returned home for a long recovery period. More than a year passed before he returned to school. Revels' illness left the family with sizable medical bills, so Susie took up domestic work outside of the home. Also, to pay the doctor for his services, she laundered his shirts.[31]

The damaging effects of the disease fortunately proved relatively minor. It partially paralyzed Revels' left arm and left leg, but in a few months they returned to normal. His left vocal cord, however, sustained minor but permanent damage. More important, psychologically the illness marked a turning point in the young man's life. Staying out of school for such an extended time nearly severed all the relationships that previously structured his life—class work, sports activities, a summer bellboy job at sea, and community ties. Only one schoolmate, a former girlfriend, came to visit, and she came just once. Revels felt isolated and alienated. Already something of a loner, he turned more within himself. He passed many hours sitting on the front porch of the apartment house, resting and reading. One day a neighbor stopped by and the two began talking. The man, an old "Wobbly" unionist (Industrial Workers of the World), gave Revels books by Jack London and Emile Zola. Soon they were spending long hours discussing literature, philosophy, and socialism.

Revels' extended convalescence held the seeds of a new beginning. His old dreams were gone. There seemed no chance of becoming a star baseball catcher like his hero, Paul Robeson, or a journalist like his father, or attending college as had his father, mother, and sister. But, as the months passed and he continued reading, his knowledge of socialism grew and new visions were born to him. He became passionate about the principle of equality between the races, and began to see himself as an idealist, like his father, but one devoted to militant action. All his life Revels had been told he was special—that, as a Cayton, he had special obligations to his race, community, and society. Now, he began to envision a unique role for himself as a fighter for a better society under a socialist system, free of racism and the exploitation of workers.

He emphasized, "By the time I got off that porch I was a socialist. I found it reasonable and sensible that the only way that blacks were going to get free would be in conjunction with the working class." If capitalism were defeated, he believed, then competition for jobs would be eliminated, and this would end racial prejudice. When Revels returned to Garfield High School, having recovered from the rare brain disease and now talking about socialism, the reception was predictable. His classmates, recalled Revels, said "That boy went to sleep and woke up crazy!"

Revels' developing knowledge of socialist philosophy restored his self-confidence and he began to assert himself intellectually. Horace Jr., however, was bothered by the prospect of his younger brother feeling equal to him and having a mind of his own. The long-gathering tension between the two broke into the open one day when Revels arrived home from school. As he walked up the stairs, Horace Jr. started taunting him. Revels spun around, hitting him with his briefcase. Horace Jr. staggered back down the stairs. Months passed before the brothers spoke to one another. Even then, the relationship remained cool. "I held him sort of at arm's length," said Revels, "because I was afraid of his dominating me. He wanted to do to me what he did to Madge."[32]

In June 1929, Revels did not spend high school graduation night with classmates. Instead, he wandered among working men on Skid Road near Pioneer Square. Gathered here were various radical political speakers, each on a soapbox surrounded by small crowds who listened to railings against the "capitalist exploitation of the working class" or the mocking of nearby Salvation Army workers as "dupes" of the existing social order. Here on summer evenings, there was a ready audience of several hundred mostly young working men—a floating population of loggers, fruit pickers and other agricultural workers, miners, railroad workers, fishermen, seamen, and jobless men who had no better place to go. Soon, their ranks would swell as the Great Depression hit Seattle.

Revels looked forward to returning to shipboard life. For the time being, however, he was too weak to work. Like his brother, Revels had grown quite independent of the family, though he maintained a close bond with his mother and Madge. When Revels finally regained his physical strength, he shipped out again as a bellboy. He felt an even closer kinship to his shipmates than before, yet he still longed to go to college. With his poor high school record, however, he stood little chance of ever attending the University of Washington. Revels said he sharply felt "the whip" of his family heritage that demanded he "be educated, [and] follow the Cayton tradition."

The Hiram Revels family, ca. 1885. Front row: Hiram, Phoebe, Emma, Lillie. Back row: Maggie, Dora, Susie. *(Courtesy of Revels Cayton)*

The Hiram Revels home in Holly Springs, Mississippi, ca. 1885. Phoebe is at the far right. *(Courtesy of Revels Cayton)*

Horace Cayton and Susie Revels Cayton about the time of their marriage, 1896. *(From* Headlines and Pictures, *July 1945)*

The Cayton residence at 518 14th Avenue on Seattle's Capitol Hill near Volunteer Park. The family lived here from 1903 to 1909. *(From* Seattle Republican, *September 3, 1909.)*

The Caytons pose for a family portrait on their front porch in Seattle, ca. 1904. Left to right are Emma (Susie's niece), Susie holding baby Horace Jr., Horace standing above Madge (seated), and front left is Ruth (blurred). *(Courtesy of Vivian G. Harsh Research Collection of Afro-American History and Literature, Chicago Public Library [VGHRC, CPL])*

The Republican State Central Committee, 1908. Ellis DeBruler, chairman, is on the left at the table and inset. At the right of the table and inset is the committee's secretary, J. Will Lysons. Horace Cayton sits behind and to the left of DeBruler, just above the inset. (*From* Cayton's Campaign Compendium of Washington, 1908)

This special edition of the *Seattle Republican* was given free to African American visitors to the Alaska-Pacific-Yukon Exposition, held in Seattle in 1909.

Madge at age 6, 1907.
(*Courtesy of Revels Cayton*)

Ruth at age 18, 1915. *(Courtesy of Susan Cayton Woodson)*

Madge's high school graduation picture, 1919. *(Courtesy of Susan Cayton Woodson)*

Revels Cayton at about age 12, in front of the Laurel Apartments, 1919. *(Courtesy of Revels Cayton)*

Bonnie Branch, Horace Cayton Jr.'s first wife, 1929. *(Courtesy of VGHRC, CPL)*

Horace R. Cayton in 1920, age 61. *(Courtesy of Susan Cayton Woodson)*

Horace and Susie Cayton walking near Lake Washington, 1935. When Horace Jr. and Irma were first married Susie sent this photo to introduce herself and Horace's father to their new daughter-in-law. *(Courtesy, Irma Cayton Wertz)*

Revels speaking to seamen on the S.S. *America* for the Maritime Federation of the Pacific, San Francisco, 1939. *(Courtesy of Revels Cayton)*

Horace Jr. and second wife, Irma, in their basement apartment of the Rosenwald building in Chicago, 1939. *(Courtesy of VGHRC, CPL)*

Horace Jr. meeting with CIO head John L. Lewis, ca. 1939. *(Courtesy of VGHRC, CPL)*

During one of his visits to Parkway Community House, Richard Wright autographs a copy of *Native Son* for Horace, 1940. *(Courtesy of VGHRC, CPL)*

Langston Hughes (left), Horace Cayton, and Arna Bontemps at Parkway Community House, May 27, 1947. *(Courtesy of VGHRC, CPL)*

Revels (right) with Paul Robeson (center) and Percy Llewlyn (left, Regional Director, UAW-CIO) at National Negro Congress convention, Detroit, 1947. *(Courtesy of Revels Cayton)*

Lillie at age 12, 1926. *(Courtesy of Susan Cayton Woodson)*

Photo studio portrait of Lillie, ca. 1942. *(Courtesy of VGHRC, CPL)*

Susan (Sue), ca. 1949. *(Courtesy of VGHRC, CPL)*

Revels and Lee, with baby Michael (Revels, Jr.) in New York, 1949. *Courtesy of Revels Cayton*

Horace Jr. and Ruby enjoy an evening at a Chicago nightclub, 1947. *(Courtesy of VGHRC, CPL)*

Revels sent this photo to brother Horace, ca. 1968. *(Courtesy of VGHRC, CPL)*

Horace's "Happy New Year" card sent to friends and family from Paris, shortly before his death, January 1970. *(Courtesy of VGHRC, CPL)*

CHAPTER 6

The Torch is Passed

The Cayton Family, 1931–1943

THE DEPRESSION YEARS proved extremely difficult for Susie and Horace Cayton Sr., as they were for so many elderly Americans. The Caytons, like other unemployed African Americans, were forced to rely on government relief programs implemented under Roosevelt's New Deal to help mitigate some of the effects of the Depression. Horace Sr. would walk down to the King County relief station and stand in the "dole lines" for hours. Eventually he strolled home with a small sack of bread, cheese, and potatoes; this upset Susie to the point of tears. "What they have done to him," she would say shaking her head, "what they have done to him. They broke him, just like you take a stick and break it over your knee."[1]

Without warning in mid-winter 1933–34, the Cayton family found themselves taken off the relief rolls. Revels' militant activities of the past couple of years had gained the attention of numerous state authorities. He was what they called a "marked agitator." Local bureaucrats found his family a convenient target for harassment. On learning this news, Revels stormed into the King County relief office, demanding that his family be reinstated. "We don't have anything to eat," he hollered. "I don't care what you do to me, but you're not cutting my family off relief, and I'm not leaving here until they're on. I don't know just what I'm going to do, but we're going to have a ball here if you don't put 'em back on." The tactic worked. The family, except for Revels, returned to the support rolls.[2]

In a few short years, Revels had moved from being a drifting shipboard worker—disinclined to pursuing academics, and unsure of what he wanted in life—to becoming a self-possessed, skilled, community organizer, a leader in Seattle's burgeoning maritime union and communist movements. The turnaround in young Revels' life began when he started to unofficially audit classes at the University of Washington. There he encountered Marian

Tayback, a friend who recently had given him a pamphlet about the Scottsboro Boys, nine young black men who had been arrested in 1931 in Alabama and charged with raping two white girls. Marian, it turned out, was a member of the Young Communist League (YCL), and soon Revels started attending meetings in a University District home.

At these social gatherings, Revels met other bright, idealistic young people like himself. Here he found acceptance and a special regard, which he had lost entirely at school and largely at home. "I found refuge in this Young Communist League," he recalled. At first, "I didn't learn anything about Communist theory or anything like that. All I knew was that I found a group that I fit into." He felt a natural gravitation to this "little island of decent people who had an ideological base not to be prejudiced." It was a good match. As the only African American, and being from a prominent Seattle family, he quickly gained respect and recognition. He thrived on the special attention, and at the same time his intellectual strengths and personal skills adapted him well to left-wing activism.

Soon, like most YCL members, Revels became a member of the International Labor Defense (ILD). The New York-based organization was established in 1925 by the Communist Party for the legal defense of radicals and the working class, and, since December 1929, it had made the struggle for "Negro rights" a first priority. It was the ILD's work in defending the Scottsboro Boys that initially impressed Revels. After a bitter two-year struggle with the NAACP, the ILD managed to take over the Scottsboro Boys case in March 1933, which became the ILD's most celebrated cause in the early 1930s. The progress of the Scottsboro affair through a series of court appeals provided a dramatic example to the nation of the denial of equal justice to African Americans.[3]

The Great Depression caused many Americans to rethink long-held assumptions about political and social institutions. Many turned to the radical left, hoping for solutions to the nation's economic troubles. For large numbers of African Americans, who faced the additional burdens of discrimination, the times appeared conducive to making dramatic changes in American society. To the Communist Party, the oppressed black masses— the large majority of whom were of the working class—seemed ripe for revolution. The party, styling itself as the champion of the oppressed, made a special effort to boost black membership, and it launched an aggressive public campaign against "white chauvinism," which the communists considered to be clear proof of the failure of the American capitalist system.

During this period, even moderate groups such as the NAACP and the Urban League became radicalized to some degree.

In Seattle, Revels soon was positioned to play an important role in the radical movement. As a militant organizer and leader from 1932 to mid-1934, the energetic young Cayton quickly learned to apply the ILD's dual tactic of using legal procedures and mass protests in attempting to achieve the organization's aims. As head of the ILD's regional office, Revels traveled to a dozen or more Northwest towns, speaking on the Scottsboro topic. "It was so interesting to see these people, where there was hardly a Negro in the town, get up and talk about the injustices to the Scottsboro Boys," he recalled. "This was a dream."

In August 1933, Revels made another tour of the region, this time with ILD President Richard B. Moore and "Mother Patterson," whose son was one of the Scottsboro Boys. In 1934, Revels repeated the tour accompanied by "Mother Wright," also the parent of one of the boys. Revels was deeply impressed by Richard Moore, and carefully observed the ILD president's dynamic speaking abilities to see how political rhetoric could be fused with passion to bring audiences to their feet and rouse them to action.[4]

Most Seattle citizens, however, did not share Revels' enthusiasm for the Scottsboro case and other International Labor Defense causes. The ILD in this district, in his words, "was just about as dead as the undertaker parlor." This reflected the climate of race prejudice in Seattle. Also, the ILD's ties to the Communist Party put off many people. Most were more interested in their own immediate needs, particularly food and shelter for themselves and their families. Still, Revels championed ILD causes, spurred on by his zealous devotion. He rapidly developed impressive skills as a public speaker, aided by his natural friendliness and genuine interest in people. His unassuming manner, quick wit, and ability to think on his feet, combined with his party loyalty and, by then, a grasp of basic Marxist theory, made him a gifted speaker who engaged the hearts and minds of audiences. Revels moved quickly up through the ILD ranks, first regionally and then at the state level, eventually becoming the ILD state committee chairman. At one point, Revels moved the downtown District 12 office to the house his father owned on Second Avenue, just two doors from the Laurel Apartments.

Revels formally joined the Communist Party on the advice of a friend, who explained, "If you have influence in the party, your work will be much easier in the ILD."

Revels actively and openly supported the Communist Party. In his later years, he reflected on the decision to become a party member:

> At the beginning, the attraction of the Party for me was its fight on behalf of the Scottsboro Boys and its concern for blacks (we called ourselves "Negroes" in those days; most people were still referring to us as "colored"). Everything I heard from the CP about the plight of my own people fell right in with the talk I had heard from my family since I could remember. I was hearing my own family history brought up to date.
>
> Later I would be excited by the ideals I associated with socialism, but in the beginning I was drawn to the Party because I believed that in a socialist system there would be no racism. When I first began to hear about "the struggle against capitalism and imperialism," the idea had very little impact on me. I figured if the whites fight among themselves there might be a chance for blacks to get a more even break. But as my education in the Party progressed, I had much broader views and became much more class conscious. From a black orientation I moved to a place that also encompassed my class consciousness.
>
> Membership in the Party gave me a sense of identity, a direction, a purpose. It also continued the education cut off by the sleeping sickness that kept me out of school for over a year, because the Party required members to be reading, and studying, and keeping up with political events at home and abroad. Above all, there was the comradeship with bold and fearless men of vision.[5]

Revels and other communists took a leading role in attempts to organize the unemployed. In Seattle, as elsewhere in the country, Unemployed Citizens Leagues were formed to represent and focus the needs of the jobless. Members of the Communist Party and the ILD were active in these leagues, shaping demands and political action through committee work, demonstrations, and hunger marches.

Revels soon was taken under the wing of one of the main organizers in the western region, Morris Rapport, whom the party sent from San Francisco to Seattle to be district secretary. "Rap" was a long-time party ideologue, a theoretician, a shrewd Marxian social analyst, and a masterful politician. With Revels he toured many of the little towns in the Northwest, teaching the young man Marxist social-political theory and political maneuvering skills. These became the basis of Revels' training as a "mass leader," one who gives leadership in a mass organization.

Revels was involved in numerous protests over the course of two years, the most dramatic occurring on March 1, 1933. A statewide coalition of unemployed leagues and labor groups, called the "United Front Unemployed,"

organized a mass march on the state capitol in Olympia to press the governor for action. A caravan of two hundred autos and trucks from Seattle
were joined en route by others from eastern Washington. When the three-
thousand jobless demonstrators and their supporters—representing over
one hundred working class organizations—arrived on the outskirts of Olympia, they found the highway blocked by two hundred policemen and a
thousand members of the hastily organized "American Vigilantes of
Thurston County."

When the hunger marchers refused to turn around, police diverted
them into nearby Priest Point Park. As they moved off the highway, Revels
suddenly found himself surrounded by a hostile, armed mob of white
American Vigilantes, chanting, "We got the nigger, we got the nigger!"
They closed in on him, but at the last moment friends managed to spirit
Revels to safety. A cold rain fell during the night, turning the park into a
virtual sea of mud. While some marchers spent the night in cars, Revels
and others huddled around large bonfires, sipping hot coffee and singing
protest songs and the Communist International. The following day, the
demonstrators—wet, cold, and disappointed at having failed to see the
governor—left Olympia.[6]

During the next few months, Revels and other ILD members under-
took another protest action that was simple and direct. They walked up
and down Seattle streets, removing many of the "Whites Only" signs. Revels, known in Seattle as "the Cayton boy," carried the signs into every church
in the African American community. As his father before him, Revels urged
blacks to rally together to bring about change. His impassioned speeches
focused on the simple message of resisting. "Yeah, we're radical, and they
call us Reds," he would say, holding up the offensive signs, "but I think
you need some more radicals and Reds around here in places of influence
and maybe you won't have so many of these!" Revels' courageous actions
made him popular and earned him a reputation as a fighter in the local
community.

With typical Cayton determination, Revels carried his campaign into
the mainstream Seattle political arena. At the beginning of 1934, Revels
filed as a Communist Party candidate for a seat on the Seattle City Council. Along with other communist office seekers, he would be soundly defeated in the March primary, receiving only 1,737 votes. At a community
forum, where city council candidates presented themselves and their plat-
forms, the Republican and Democratic candidates gave their "usual promises." Revels arrived with an armful of signs, and his blunt, fervent speech

brought the same reaction it had from the church congregations. "The whole place just burst out hollering," he recalled. But to Revels, the most important part of the evening came after the meeting. His father had attended the forum and the two Caytons strolled home together. Revels remembered their conversation as one of the high points of their relationship. "My Dad said, 'Son, you did a wonderful job. You really put it to them. I don't agree with anything you said, but I was very, very proud of you.'"[7]

The most memorable—and terrifying—incident in this period for Revels happened in mid-April 1934, when a visiting professor and his wife from Oxford University in Britain, Mr. and Mrs. E.M. Hugh-Jones, took Revels on an automobile tour of the area. In the little coal mining town of Roslyn in the mountains of central Washington they encountered a bitter and violent miners' strike. Revels' reputation as a radical and "a marked agitator" landed him in jail when the State Patrol spotted him less than an hour after his arrival. The police grilled Revels for five hours, threatening to carve a swastika in his scalp and lynch him. Local vigilantes crowded around the jail cell. Only Hugh-Jones' persistent telephone calls to the British Consulate and the governor's office secured Revels' release. Once again he narrowly escaped serious trouble. The English professor's report on the incident in the *New Republic* described Revels as "courageous," noting, "[T]he lad…would certainly not have emerged undamaged, and, being a Negro, would have been lucky to emerge alive."[8]

Revels' efforts began taking him in other new directions. In August 1934, he dropped ILD activities to help promote the Seattle chapter of the League of Struggle for Negro Rights (LSNR). The LSNR was intended to be a "mass organization" of, and for, African Americans. At the Seattle group's first meeting, the discussion focused on the anti-segregation movement. Revels delivered a lengthy presentation, addressing the status of black workers in America and emphasizing "militant mass action as the way to force concessions." Over the next ten months, Revels energetically supported the LSNR, but with limited success. He led protests against segregation and discrimination as well as other efforts aimed at heightening community awareness of the league and its goals.[9]

In April 1934, however, Harry Haywood had replaced Richard B. Moore, then the national president of the LSNR. Moore and those who supported him were ousted by a Community Party offensive to root out "petty bourgeois nationalism." This had followed the Communist Party's Eighth National Convention, where the party leadership's goal of eliminating "black nationalism" was given almost the same attention as eliminating white chauvinism. By mid-1934 when the Seattle LSNR had begun to be formed, the party and the ILD leadership had little interest in assisting in its development or that of any other "nationalistic" organization. Revels eventually would give up trying to sustain a branch of the LSNR and focused instead on the "world unity of black and white proletarians."

In September 1934, the Communist Party nominated Revels as its candidate for state senator from the 37th District. The left-wing weekly, *Voice of Action,* gave him front-page attention, including full pictorial coverage, as a "prominent Negro leader." That fall, Revels also organized a community protest against the formation of a "colored Girl Reserve group" at Washington Grade School, where Susan was a student. Revels blasted the Reserve group organizers—the YWCA's Idell Vertner, the Urban League's Joseph Jackson, and the school principal—calling them "misleaders" for participating in a Jim Crow organization that could lead to segregated lunchrooms and classrooms. The protest aroused little public interest and the Girl Reserve continued to function. Among those who joined was Susan Cayton, along with many of her friends.[10]

In December 1934, the League of Struggle for Negro Rights hosted a banquet in honor of Angelo Herndon, a young Communist organizer arrested in Atlanta for leading a 1932 unemployed workers' protest. Charged under an archaic law for inciting insurrection and sentenced to twenty years on a Georgia chain gang, Herndon was released on bail in 1934. The ILD had publicized the case and Herndon gained national recognition for his cause, which involved free speech and assembly issues. Revels penned an article for the *Voice of Action,* calling Herndon a "fearless leader" in the struggle for justice and workers' rights. When visiting Seattle, Herndon stayed at the Cayton home, where Susie took a liking to the twenty-one year old, whom she thought was "sweet" and "charming."[11]

Revels' final LSNR activity of note occurred in early 1935. Dorlan Todd, a King County state representative, introduced an anti-intermarriage bill in the legislature. Immediately, the African American community banded together to form a citizens' committee with representatives from such diverse groups as the LSNR, NAACP, Urban League, and an array of churches, clubs, lodges, and women's societies. The House of Representatives in Olympia was deluged with letters of outrage from people and organizations of all races, including a host of white churches, labor unions, and liberal organizations. Within six weeks the bill died. In the *Voice of Action,* Revels praised the bill's defeat as a "victory of unity between white workers and Negro people." Applauding the citizens' committee as a "united front," he called for continued action and mass protests, "to keep fascism from coming to America, free the Scottsboro boys, and break down the entire system of lynch terror and oppression."[12]

Revels' ILD and LSNR work had received regular coverage and support from friends publishing the *Voice of Action,* many of whom Revels had known since his Young Communist League days. The newspaper's staff included editors Lowell Wakefield and Allan Max (who had lived with the Caytons for an extended period, and led one of the hunger marches on Olympia), and business manager Arlene Randall. All of this energy, talent, and support notwithstanding, Seattle's LSNR chapter was destined for a short life.

Over the years, Revels had tried to maintain ties to workers in the shipping industry. Because of his radical activities, however, the company-directed black seamen's union blackballed him. The Colored Marine Beneficial Association controlled all hiring for the Pacific Steamship Company's Admiral Line, the only coastal shipping firm that hired African Americans. In 1934, as the LSNR faltered, Revels started directing his attention toward waterfront issues. When a massive maritime strike began that year, Revels attended meetings in Astoria, Oregon, connecting him with West Coast workers' activities. He began organizing for the left-wing Marine Workers Industrial Union (MWIU). During the marine strike, the number of unemployed workers recruited as strikebreakers was remarkably low. One leftist writer claimed, "nowhere on the 2,000 mile strike front was there greater solidarity between strikers and unemployed."[13]

After the strike ended, Revels began seeking further opportunities in the labor movement. The future for him appeared to lie in San Francisco, where the Marine Cooks and Stewards Union had its headquarters. In May 1935 he left Seattle for San Francisco, where the maritime workers' struggle would play out in a dramatic and often violent fashion over the next decade.

+≒≒+

As the older Cayton children grew up and left home in the 1920s and 1930s, Lillie and Susan were left to take care of Horace Sr. and Susie, who now were getting on in years.

From an early age Lillie seemed to fall outside of the family mold and expectations of its children. Lillie was slow in school and a weak personality, easily pushed around by others. When she was about 16 or 17 years old (ca. 1930–31), Lillie suffered a life-changing trauma: she was attacked and gang-raped by a group of young men. She kept the violent sexual assault secret from her sisters and brothers, and perhaps her parents. After the incident, Lillie increasingly strayed from the Cayton home. She began to lead her own, difficult life. In 1933 she dropped out of Garfield High School, before the end of her second year. She found work as a waitress and cashier, and her life began to center around the "sporting world" down on Jackson Street. Lillie spent little time at home and finally moved to a house near Jackson and Lane streets. By 1937 she had married a man named Romey. For a time they lived just down the street from the Caytons, then they moved from Seattle. In March 1938 Lillie returned to town, in the process of obtaining a divorce. Within another two years she had remarried. Although her lifestyle distressed her family, there was little they could do to intervene.[14]

More and more, Horace Sr. lived in the past. Susie complained to the children that all he wanted to do was talk about Reconstruction and the old days. He did more than just talk about the past, however; he also preserved family history for posterity. In 1937, Horace Sr. released a brief autobiography of Hiram Revels, which the former senator had dictated to one of his daughters in 1897. The original fourteen-page document, which Cayton termed "a more or less disjointed story," was placed in the Schomburg Collection in the New York Public Library. Horace Sr. also began writing his autobiography, an effort that occupied much of his final three years, and he still dashed off occasional letters to editors when racist comments appeared in the press.[15]

Horace Sr. also wrote to W.E.B. Du Bois, offering a rather condescending review of Du Bois' book, *Black Reconstruction*. Cayton said that the book conceivably might be of benefit to African Americans, but if so, he was "at a loss to decipher how." Horace Sr. claimed the work was based on an erroneous assumption: "It is absolutely preposterous to think of the Negro in the United States in the light of a distinct individuality, to say nothing of a separate nationality." Black people were denied the opportunity to assert their individuality, and thus were "without a cause or a country." Cayton felt the race was facing extinction, either by amalgamation or by violence. He closed respectfully, calling Du Bois "one of the foremost writers" in America, and ending with "May your literary star grow bigger, better and brighter."

Du Bois replied to this highly critical letter with courtesy and restraint. He suggested that Cayton had made the common mistake of "minimizing the importance of careful knowledge and a study of the past," the only way by which we could "be wise for the future."[16]

Susie reacted to the strains of aging and living in poverty quite differently. While her husband's attention narrowed to recording and preserving the past, her vision broadened outward and forward. She read voraciously and talked about the daily news, current ideas, and the future. As the parent closest to Revels, she watched his blossoming interest in socialism, and hers grew with it. Susie attended every meeting Revels organized in the Madison area about the Scottsboro Boys. Although her husband had long since stopped participating in the NAACP, Susie joined the Seattle chapter so she could have yet another avenue for working on community issues. As the Depression deepened and Seattle's unemployed workers began to organize for action, Susie became involved in this effort, too. She served as secretary of the Skid Road Unemployed Council for a time. As the only woman in the movement, she quickly earned the respect and love of many, who called her "Mother Cayton." At some point in the mid 1930s, she became a member of the Communist Party.

Although a communist late in life, Susie remained a devout Christian. She had many conversations with Revels about the Marxist view that religion was the "opiate of the masses." Following one of their discussions about the local churches' lack of involvement in the unemployed struggle, Susie decided that she had to agree with her son. Revels smiled as he recollected their conversation:

> One night she came in and woke me up, and she said, "Son, I agree with you. The church is not doing its job, and it's not really a social factor for good"…And I said, "Mama, that's just great. Now, let's see about this fellow Jesus Christ."
>
> Well, mother started laughing. She burst out and said, "Now, look, young fella, don't you start talking about Jesus Christ, as old as I am. The minute I say I agree with you about the church, here you come about Jesus Christ. You just leave Jesus Christ alone. I'm too old for that talk. I've got to die, you know, and I don't want to have any trouble from him."

As a result of her community activist reputation, one day Susie answered a knock at the front door. A large, tall man nearly filled the doorway. "I'm Paul Robeson," he said. "I'm on concert tour here, and so many people have told me about you that I just wanted to come up and see you."

The two sat in the kitchen and talked for hours, stimulated by their mutual enthusiasm for books, contemporary social issues, and world problems. Thus began Robeson's long-time friendship with the Cayton family that lasted until his death over three decades later. On a later visit in Seattle, Robeson even took the time to talk to Susie's sewing club. Of course, with Susie as its leader, this was no ordinary sewing club. To Susie, piecing quilts together for the needy provided a good rationale for gathering a dozen women together to discuss social and political issues. Susie cut out newspaper articles to read to the group, and then led a discussion. She called it, "educating the neighborhood."[17]

Susie also brought Langston Hughes into the family's circle of friends when, in May 1932, Hughes passed through Seattle. He, too, began regularly stopping at the Cayton home when visiting the city. This greatly pleased Madge and her girl friends, who were excited about spending time with the young poet whom her brother Horace Jr. described as "extremely good looking, a beautiful brown color."[18]

As the 1930s neared an end, Horace Sr. worked on the final draft of his autobiography. Susan Cayton Woodson remembers evenings as a young woman listening to him read the manuscript aloud as she sat perched in bed next to Mother Susie. By early 1939, the project was finished; the manuscript numbered over four hundred typewritten pages, plus several illustrations. Horace Sr. immediately wrote to Langston Hughes, asking him to recommend a publisher, but Hughes could not. With high hopes, Cayton then sent the manuscript off to Horace Jr. in Chicago, who had promised to find a publisher. The old man anxiously awaited word from his son. "Every day he went through that mailbox, looking for a letter, and it hurt," recalled Susan, who was a high school senior at the time. "Dad was hurt; Mama was hurt. I didn't have enough sense to be hurt, but I knew the drama that was going on."[19]

Horace Jr. may not have tried seriously to find a publisher. Apparently, he considered the manuscript's style "too flowery." At any rate, in this period most presses were content to publish works focusing on interests of the white majority; there was little or no market for an ex-slave's autobiography. The failure to find a publisher was the final disappointment of Horace Sr.'s life.

Horace Sr.'s last two years brought the ravages of advancing age. On good days he was fairly cheerful, but on bad days his company was almost unbearable. He insulted Susan's houseguests, and once killed one of her cats with a rock. In early 1940, Horace Sr. wrote to Madge, by then living in Chicago, apologizing that poor health had prevented him from writing earlier. At eighty-one years old, he no longer had the strength to turn earth in the garden that spring. The chores, cooking, and chopping wood for the stove had passed to Susan. On most days, he spent long hours in a rocking chair at a window or listened to the radio. In May 1940, Susie wrote to Madge, informing her: "Your dad is not doing well. He grows more and more feeble. He let Lillie go to the market yesterday for him—that speaks for itself. One can never tell—he may live for some time and again I would not be surprised if the end came at any moment."[20]

The end came three months later on a summer afternoon, August 16, 1940. The physician recorded Horace Sr.'s official cause of death as carcinoma of the stomach, which had afflicted him for two-and-a-half years. A small funeral was held at Angelus Mortuary, with only family members and a few old-timers in attendance. Although the Caytons owned plots at Lakeview Cemetery, they could not afford a coffin, burial, and the grounds keeping. Horace Sr. was cremated and Susie later spread his ashes over the waters of Puget Sound.[21]

In the years before his death, Horace Sr.'s struggles against ever-present poverty, the loss of social and political status, the failure to get the book published, and the debilitating challenges of old age and poor health had all sapped his spirit. He bore the yoke of second class citizenship with great reluctance. Although his spirit suffered severely, Horace Cayton Sr. never gave up entirely. On his deathbed, the ex-slave who had come so far from Reconstruction-era Mississippi said to his son, Revels:

> The real test is whether you can live a good life—whether you can live among men as a man, and have no real deep regrets about anything. I've lived a good life. Really, I've lived a good life, and I've got good children to show for it, and a wonderful wife. That's all one can expect. So, when I die the light will be gone. I will have done my part for the world.

The leading regional African American newspaper, the *Northwest Enterprise,* carried a front-page obituary with the headline, HORACE CAYTON, PIONEER, PASSES AWAY. The King County Colored Republican Club issued a special resolution honoring Cayton with "grateful remembrance" as one of its founders and most active workers, and praised his "ability and keen judgment...his manifold service, contributions, and counsel." The white press considered Horace Sr.'s passage of little consequence. The *Seattle Post-Intelligencer* buried an abbreviated version of the obituary on page twenty-two. Not until the late 1960s would Seattleites "rediscover" Horace Cayton Sr. and begin to balance the region's history by drawing upon his many publications for evidence of the contributions made by African Americans in the Pacific Northwest.[22]

＋＝＝＋

After Horace Sr.'s passing, Susie sent twenty-two-year-old Susan to Chicago to live with Madge. Lillie remained with Susie in the house on Twenty-first Avenue. For a while, Lillie was attentive to her needs and would "make a fuss" over her mother. She drove Susie about town to her many meetings. Lillie also took care of some neighborhood children who had been deserted by their mother. Susie wrote to Susan telling her how pleased she was with Lillie, noting that the children had greatly improved under her care. "She is very kind to them, but compels them to obey," wrote Susie, and "they love her dearly."[23]

Throughout her sixties, Susie maintained a schedule hectic enough to outpace most people half her age. Though slowed by some physical ailments, including diabetes, she continued to devote energy to community work. In one of her letters to Madge, written when Susan yet attended Garfield High School and Horace Sr. was still living, Susie described her schedule:

> Now I will give you some idea of my activities and nothing but shortage of car fare ever keeps me from pursuing them.
>
> Monday night: P.W.U. Local, A.F. of L. (now merged with the Worker's Alliance). Meets in one of the Minor School portables (walking distance).
>
> Tuesday night: The Negro Workers Council, meets in a portable at the Horace Mann School. I'm Vice Pres. and our Pres. is out of the city at this time.
>
> Wens.[sic] Night: stay in and read late.
>
> Thursday: Party Unit always meets. (Some times walking distance, some times not.)
>
> Friday night: Stay home or visit in the neighborhood.
>
> Sat.: The Harriett Tubman Club meets . . .
>
> Sunday night: The Worker's Forum, 94 Main Street.

> Besides, I try to attend the Legislative Council which meets every first and third Monday in the Mo. also the P.T.A. at Garfield, which meets every third Thursday in the Mo. Of course, there are mass meetings, dances and what not that come in at times. I'm having the time of my life and at the same time making some contribution to the working class I hope.[24]

Her husband's passing did not seem to slow the pace of Susie's life. In an October 1940 letter, she again provided the children living in Chicago with an update of her activities. Susie said she would soon attend a banquet hosted by the King County Colored Republican Club at which all wives of past presidents were to be honorary guests; and, she had visited a "white comrade friend" in Harborview Hospital. She also recently had attended a Sunday Night Forum featuring a young democratic congressman, Warren G. Magnuson, who spoke to a full house audience. Here, Susie paused to add that the Sunday Forum's Executive Board had presented her with a large floral piece at "Mr. Cayton's" funeral. "That token of love and respect from an organization of, largely, unemployed men to a fellow worker," Susie wrote, "was a thing that money could not buy."[25]

Susie remained an active member of the Communist Party. When she went to see the Russian film, "We Are from Kronstadt," she was deeply moved. The movie prompted her to reflect on changes in the local Communist Party in the preceding seven years:

> Saw quite a few party members that I knew. So many of the old-timers have dropped out. Two things, in a way, I noted: good warm clothes, shoes on the workers, and dollars instead of dimes in the collection box. Quite a change from '35, '36, '37, etc.[26]

In early 1941, Susie was renting one room of the house to Lillie, who was supporting herself with day work and filling in part-time at the Court Hotel bar. At the time, Lillie was separated from her second husband, Otis Grey. Lillie's divorce case went to court in August of that year. Soon afterward, Lillie moved out of the Cayton family home and began working as a hotel maid at twenty-five dollars a week, while taking classes in shorthand and improving her typing skills in hopes of finding secretarial work.

In late winter 1942, Susie's health took a downturn, and Madge arrived to take her mother back to Chicago, where the Cayton children—Madge, Susan, and Horace Jr.—could look after her. Sixteen months after leaving Seattle for Chicago, in July 1943, Susie died of complications from diabetes. When news of her death reached Seattle, Susie's long-time friend from the Skid Road Unemployed Council, Byrd Kelso, responded with a letter of glowing tribute.

Susie Revels Cayton, he wrote, was one of the "grandest ladies" he had ever known, and "always such an inspiration to all of the poor folks here, no matter their color, religion or nationality." The workers loved Susie for good reason. "Many times, during that bitter depression," Kelso emphasized, "we worked together to help HUNDREDS if not THOUSANDS of poor people here and actually kept them from starving to death."[27]

Some weeks later, Susie's children spread her ashes, like those of her husband before her, in Puget Sound. Not long after their mother's funeral, Lillie visited Chicago. She wanted to stay, but the family refused her. Madge had enough family responsibilities at the time. To her siblings, Lillie was an alcoholic, who attracted drunks and "riff-raff." They put her on a bus back to Seattle. A year later, this scene was repeated. Again, the family cast Lillie adrift. In the coming years, Lillie descended into the miserable, chaotic life of an alcoholic, marrying four more times and bearing four children that she increasingly became unable to care for.

Preoccupied with their own careers and personal lives, Lillie's brothers and sisters took as little interest in her now, as when she was a child. Later, Revels hardly could recall Lillie in those years. The same is true of Susan, who laments, "I lost Lillie somewhere along the line." Lillie had not received the same attention that her parents had given the rest of the children. Lillie grew up, she later said, feeling like "the outcast" of the family. Many years later, her eldest daughter, Madge (Thompson), noted that Lillie "never talked about her family much… A few times she told me who Hiram Revels was. That's all… She didn't have much love in her for the family. She felt hurt because they wouldn't associate with her…they were just never there for her."[28]

As adults, what separated the Cayton siblings from Lillie was more than a simple age gap. Madge, Horace Jr., and Revels did not see Lillie leading a life that their father and mother would approve of. They saw no achievements or community contributions coming from her, no civic works to benefit others, no membership in organizations that aimed to further "the uplift," no participation in the struggle against racism and discrimination. Unlike Madge, a social worker, Horace Jr., a student of black urban culture,and Revels, a labor rights advocate for African Americans and working class whites, Lillie did nothing to "educate the neighborhood."

For many years, the Caytons turned their backs on Lillie. Yet they felt that Lillie had turned away from them, too, by flouting family tradition and rebelling against the middle class ethics and Victorian moral standards that they had inherited from their parents. Lillie seemed far removed from being "a Cayton." The name, the family status, and the commandment to "go out and achieve" apparently meant little to Lillie. As far as they were concerned, the proud family tradition in Seattle had come to an end, and the Caytons' future lay elsewhere.

CHAPTER 7

A Black Metropolis

Horace Jr., Madge, and Susan, 1931–1943

S USAN CAYTON WOODSON clearly recalls the day she arrived in Chicago
in 1940. She stood on the corner of 47th Street and South Parkway
with Paul Robeson and family friend Gene Coleman, feeling frightened by
the immensity, the newness, the rawness, and the blackness of her new
home. Twenty-two-year-old Susan was shocked by her encounter with
Chicago's South Side, just as her uncle, Horace Jr., had been when he
arrived nine years earlier. The Caytons had plunged into a sea of ebony, a
world vastly different from the uncrowded, genteel, and very white Seattle
in which they had been raised.

In their landmark study, *Black Metropolis* (1945), Cayton and St. Clair
Drake characterized the busy Chicago intersection as "the urban equiva-
lent of a village square":

> Stand at the center of the Black Belt—at Chicago's 47th St. and South
> Parkway. Around you swirls a continuous eddy of faces—black, brown,
> olive, yellow, and white… In most of the stores there are colored sales-
> people… In the offices around you, colored doctors, dentists, and law-
> yers go about their duties. And a brown-skinned policeman saunters
> along… On a spring or summer day this spot, "47th and South Park,"
> is the urban equivalent of a village square… There is continuous and
> colorful movement here—shoppers…insurance salesmen…club
> reporters…irate tenants…job-seekers… At an exclusive "Eat Shoppe"
> just off the boulevard, you may find a Negro Congressman or ex-Con-
> gressman dining at your elbow, or former heavyweight champion Jack
> Johnson…in the next room there may be a party of civic leaders, black
> and white, planning reforms.[1]

When Horace Jr. and Bonnie had arrived in 1931, Chicago's African
American population of over two hundred and thirty thousand was con-
centrated in the Black Belt, a rigidly segregated strip of land some seven-
and-a-half miles long. Over the next decade, forty thousand migrants, most
from the South, crowded into the small, already saturated area, which

became known as Bronzeville. Bonnie and Horace settled into a one-room kitchenette apartment near the University of Chicago.[2]

Horace came to know the culture of this "black metropolis" intimately over the next decade as a participant-observer, as both civic leader and social scientist. In the dozen years from 1931 to 1943—from his arrival in Chicago to the eve of the publication of *Black Metropolis*—Cayton would reach the peak of his professional career. His work as a sociologist, teacher, writer, and civic leader brought him recognition from a variety of circles, and he associated with many of the leading figures of the period. By 1946 his name began to appear in *Who's Who* and *Current Biography*. At the same time that he was achieving success in his professional life, he was descending into an emotional turmoil that led to marital problems, a growing dependence on alcohol and drugs, and eventually, an estrangement from his brother Revels.

Upon arriving in Chicago, Horace immediately began to grapple with comprehending this strange, new environment. Bronzeville was experiencing serious social and economic problems, including a severe housing shortage, high crime, police brutality, and a host of other "ghetto conditions." The press regularly reported on eviction riots, and just weeks after his arrival, Horace witnessed a rent strike. He was moved to put the dramatic event into words: "The Black Bugs," his first published article, appeared in the September 9, 1931, edition of the *Nation*.

It was the appeal of sociology and the encouragement of renowned sociologist Dr. Robert Park that had drawn Horace to Chicago in the first place. Cayton vaguely expected the sociological perspective to help him understand himself and his place in the world. Sociology seemed more than a career; it was a calling. He believed it would not merely provide him with a profession, but, as he later declared, it "would solve my own racial and social problems as a Negro trying to find an at-homeness in American society."[3]

In the summer of 1931, Horace began graduate studies at the University of Chicago. He eagerly set about learning the academic discipline that he hoped would provide answers to his questions about his identity as an African American. The sociology department had a prestigious national reputation, counting among its esteemed faculty Robert Park, Louis Wirth, and Ernest Burgess. They took an interest in Horace and his academic career, particularly Wirth, who became his major mentor. Horace was a full-time student for two years, taking graduate classes in sociology, economics, and political science. He then held various "research assistant" positions over the next six years, but he did not receive a degree. As a research assistant to political science professor Dr. Harold Gosnell, Horace interviewed black policemen, providing most of the material for one chapter of Gosnell's study, *Negro Politicians: The Rise of Negro Politics in Chicago,* published in 1935.

Upon the Caytons' arrival in Chicago, Bonnie started working as a social worker with United Charities at a new emergency relief office in the heart of Bronzeville. There, as a caseworker under Mary Wirth, wife of Horace's mentor, Louis Wirth, she aided newly arrived migrants from Southern states who were desperately seeking food and housing assistance. "I loved my work and felt we were helping people in great need," she recalled. "Thus began several exciting and rewarding years of mental and cultural stimulation and growth for both Horace and myself." They made many friends, black and white, and felt genuinely welcomed. After their first year in Chicago, the Reverend Dr. Curtis Reese, director of the Abraham Lincoln Center, invited the couple to live there. It was the one place in the city where mixed race couples were accepted and could feel at home, and their time at the center was the best that Horace and Bonnie would know.[4]

In June 1932, after the end of Horace's first year at the university, he was offered a summer position at Tuskegee Institute in Alabama. At the urging of Robert Park, he accepted. Advised not to take a white wife to the Deep South, Horace left Bonnie behind in Chicago. To his disappointment, his duties at Tuskegee were unchallenging and the summer was uneventful, except for one occurrence he never forgot: a caravan of cars speeding past campus in pursuit of "a young Negro accused of insulting a white girl." It was his first sight of a lynch mob. Shaken and anxious to return to Chicago, Horace later noted, "The ignorance of the South, its sudden violence, and the hopelessness of its people had thoroughly disheartened and discouraged me. I had felt like an alien in a strange country."[5]

When he returned to the University of Chicago, Horace began a research project with Wirth, assisting in a study of teen suicide for the National Resources Committee. Midway through the academic year, Dr. Charles S. Johnson, noted sociologist at Fisk University, offered Horace an appointment as "special assistant" to U.S. Interior Secretary Harold Ickes on a research program under Johnson's general direction. Horace accepted the job, and for the next year he worked with George S. Mitchell, a professor at the University of North Carolina. They surveyed the effects of the National Recovery Act on African American workers, assessing their economic status and union participation, and documented the organizing efforts of the CIO (Congress of Industrial Organizations).[6]

For five months Cayton toured the Northeast and Midwest, visiting almost every important steel producing center and meat packing plant in those regions, while Mitchell covered CIO organizing in selected sites in the South. The work and travel schedule was intense. In July 1934, after only four months on the project, Horace wrote to Wirth that he had covered the cities of Nashville, Washington D.C., New York, and Pittsburgh, with Maryland, upper New York State, eastern Pennsylvania, and Ohio still to come. He expected to finish up in the steel center of Gary, Indiana. Cayton and Mitchell interviewed some six hundred factory workers, union officials, plant managers, and foremen; an additional three hundred workers were interviewed in 1937 and 1938. This effort eventually resulted in Cayton's first book, *Black Workers and the New Unions,* co-authored with Mitchell and published in 1939.[7]

The grueling pace took a toll on Horace's health; he suffered as well from troubles in his personal life. His academic and professional advancements contrasted sharply with the disintegration of his relationship with Bonnie. The extended separations, starting with Horace's summer in Tuskegee, severely strained the marriage. More damaging to the relationship, Horace had been seeing other women and developed serious drinking and prescription drug abuse problems. Under the effect of the sedative Nembutal, he experienced blackouts and episodes of crawling in a stupor on the floor. Finally, in September 1934, Bonnie walked out. Horace became severely depressed, even suicidal.[8]

By the fall of 1934, his condition was obvious to all. Dr. Johnson wrote to Horace, "I learned just before leaving Chicago that you were showing some of the effects of this sustained drive in your physical condition...I feel that I should repair this earlier omission by insisting that you take at least a couple of weeks in a sanitarium and follow this with at least a couple of weeks of less arduous labor, perhaps in the Department at Fisk."

With assistance from Mitchell and his wife, Cayton headed to Canada, staying for some time at Limberlost Lodge, one hundred and fifty miles north of Toronto, Ontario. Shortly after his arrival, Horace penned a note to Wirth, apologetically saying, "My hand is still a bit unsteady for writing." Horace expressed his deep appreciation and affection "for your interest in me during this last escapade." When Cayton returned to Chicago, he dropped out of school and out of sight for nearly eight months. During this period of recuperation, Madge came to live with him in Chicago, staying nearby in the Abraham Lincoln Center where she could provide some support for her younger brother.[9]

In the spring, Horace was well enough to resume his duties as a research assistant for the last few weeks of the academic year. For some time he had been living with a young white woman, Elizabeth Johns, one of Wirth's graduate students. In mid-summer 1935, Horace, Elizabeth, and one of her friends (a Swedish exchange student named Torsten) took a three-month trip to Europe. Horace stayed much of the time in Paris, which he soon grew to love. His letters to Wirth were filled with descriptions of his daily activities: taking long walks through the city with stops for food or drink at sidewalk cafes; attending a writers' conference; experiencing the political scene; and living in the Latin Quarter, where he met intellectuals, artists, and students. To Horace Jr., the French were "the most charming and delightful" people he had ever met, and he proclaimed Paris "the most wonderful city in the world."

Among the memorable experiences for thirty-two-year-old Cayton was an encounter with shipping heiress and noted "Negrophile," Lady Nancy Cunard, whose book *Negro* was published the year before. "She took me around to see the night life in Paris," he told Wirth, wryly adding, "interesting but not what it is cracked up to be."[10]

From Paris, Horace traveled to England, Belgium, Germany, Switzerland, and Sweden. In Stockholm he enjoyed a dinner with sociologist Gunnar Myrdal. Like Paul Robeson, who visited Germany a few months earlier, Cayton had found travel in the new Nazi state an unpleasant experience. "Leaving Germany was a relief," he wrote Wirth from Lucerne. "I felt terribly tense all of the time I was in Germany. Heidelberg, which was the seat of culture, is now the —hole of creation. People on the street were very antagonistic. One night in a restaurant had a close call. Refused to return the Nazi salute… I only got out by playing dumb."

Back in Paris, Horace pondered his future. Nearly a year had passed since he had left work and school, and he felt ready to resume his studies at the university. "I believe that I am now in a condition to do some work," he wrote to Wirth. "I would request only that you give me a three months appointment to see what I can do and if I do not make good I will willingly get out of academic life altogether. I think I have got a belly full of this neurotic business and am ready for good hard work—which I have on occasion done."[11]

No sooner did Horace arrive back in Chicago on October 1 than he found himself on the way to Nashville, Tennessee. Wirth and Johnson had arranged a one-year position for him at Fisk University, teaching courses in economics and labor. One of the leading "Negro colleges" in the country, Fisk was known for its social science department, which boasted a number of prominent scholars on race and culture, including Charles S. Johnson, James Weldon Johnson, E. Franklin Frazier, and Robert Park. Despite his dislike for the South, Horace quickly settled into the routine of his work.

One young woman on campus, Irma Jackson, immediately caught Horace's eye. The daughter of a well-to-do physician from Brunswick, Georgia, Irma was working as a social science department assistant while studying for a master's degree in social work. She was a vivacious Southern belle, a "handsome, light-complexioned girl," as Horace later described her. They fell in love and six weeks later, on November 18, 1935, married during a weekend trip to Chicago.[12]

At Fisk, Cayton had the opportunity to further develop a relationship with his University of Chicago mentor, Dr. Robert Park, who had taken a visiting lectureship at Fisk. Park had been interested in Cayton since their first meeting in Seattle, and he challenged Horace, sometimes with kindness, sometimes with what seemed like cruelty. Park was a father figure to young Horace and exerted a strong influence on him. Horace praised his professor as "brilliant" and admired his "rugged mind and intellectual honesty." Although the two men had offices next door to each other and spent many hours engaged in lively debate, Park remained "the great professor" and Cayton "his humble student."[13]

Horace began developing ideas for a master's thesis or doctoral dissertation focusing on the economic and social stratification of blacks in America. Park was intrigued by Cayton's work. He invited Horace to sit in on his "Race and Culture" seminar and to present papers to the group. By late spring, Horace wrote enthusiastically to Wirth, "I am spending all of my spare time on it and hope to use it for my thesis. In it I hope to trace the development of a group from a caste to what Dr. Park calls a Minority Group, i.e., a group with functional economic upper classes. I also hope to describe the social world of the Negro upper classes and their struggle to create this world apart from both the black masses and the unaccepting white community." It represented his first formal academic attempt to comprehend his personal experience in terms of Parkian sociology.[14]

Bolstered by his teaching success at Fisk (he reported "getting good results in my classes, and have quite a little student following") and by Park's encouragement, Horace was eager to resume studies at the University of Chicago. As the end of his term at Fisk approached in the spring of

1936, Horace wrote to Wirth about his plan to become a high school teacher.

> And now I believe I want to settle down and perhaps raise a family. Maybe I'm getting old, but I've lived an eventful life after a fashion and now I want a bit of security, economically and otherwise... I hope that within the next year and a half I can get my degree and with a Ph.D. ought to be able to break into the school system and then live a rather quiet life as a respectable, middle class, colored gentleman—occasionally serving on interracial committees and slipping the Communists a dollar or two on the side."[15]

Horace and Irma returned to Chicago and shared Madge's small apartment in a private home for the summer. In the tight Chicago housing market, the couple had to pull strings to get a place of their own. Irma knew the manager of the Michigan Boulevard Garden Apartments, known as "the Rosenwald." The 421-unit complex had been built by Julius Rosenwald in 1929 to provide housing for middle- and upper-income African Americans. The manager, Irma's ex-fiancé's brother, arranged for the Caytons to have the next available apartment.

+≡≡≡+

Horace resumed working in the fall of 1936, accepting a research assistantship in the anthropology department. His acquaintance with professor W. Lloyd Warner, who taught both anthropology and sociology, led to discussions about a government-funded research study of Chicago's African American population. The WPA—established as the Works Progress Administration in mid 1935, and later changed in July 1939 to the Work Projects Administration—had become the leading federal agency for financing work relief programs, including engineering and construction projects, community services, historical records surveys, the Federal Arts, Federal Theater, and Federal Writers projects, social research and statistical studies, and a great many others.

Warner and his colleagues at the University of Chicago submitted a project proposal to the federal government. Consequently, in November 1936, Cayton was named superintendent of the first of a series of funded research programs administered by WPA District 3, Chicago. The post, which Horace held until 1939, shaped his life for years to come. As a graduate student, it was a "dream come true" to be paid to assemble data for his planned study of black social stratification, which presumably would lead to an M.A., or possibly a Ph.D., in sociology (though in the end, an advanced degree eluded him). Furthermore, the position allowed Horace to engage in social activism, it spurred his growth as a sociologist, and provided an enormous bank of raw material for articles and books. The WPA position also brought Horace into contact with many scholars and writers, most notably Richard Wright and St. Clair Drake. His partnership with St. Clair Drake led to *Black Metropolis* in 1945, and the friendship with Wright became one of the most influential associations of Horace's life.

Under sponsorship of the Institute for Juvenile Research and Professor W. Lloyd Warner, Cayton launched the first project, a study focusing on the cultural and social factors contributing to juvenile delinquency. Cayton and Warner shared an interest in social and class stratification in the African American community. They decided to take advantage of this unique opportunity and broaden the project's focus, proposing to answer the questions of how and to what degree blacks were "subordinated and excluded in relation to white society," and what the effects were on African Americans.[16]

Using the juvenile delinquency study as a springboard, Warner and Cayton initiated what eventually became a series of in-depth studies of Chicago's African American community, financed by the WPA, county and state agencies, and individual sponsors. Establishing the project headquarters in the basement of the Good Shepherd Congregational Church, within a year Cayton was supervising a staff of just over one hundred people (90 percent of whom were black), including forty field workers who conducted interviews. Among the nineteen graduate students that Horace hired to collect and organize data was a young Chicago doctoral student in anthropology, St. Clair Drake. Cayton considered Drake, an instructor on leave from Dillard University, "by and large a poor executive," but "by far the most creative supervisor." Cayton admired his prodigious energies, which made him an excellent choice for directing the research methods and procedures for compiling information.[17]

During his tenure with the WPA, Cayton supervised at least ten major programs. The initial juvenile delinquency project was followed by studies on migration and mobility, churches and other social associations, and the occupational status of Chicago's blacks. Over the next three-and-a-half years, Cayton's staff assembled a massive volume of demographic information—statistics, charts, maps, and various data from libraries, newspapers, and other sources, plus personal histories from interviews. The information and materials produced under Cayton and Warner's direction were impressive and unprecedented. Along with a WPA-funded Illinois Writers Project, the "Negro in Illinois," the Cayton-Warner studies—the only research of its kind in the country at the time—stand among the finest products of the WPA's nationwide efforts. They provided the bulk of raw data for a number of significant reports, scholarly studies, and publications. The research files that survive, although constituting a small percentage of the original output, continue to be a legacy of enduring value to a host of scholars, students, and citizens.[18]

Cayton devoted himself to general administrative concerns, including resolving wage issues and other matters with the Communist-dominated WPA union, and raising funds for the sponsoring body, the Institute for Juvenile Research. His sense of working hard but having fun, punctuated with frequent informational meetings plus parties, created an *esprit de corps* among the project's African American and white staff. As project superintendent, Cayton received recognition from numerous public and professional sources. Accolades came from his staff, too. Mary Elaine Ogden, a research assistant and author of one of the project's published studies, closed the preface to her volume with a brief salute: "To Horace R. Cayton…all of us owe a great debt of gratitude, for his wise direction and human insight, the unusual combination of administrator and friend which won not only our respect, but also our affection."[19]

Many years later, St. Clair Drake fondly recalled Horace's contributions:

> [The] W.P.A. project out of which *Black Metropolis* came was a "natural" for his talents. His "cool," his sense of humor, and his negotiating skill held together a varied group of human beings on a research project for four years against the illegitimate pressures of gangsters (and conmen on the project and off) as well as the legitimate pressures of a militant union, the idiosyncrasies of academics, and the close scrutiny of government auditors. He created and maintained a framework of co-operative relations within which we were able to gather, analyze, and write up an incredible mass of material.[20]

In May 1937, Horace received news that he had been granted a prestigious Rosenwald Fellowship in sociology and statistics. The award was intended to allow him to pursue his proposed thesis topic, the "social and economic stratification of the Negro," at the University of Chicago, while continuing to supervise WPA projects. Horace used the fellowship to complete some final interviews and write his sections of *Black Workers and the New Unions,* published with co-author George S. Mitchell in 1939.[21]

Irma proved to be an asset to Horace in his WPA work. Attractive and intelligent, she felt equally at ease among Horace's white academic associates and in South Side social circles. She attended the Chicago Academy of Fine Arts, and found employment as a social worker. With Horace's job paying two hundred and fifty dollars a month, the Caytons lived comfortably in Bronzeville's middle and upper class area. In money matters, Horace was frustratingly irresponsible, so by mutual agreement Irma managed the couple's finances and their apartment at the Rosenwald building. A thoughtful editor, Irma worked side by side with Horace on *Black Workers and the New Unions,* organizing and rewriting his voluminous notes into readable form and making other contributions. Horace and Irma brought a sense of class and style to the WPA projects. Those years, recalled Irma, were "exciting, adventuresome and often reckless."[22]

As more and more documentation of the vicious repercussions of racism and segregation accumulated in the project's files, Cayton increasingly felt impelled to take action. Horace's position, as the only African American heading a major white-collar WPA project in Chicago, afforded him a unique platform. Armed with the latest data, Horace helped push long-smoldering issues to the attention of the populace and the press. The first fruits of the Cayton-Warner research projects were public speeches and articles in newspapers and magazines, intending to rouse readers to action. The project's massive data presented a clear picture of the black community's problems.

In December 1937, the first installment of Cayton's "Negroes Live in Chicago" appeared simultaneously in *Opportunity; Journal of Negro Life* (edited by Charles S. Johnson) and in Chicago's liberal monthly, the *Beacon.* Part two followed in the next month's issue of each magazine. Horace became a frequent speaker at clubs, churches, and other community organizations, and on local radio. Though occasionally addressing broader topics, such as "Abolishing the Black Belts in American Cities," he kept his main attention focused on the most critical, long-standing problem on the South Side—housing. With the humanist's compassion and the sociologist's insight, Cayton quickly emerged as a leading community spokesman, earning a reputation as a "crusader."[23]

On the South Side the number of blacks living in substandard housing was steadily increasing, while at the same time property owners and realtors were demolishing residential buildings for speculative aims. Meanwhile, restrictive housing covenants adopted by white homeowner associations in the surrounding communities prevented blacks from dispersing to outlying areas. The result, in Horace's words, was the creation of a de facto "legal ghetto." Chicago's federal housing projects initially were expected to bring some relief, but African American tenants were not being accepted, nor did city officials show any interest in addressing the problem or in appointing even one black person to the Chicago Housing Authority.

A crisis was imminent by the winter of 1937-38, and Horace stepped forward as one of the leading spokesmen calling for action. In a speech titled "Ways and Means of Securing Adequate Housing for Negroes in Chicago," he called upon trade unions and community, church and political groups to join in "aggressive and unified action." In an article, "Negro Housing in Chicago," Horace charged University of Chicago officials with supporting residential restrictions; and, in the follow-up "No Friendly Voice," he aroused a wave of community resentment against the university. Next came a piece co-authored with Estelle Hill Scott focusing on a new federal housing project, the Jane Addams Homes. Published in the *Chicago Defender,* the article used stark population statistics to dramatically demonstrate that, by proportionate measures, at least two hundred and twenty-five black families deserved homes in the project.[24]

In February 1938—after numerous community meetings, widespread protests, and requests to the secretary of the interior and the Federal Housing Authority for an investigation—the Chicago City Council finally began to hold hearings on the housing problem. Cayton's appearance before the Council Committee received front-page coverage in the *Defender.* Asking the city to act before people took matters into their own hands, he warned, "People will put up with these intolerable conditions only so long, then they will go and take what they want. If you do not want the bombings and murders which characterized the southward expansion of Negroes several years ago, do something to relieve the situation now."

The *Chicago Defender* and various civic organizations supported Cayton for appointment to the Chicago Housing Authority, but the city mayor appointed Robert Taylor, whose views were more conservative. By the end of 1938, the CHA and FHA signed an agreement to construct low cost housing on the South Side. The mayor and council promised other action, but little more was done.[25]

Some of the first academic papers resulting from the Cayton-Warner projects were given by Cayton, St. Clair Drake, and Estelle Hill Scott at the University of Chicago's "Annual Institute of the Society for Social Research," held in the summer of 1938. Horace Jr., W. Lloyd Warner, Elaine Ogden McNeil, and others also presented findings at other conferences and eventually published in academic journals. The first official publications from the WPA research projects appeared in December 1939. The WPA issued three project monographs in mimeograph form: *The Chicago Negro Community, A Statistical Description* by Mary Elaine Ogden, Estelle Hill Scott's *Occupational Changes among Negroes in Chicago,* and St. Clair Drake's *Churches and Voluntary Associations in the Chicago Negro Community.* Two years later, the WPA mimeo-published *Subject Index to Literature on Negro Art.* These and other manuscripts, interviews and data gathered by the projects were used by Cayton for various articles during this period. The Cayton-Warner projects also provided the bulk of data for three books published in 1941: W. Lloyd Warner's *Color and Human Nature* (he referred to the "Warner-Cayton research"), Charles S. Johnson's *Growing Up in the Black Belt,* and Richard Wright's *12 Million Black Voices.* In addition, the project data supported academic studies by at least ten graduate students (mainly at the University of Chicago) who completed master's theses, doctoral dissertations, and journal publications. Most of the students had worked on the projects as research assistants. Another product of the WPA research was a series of twenty articles published by the *Chicago Defender* (with "invaluable assistance" from Cayton) from July to November 1939, boldly headlined "Is the South Doomed?" In August 1940, Cayton made use of project data to prepare a statement on "Negro Migration" that he presented in Chicago at a hearing of the U.S. Congressional Committee on Interstate Migration. Later (in September 1941), Cayton and Elaine Ogden McNeil published a summary of their WPA efforts, "Research on the Urban Negro," in the *American Journal of Sociology.*[26]

At the end of the WPA project's second year, Cayton and the staff held an open house exhibition at the Good Shepherd Center in January 1939. The week-long event attracted over five hundred visitors—a rather impressive turnout for a government program's presentation of maps, charts, statistical tables, and typed manuscripts.[27]

In 1939 Warner and Cayton had a falling out over Warner's decision to exclude Cayton from a Washington D.C. trip to report on the program's progress. The slight was "an injustice," Horace pointedly wrote to Warner. "In view of this and a number of other misunderstandings in the past," he declared, "I feel quite definitely that I would like to work independently in the future." Cayton planned to remain until the WPA projects under his supervision were completed and the new ones successfully launched.[28]

In a May 1939 eleven-page memorandum, Cayton summarized the results of his two-and-a-half years of effort in Chicago. The staff had conducted eight thousand interviews, collected and transcribed twenty-five life histories, and amassed statistics covering over ninety years of African American community development from 1840 to the late 1930s. A month after writing the memorandum, Horace Jr. received perfectly timed news: he had been selected for another Rosenwald Fellowship. This would allow him to resign his WPA post and finish graduate studies at the University of Chicago. Cayton resigned and hastily made plans to sail for Europe to study low-cost housing in Amsterdam and London.[29]

During this time, Horace Jr.'s *Black Workers and the New Unions*, co-authored with George S. Mitchell, came out. In one of Horace Sr.'s last letters, written on July 4, 1939, the old newspaperman informed Madge that the book was "causing quite a sensation" in the Northwest. Horace Sr. beamed with pride over his oldest son, declaring, "There is no doubt but that he is going some where and in his Sunday clothes." Also in the letter, Horace Sr. noted that Susie, despite some difficulty in walking, was still actively "lending moral support to 'the cause,'" Susan was working as a waitress at Mrs. Smith's restaurant, and of himself, he told Madge dryly, "I am still under Dr. Hunter's care and he says he thinks he will be able to keep [me] patched up for some time to come though I seriously doubt it."[30]

＋══╪＋

Horace and Irma sailed on July 20, 1939, from Montreal for Glasgow, Scotland, with Mrs. Mae Barnett, his secretary at the time. Upon arrival in Scotland, they proceeded to Edinburgh, where Cayton met with African students at the university. After a few days, they moved on to London and Horace made observations on race, status, and class among the English. While in London, the Caytons enjoyed talking politics and visiting cabarets with Paul Robeson and his wife Essie, whom Horace had met at Fisk University.

By late August, Europe was nervously edging toward war. Undaunted by London blackouts and store closings, Horace and Irma gaily headed for Paris. Only days after their arrival, they were stunned by Hitler's announced intention to invade Poland. Barnett departed for the United States, while the Caytons stayed on, reluctant to leave Horace's favorite city and hopeful that the political situation would settle down. Hitler's invasion of Poland on September 1, 1939, threw France into confusion as the country strained to mobilize its military forces virtually overnight. When France and Great Britain declared war on Germany two days later, the U.S. embassy in Paris advised Americans to leave immediately. Horace and Irma, still optimistic, lingered. They stayed as guests in the luxurious apartment of Lydia Jones, wife of a Chicago millionaire who had sent his children to be educated in Paris.

By the second week of September, many restaurants and theaters had closed and travel was becoming difficult. Horace and Irma knew the time had come to leave. Passage to America, they soon discovered, was available only from one port, Bordeaux, located several hundred miles south. Forced to leave most of their luggage at the Paris station, they endured a thirteen-hour ride standing up in a packed train. In Bordeaux the Caytons found the waterfront teaming with thousands of other stranded travelers, struggling to secure passage. Several days passed before they managed, through good fortune and the assistance of an Englishman whom they earlier had befriended, to obtain tickets on the *President Roosevelt*, sailing on September 19. The weary travelers arrived ten days later in New York. The Caytons' dramatic departure from Europe drew the attention of the *Chicago Defender*, which ran a feature story and a photo of Horace, under the headline "Vivid Account of Mad Scramble of the Americans to Flee the Wrath of War."[31]

Horace returned to the University of Chicago and resumed his Rosenwald Fellowship research, but not for long. For the previous three years, the Cayton-Warner WPA projects had been housed in the basement of the Good Shepherd Congregational Church. Led by Pastor Harold M. Kingsley, the church also was one of the major focal points for community support during the Depression. The church's outreach center, recently named the Good Shepherd Community Center, had been organized in 1936 with aid from the WPA and sponsorship by the Chicago Board of Education. It provided several hundred South Side residents with daily educational and recreational activities. In December 1939, the center's board of directors announced plans to implement new programs and to start construction of a new facility next to the church. They selected Horace Cayton to direct the center and administer its eighteen-thousand-dollar annual budget. With an annual salary of thirty-six hundred dollars, the job provided Horace Jr. with a stable financial base, plus an office and secretary. He resigned from the Rosenwald Fellowship and assumed his new post.[32]

For Horace Jr., the directorship represented the culmination of his professional career and of an "uncommon" work history. In his younger years, he had worked at various jobs aboard ship and as a shoe shine boy, cook, railroad worker, coal miner, cab driver, deputy sheriff, jail guard, and a "go-fer" in an Alaskan brothel. He also had traveled to Europe twice, taught college, conducted large research projects, received two Rosenwald fellowships, and published a book. Now, at the age of thirty-six, he headed the largest African American settlement house in the world.

Within months, he became a regular columnist for the *Pittsburgh Courier,* the nation's largest black newspaper. The new post offered Horace unique opportunities and goals, as he explained to the press in 1942:

> Instead of sitting in an ivory tower and making my investigations, I am trying to do three things in a practical way. First, I am applying socio-logical principles to a particular place; second, I am working toward the greater participation of the Negro in American culture; and third, I am attempting to discover how an underprivileged, urban population can best be served by institutional, recreational, and welfare agencies, both white and black.[33]

While Horace initiated the center's expanded program, he never lost sight of his academic goals, one of which was to write another book using the WPA material. For several months in early 1940, it appeared he might get the chance. The door of opportunity was being opened by Horace's friendship with Swedish sociologist Gunnar Myrdal, who he had visited in Europe. At the time, Myrdal was within months of completing his "Study of the Negro in America," later published as *An American Dilemma*. In early 1939, Cayton proposed a cooperative exchange, making his expertise and portions of the Cayton-Warner research materials available to Myrdal and his staff. Myrdal responded positively. In February 1940, after a meet-ing between the two men in New York, they began an intense discussion about how to conduct a mutually beneficial collaboration.

Horace was excited about the project, as it gave him "an opportunity to reap some benefit from three and a half years of tremendously hard work." But to do the job right, he would need to take a leave from the Good Shepherd Center to organize the WPA data for Myrdal's use. Horace asked for a modest stipend, but Myrdal refused and repeated his request that the WPA materials be shipped to him right away. By March 1, 1940, the two still had not reached an agreement. Horace complained to Louis Wirth: "He has been very unfair and I will do all I can to keep him from getting any of our data unless he shows some willingness to compensate me in part for the money and work that I have put into this study."[34]

By early April, with Myrdal's manuscript submission deadline rapidly nearing, Cayton concluded that a collaboration was impossible. "Our negotiations so far," he wrote to the Swedish sociologist, "have been a 'comedy of errors.'" When Myrdal's *An American Dilemma* appeared in late 1944, its coverage of Chicago—the city with the country's largest African American population—relied heavily on older, previously published sources. [35]

Under Cayton's leadership, the Good Shepherd Community Center became an increasingly vital institution on the South Side. "I have got something here," Horace wrote to a friend, "that with luck I can develop into a unique institution." In October 1940, the center announced its purchase of six spacious buildings and the grounds of the Chicago Orphan Asylum to serve as Good Shepherd's new headquarters. The property at 51st and South Parkway, including a rambling Georgian structure, reportedly was valued at a half-million dollars, but was made available at the "moderate cost" of just over twenty-two thousand dollars. What had been a small church center serving a local neighborhood now assumed the role of a community-wide institution. Supported by the Chicago Congregational Union, the Community Trust, and hundreds of individuals and organizations, the Good Shepherd Community Center (soon to be called the Parkway Community House, though the official name change came in late 1942) pursued a dramatically expanded program of activities and services. By 1941, after renovations, it housed a mother's clinic, a birth certificate bureau, a relief office, a selective service office, the Henry George School of Social Service, and an auxiliary servicemen's center. [36]

The center also offered a wide variety of free instruction in arts and crafts, sewing, music, dramatics, and writing. It provided workshops for handicapped persons and literacy classes for the general public. The center, too, taught disabled persons how to make saleable articles. A new game room for ping-pong, archery, and other activities opened in 1941. Also that year, Cayton launched a serial publication, "The Voice of the Good Shepherd Community Center," with interest spurred by "newspaper night parties." Community meetings and lectures likewise were held at the center, including a series of Labor Town Hall Forums in October 1941, co-sponsored by the CIO, AFL, and the unaffiliated unions of the Negro Labor Council.

The center sponsored special events throughout the year, including Christmas musicals and Negro History month educational programs. Performers such as W.C. Handy, "the father of the blues," and prominent authors like Langston Hughes often appeared at the center. Horace had first met Hughes in 1932 and Irma had known him from his visits to Fisk

University years before. As the Caytons' friendship with "Lang" developed, Hughes was a frequent guest at the center, often for poetry readings, and, for one five-month period, even lived in an apartment there. Hughes organized and launched the center's theater group, the Skyloft Players, which presented his musical drama, "Sun Do Move." The cast included Irma and a young aspiring thespian, Brunnetta Barnett, who became one of Horace's lifelong friends. Recalling these times, Irma explained, "Langston said he wanted to write a play in which I would be a star. Later on, he confessed to me that what he really wanted was to guarantee a place to sleep and eat!" [37]

While Horace's career steadily moved forward, he began to encounter problems in his personal life. In mid-August 1940, Horace Sr. died and this milestone shook him deeply. By September, Susie sent young Susan to Chicago to be with Horace, Irma, and Madge, bringing increased family responsibilities for Horace Jr. Meanwhile, his relationship with Irma began to unravel as each pursued separate interests. Horace absorbed himself in his civic work, administering Parkway, and writing. Irma taught Red Cross first-aid classes and became active in a Volunteer Defense Group, helping to extricate Jewish family members from wartime Germany.

Horace's marriage to Irma proved as problematic as his first to Bonnie. Following a similar pattern, Horace was unfaithful and at times he erupted in fits of anger. Once, in a drunken rage, he pulled a gun on Irma. Excessive use of Nembutal, then Secanol (available over the counter at the time), had made Horace dependent on sedative barbiturates. During one of what Irma referred to as Horace's "upper-downer" periods, she moved out and filed for divorce, which became final in October 1940. Horace drank more heavily, his depression deepened, and his work became more erratic. Some six months later, his friends Richard and Ellen Wright came to Chicago to try to help. One night Irma received a call from Wright, asking if she would consider having dinner with Horace the following evening. She agreed, and a series of intense discussions about remarriage ensued. A few weeks later Horace and Irma did remarry, but their struggles continued. [38]

+≻═≺+

By 1940, Madge had been in Chicago for five years. She was thirty-nine years old and unmarried. In Seattle she had taken over many of Susie's motherly duties, and the whole family had depended on her. Chicago was to have changed that, giving her a chance to find a decent job and some freedom and independence for the first time in her adult life. It did not in many respects. For a brief time, Madge had lived at the Abraham Lincoln

Center, then rented a small apartment in a private home. When Horace and Irma returned to Chicago and took a basement apartment in the Rosenwald building on South Wabash Avenue, Madge moved there too. Soon, Horace imposed the old pattern: he would tell Madge to prepare dinner because he was bringing guests home—Marshall Field or Katherine Kuh, or Claire Florsheim—and Madge would oblige.

Even from Chicago, Madge maintained her caretaker role toward the family back in Seattle. She mailed Susie books and magazines, and sent money for fuel to get her parents through the hard winter of 1937–38. When Susan arrived in town, Madge—seventeen years older than her niece—assumed responsibility for her, too. Susan moved in with Madge, sharing a basement apartment in the Rosenwald building. Two years later she took in her aged mother, Susie, as well. The family took Madge's caretaking for granted, and it was only after her death that they realized how heavy of a burden they had placed on her.

Madge had struggled to find suitable work when she first arrived. In Depression-era Chicago, African American women were on the bottom tier of the workforce. After much searching, she managed to get a job with the Cook County Department of Public Assistance as a caseworker. Horace's ex-wife, Bonnie, worked there at the time, and the two became close friends. Later, Madge took some graduate courses in the School of Social Sciences at the University of Chicago, which qualified her for a higher position. As a supervising caseworker in the Children's Division of the Public Assistance Department, Madge's high standards and expectations for her staff, and her sincere caring for people, earned the respect and affection of her colleagues.

For Susan, finding a job in Chicago proved as hard in 1940 as it had for Madge. At first, Madge took Susan to stores and shops up and down 47th Street, and waited outside while Susan went inside, asking, "Do you want to hire me?" Each time she desperately hoped they would say, "No," and they did. After a few months, however, Susan was hired to work the late shift at a drug store counter. Soon Horace found her a job as the Parkway House switchboard operator. Next, she took a clerical job with the Supreme Liberty Life Insurance Company, located just several blocks down Parkway Avenue. Six months later, she discovered that her connection to her well-known uncle could be a disadvantage, as well as an advantage, when she suddenly lost her job as a result of a political squabble between her employer and Horace.

Susie, while still in Seattle, had kept in touch by mail with her children in Chicago, updating them about her political activities and Lillie's romantic escapades. For several years, Lillie had been entirely beyond the control of her mother, who generally disapproved of her youngest daughter's lifestyle and considered her "promiscuous." In early 1941, Lillie was renting a room in the family house, earning enough doing day work and filling in part-time at the Court Hotel bar to be self-supporting. Susie, lamenting to the girls in Chicago, said Lillie was "like her father—I think she will always be in debt, but I have nothing to do with her debts." At the time, Lillie was separated from her second husband, Otis Grey, and was keeping busy with two boyfriends. Lillie's second divorce went to court in early August 1941. In resignation, Susie wrote to Madge and Susan, "I told her to get someone else for a character witness—I did not have the strength to go through with any more 'cases.'"[39]

By Christmas 1941, Lillie had moved out, and Susie remained in the house with two boarders. Three months later, Susie's health had deteriorated, and Horace sent Madge to Seattle to bring their mother back. In Chicago, Madge cared for Susie while she continued, with Susan's help, to cook and entertain Horace's array of guests. Many of Horace's well-known friends came especially to visit Susie. Susan vividly remembers Susie in the Rosenwald Apartments "holding court," with "all of Horace's celebrities"— Richard Wright, Langston Hughes, and other prominent intellectuals— gathered around the bedside talking to the seventy-three-year-old communist and daughter of the first African American U.S. Senator.

Hughes, in particular, visited Susie often and grew quite fond of her. On Christmas Day 1942, she wrote to him expressing her appreciation for his understanding manner and great kindness toward her since her arrival in Chicago. This might be attributed to several things, she wrote: "Maybe in some vague way I symbolized your own mother; perhaps an innate respect, affection for quite elderly persons; perchance a reflection—could I say by-product—of cordial relations with my two beloved sons." For this, she said, she loved him dearly. A few months later, in April 1943, when Hughes wrote the poem, "Dear Mr. President," he gave her the original, signing it "For my friend, Susie Cayton."[40]

During this time, Horace became acquainted with author Richard Wright. In March 1940 Horace received a telegram requesting that he meet Wright at the airport. *Life* magazine was flying the author in from New York to do a picture story about his newly published novel, *Native Son*. The two men had met only briefly some seven years before, and had no further contact until 1940. Cayton, in fact, had no recollection of their first meeting. With Wright in Chicago for the *Life* article, Cayton spent several days with him, touring the South Side. Horace had been "viscerally, emotionally and intellectually affected" by *Native Son*, and Wright was fascinated by the sociologist's analyses of the complex dynamics of urban Chicago. Their bonding and mutual respect were immediate. Also, Horace hoped that his own efforts and Wright's article in *Life* would stimulate interest in a book on Chicago, creating a fundraising base "for my Institute." It proved to be the beginning of a ten-year friendship.[41]

Horace honestly recorded his feelings about Wright's *Native Son*. "Of course, being a frustrated writer of fiction I was…surprised, envious and pleased that a book by a Negro author would gain the attention and acclaim that it did. But, most important I found that Wright and I were saying much the same thing." Cayton was struck by the fact that the two of them—one from a socially active middle-class family in the Pacific Northwest, the other from a poor, rural sharecropper's home—could think so much alike, despite coming from profoundly different environments. Horace felt impelled, he wrote later, "to compare our lives and try to find the common element of our experience as Negroes in America." Over the next few years, their work on projects of mutual interest and their personal relationship helped Horace formulate and clarify his own ideas.[42]

At the same time, Wright was deeply fascinated by Horace Jr.'s sociological expertise and because he was a former student of sociologist Robert Park:

> I did not know what my story was, and it was not until I stumbled upon science that I discovered some of the meanings of the environment that battered and taunted me…I encountered the work of men who were studying the Negro community, amassing facts about urban Negro life, and I found that sincere art and honest science were not far apart, that each could enrich the other. The huge mountains of fact piled up by the Department of Sociology at the University of Chicago gave me my first concrete vision of the forces that molded the urban Negro's body and soul.[43]

By early 1941, Horace Jr. was assisting Wright with *Twelve Million Black Voices,* opening up the voluminous WPA files and interpreting, through a sociologist's eyes, Chicago's ghetto and Northern urbanization and industrialization, as contrasted to Southern rural life. Cayton also worked with the book's photographic editor, Edward Rosskam, and the Farm Security Administration's photographs section to help select scenes from nearly fifteen hundred pictures. When *Twelve Million Black Voices* appeared in November 1941, Horace Jr. used his *Courier* column to praise the book as "magnificent in its simplicity, directness and force."[44]

In April 1941, during one of his Chicago visits gathering material for the book, Wright wrote the text of a promotional pamphlet for Parkway House. Wright's essay, "The Negro and the Parkway Community House," reflected Cayton's intellectual influences, as well as Wright's own observations. Horace felt deeply proud about this striking statement.

Drawing on Cayton's data, Wirth's concept of "secular and sacred societies," and Redfield's interpretations of "folk-urban" communities, Wright's poetic and vibrant pamphlet foreshadowed both *Twelve Million Black Voices* and, later, his introduction to Cayton's *Black Metropolis*. The opening sentence set the tone: "A great drama is transpiring in the tenements, on the pavements, and in the factories and shops of our industrial American cities, a drama of such violence, poignancy and magnitude, a drama involving the lives and destinies of so many millions, that it is incredible that so few people know of its existence and comprehend its fateful meaning."

Wright ended the essay with a direct appeal: "The Parkway Community House is the first institution equipped with scientific knowledge of the urban situation among Negroes to attempt to control, probe, and disseminate facts as to the processes, meanings, causes and effects of urbanization. Its policies and activities should merit your most urgent attention and support."[45]

+══╼══╾══+

World War II intruded dramatically on the Caytons' lives in mid 1942. In July, Irma joined the Women's Army Auxiliary Corps (WAACs, which in the following summer became the Women's Army Corps, or WACs). Horace wrote innocently to Richard Wright: "Why I'll never know." As one of four African American women from Chicago accepted for the first officer training class, within weeks Irma was headed for Ft. Huachuca, Arizona. This prompted Horace to quip to Irma, "Young men are giving their life for our country; I'm giving my *wife* for my country!"[46]

Even before America's entry into the war, Horace's civic activism and provocative writing drew the attention of the FBI. Agents began investigating Horace, and he became aware of them in June 1941. In *Pittsburgh Courier* columns, he often discussed discrimination in the military, African American demands for democracy "at home" as well as abroad (the "double victory" campaign), and federal attempts to suppress criticism of U.S. foreign policy and the military effort. Horace was put under investigation again on February 3, 1942—only five days after his column "White Man's War" appeared in the *Courier*. The FBI's final report noted that Cayton's writings might be construed as "inciting race hatred," but concluded that he did not "appear to be engaged in Communist activities."[47]

In October 1942, soon after his "Fighting for White Folks" appeared in the *Nation,* Horace Jr. was reclassified by the local draft board and ordered to report for a physical examination. With Cayton's induction into the military imminent, the Parkway Executive Board tried, unsuccessfully, to intervene. Arna Bontemps, who often exchanged letters with Langston Hughes at the time, noted, "Horace is taking his expected call rather hard, it seems to me. Drunk more than usual. And at unaccustomed hours of the day. He says it is because Irma is in the WAACs. I think his own military prospects figure in it." In the end, only the draft system's exemption from service of men over the age of thirty-eight kept Horace Jr. out of the military.[48]

Horace and Irma's second attempt at married life was failing. In October 1942, Horace Jr. confided to Wright that he and Irma were "breaking up again." Occasionally, Irma returned to Chicago from Arizona to visit Horace, which typically caught the attention of the *Chicago Defender* and its photographers. Eventually, on September 21, 1944, after nine stormy years together, they divorced for the second and final time.[49]

At the time that Irma had joined the WACs, Horace Jr. was devoting considerable energy to his "Study of the Negro in Chicago." This work was a source of emotional support during an increasingly troubled period. Determined to publish his own book after the soured relationship with Gunnar Myrdal, Horace decided that his best chance to complete the manuscript would be to acquire a reliable collaborator. Horace turned to one of his WPA colleagues, St. Clair Drake, as a co-author. With assistance from the Rosenwald Fund, they began work together on the manuscript in mid 1942. Each brought a different expertise to the project: Drake, using the social anthropologist's approach, collected data primarily on the lower class; Cayton, using a sociologist's approach, assembled information on the middle and upper classes. While in New York attempting to line up a publisher, Horace learned of his mother's death.[50]

On July 28, 1943, Susie died in Madge's bed at the Rosenwald Apartments. Being diabetic with poor circulation in her lower extremities, gangrene had set in following an accidental cut to a toe. Earlier, while Susie was yet in reasonably good health, Horace had commissioned the artist, Eldzier Cortor, to paint her portrait. He also asked Cortor to paint Madge at the same time. These portraits later became a focal point in the tensions between Susan and Horace Jr.

Madge prepared a short obituary, linking Susie's contributions to those of her husband, Horace Sr., and her father, Senator Hiram Revels. In conclusion, Madge noted, "As a person she was always interested in the larger issues which confronted the common people, white and black, and worked constantly for progressive measures which would better their living conditions." Lillie made the long trip from Seattle to Chicago. The family generally took little notice of her, and when Lillie left, everyone felt relieved. Later, Lillie returned to visit, hoping to stay, but Madge had too much to cope with already, catering to Horace, mothering Susan, and keeping up with her job. After several weeks, Madge sent Lillie back to Seattle.[51]

Many years later, Irma Cayton lovingly recalled a remarkable letter her mother-in-law had written in 1942, offering advice about living with a difficult husband. Noting that she, too, had married a man "who loved her devotedly but who was hell to live with," Susie declared she never understood Horace Sr. until after his death. She continued,

> Since it was impossible to fully unite my efforts with my husband's…I would join him whole-heartedly whenever the opportunity presented itself, *steelhandedly* pushing my own project yet comforting him when he wished it and loving him always… I concluded that the wonder is not that there are so many misunderstandings in married life but that there are not more; two unities with contrasting modes of reactions, contrasting approaches to reality and contrasting degrees of self-mastery trying to meet the complex demands of human existence in unison. It's a challenge. The question is, who is big enough to meet it?[52]

His mother's death left Horace deeply shaken. Their relationship had been seriously undermined by long unresolved conflicts. Since childhood, Horace had suffered from feelings of rejection (Revels had been Susie's favorite) and had developed a deep need for his mother's (and, by extension, female) acceptance. And, Horace blamed his mother for his alcohol and pill problems, resenting her for the time he had spent at the Chehalis reformatory. As Susie lay on her deathbed, Horace asked if he had been a good son, then begged her forgiveness. She avoided a direct reply, mentioned his broken marriages and suggested that he "check up on himself."[53]

CHAPTER 8

Dark Mirror of Our Lives

Horace Jr., Madge, and Susan, 1943–1948

A S A GUEST COLUMNIST for the *Pittsburgh Courier,* Langston Hughes described his friend Horace Jr. as the "king bee" of the busy Parkway hive, a "Genuine character, an ace sociologist, A-1 administrator, amateur psychiatrist, bon vivant, good party giver, art lover, and a man with a beard." Horace was an imposing figure, a large-chested man standing five-feet-ten inches and weighing over two hundred pounds. "One of his strongest assets," author Margaret Walker later noted, "was his physical appearance— portly, stalwart, with a touch of arrogance." Horace's longtime friend, Brunetta Bernstein, remarked that he was "truly a humanitarian, a humanist in the sense that he 'ate, drank and slept' people." The Parkway's programs and facilities, and its director's energetic personality, attracted a dazzling array of intellectuals, artists, writers, actors, dancers, painters, and social activists. For those visiting from out of town, the Parkway became *the* place to stop at in vibrantly social Chicago.[1]

Whenever Horace attended a party or gave one, Hughes said, "something happens for folks to remember a long time and repeat to others, and no party is ever the same again once he arrives." Parkway's social gatherings always were an interesting mix of people. One might see white university professors in the crowd, as well as South Side notables such as Claude Barnett of the Associated Negro Press, attorney Cy Colter, and Sidney Williams, head of the Chicago Urban League. Among the celebrities there were the likes of Paul Robeson, Richard Wright, Arna Bontemps, Katherine Dunham, Langston Hughes, Chester Himes, Ulysses Kay, and Frank Marshall Davis. But, at center stage stood Horace Cayton Jr. His colleague and long time friend, Sidney Williams, later described the scene: "His room was long, and Horace would put on his white pants and his Hawaiian jacket, and then he would have that ascot around his neck. He would stand in front of that mantel and hold court!" Years later, Williams' wife, Ruth, vividly recalled her first encounter with Cayton when Sidney brought him home one day—the two men walked up Dorchester Avenue, with

Horace Jr. sporting a wide-brimmed straw hat, a cane, and a cigar in a long holder.[2]

Among those drawn to Parkway House were some women who found Horace Jr. irresistible, and he spent no small amount of time and effort enjoying their company. By his own boasts and the gossip of those around him, he attracted and charmed a long list of females, from Bronzeville socialites, such as Marva Louis (former wife of boxing champion Joe Louis), to white society women like Nancy Cunard, Claire Florsheim, and Katherine Kuh. Years later, when word got around that Horace Jr.'s autobiography was about to be published, one of Susan Cayton Woodson's friends told her, "There's a whole lot of women shakin' in their boots around here."

Socializing and entertaining, for personal pleasure as well as for fundraising, occupied much of Horace and Irma's time at the Parkway House. Horace's love of art was well known, and his collection included works by Charles White, Eldzier Cortor, and Charles Sebree. His passion for music ranged widely, from jazz, swing, boogie woogie, and blues, to Gilbert and Sullivan, Beethoven (especially the "Ninth Symphony"), and Bach. He considered music his only real "hobby," and amassed a collection of over a thousand records.[3]

His friends came from all walks of life—young and old, rich and poor, well educated and illiterate. In this, Horace was more like his mother than his father. With wit, charm, and curiosity, he approached people with surprising directness if he so chose. Former *Chicago Defender* columnist Doris Saunders described Horace as having "no difficulty in asking perfect strangers most revealing questions and getting careful and truthful answers."[4]

Though urbane, articulate, and charming, Horace also could be opinionated, arrogant, and impatient. Sometimes he revealed a violent temper, and disagreements could erupt into ferocious arguments. "Anyone who knows him," said Cy Colter, "knows that he'd fight at the drop of hat—and he'd drop it himself." If challenged regarding his strongly held convictions, he conducted himself much like his father. "I take my stand," was an often-heard Caytonism. He would not yield "one iota," just as his father used to say, to anyone who gave the slightest indication that Horace Jr. did not merit respect or treatment as an equal.[5]

+=≈=+

In the 1930s and 1940s, the cultural vitality of Chicago's South Side rivaled that of New York's more famous "Harlem Renaissance" of the 1920s. The period was unique in Chicago's and the nation's social history. A host of talented writers and other creative artists, civic leaders, political activists and institutions contributed to the vibrant scene. This "flowering of African American arts and letters" grew out of the distinctive events and circumstances that shaped South Chicago, the same milieu that influenced, nurtured, and challenged Horace Cayton. The extraordinary combination of personalities, events, and institutions produced a heady atmosphere of stimulating, dynamic energy. It was a time of enhanced opportunities for artistic and intellectual expression. The Chicago Renaissance developed an internal momentum of creative cultural upsurge, the achievements of which reverberated loudly in Chicago and nationally.[6]

In literature, art, music, journalism, and the social sciences major figures emerged. Many of them had been involved with the various WPA programs, especially the Illinois Writers Project. The most notable names included Arna Bontemps, Richard Wright, Margaret Walker, Katherine Dunham (better known as a dancer and choreographer), novelist Frank Yerby, playwright Theodore Ward, poet Frank Marshall Davis, novelist Willard Motley, and poet Gwendolyn Brooks. Some national figures, notably Langston Hughes, also made their mark on the Chicago Renaissance. In art a small group of emerging talents dominated the scene, including Charles White, Charles Seebree, Eldzier Cortor, George Neal, Margaret Taylor Goss (Burroughs), Bernard Goss, Charles Davis, William Carter, Earl Walker, Henry Avery, Fred Hollingsworth, Vernon Winslow, and sculptor Joseph Kersey. The 1940 American Negro Exposition in Chicago offered the most comprehensive exhibit of their work to date, marking a milestone for African American artists.

Among the key institutions influencing the renaissance were the WPA, the University of Chicago (especially the sociology and anthropology departments), the Hall Branch of the Chicago Public Library, the Julius Rosenwald Foundation, the South Side Community Art Center, and the Parkway Community House. The University of Chicago's national prominence in sociology and anthropology formed an integral component of the intellectual milieu of the period. Social science informed government plans and policies, structured social events, and influenced cultural developments. It is emblematic of the times that Richard Wright embraced sociology as enthusiastically as Horace Cayton embraced literature. Historian Robert Bone calls Horace Cayton "the crucial link between the Chicago School of Sociology and the Chicago School of African American writing." True, but Cayton was much more.[7]

Horace Cayton played an exceptional and largely unrecognized role in the Chicago Renaissance. By virtue of his personality, his experience and activities, as well as the positions he held, Cayton served as a participant, a link, and a catalyst in the cultural processes that unfolded in Chicago. As a graduate student and research assistant at the University of Chicago, as supervisor of the WPA projects on the South Side, as a journalist and author, as a civic activist, and as director of the Parkway Community Center, Cayton made major contributions to the Chicago Renaissance. His institutional affiliations and his individual activities were unique. He was, it can be argued, the most central, representative figure of the Chicago Renaissance.

Cayton formed personal and professional relationships with some of the most influential academic figures of the Chicago School of Sociology: Robert E. Park, Charles S. Johnson, E. Franklin Frazier, Louis Wirth, Ernest Burgess, and W. Lloyd Warner. These connections continued during the WPA projects, where Cayton also directly influenced numerous graduate students who produced a sizeable body of academic studies based on the WPA research. During his years at the Parkway House, Horace routinely facilitated graduate student research. He also continued to involve Louis Wirth particularly, often inviting Professor and Mrs. Wirth to various social functions and house activities.

Cayton's work as a sociologist, journalist, and author provided some of the most distinct national impacts for the Chicago Renaissance. Most notable is his authorship with Drake of *Black Metropolis.* One could also include his earlier *Black Workers and the New Unions* (co-authored with George Mitchell) for its emphasis on current "social realities" and issues. As a journalist, Horace's numerous magazine articles and years as a columnist for the *Pittsburgh Courier* presented his most frequent and widespread contributions to the literature of the Renaissance.

In his writing, speeches, and civic activities Horace Cayton reflected and propagated the Chicago Renaissance's intellectual debt not only to the prominent white scholars of the Chicago School, but also to black sociologists, especially W.E.B. Du Bois, E. Franklin Frazier, and Charles S. Johnson. At a 1998 conference on the Chicago Renaissance, sociologist Aldon Morris contended that "the intellectual influence of W.E.B. Du Bois, and the experiences of the Black sociologists *prior* to their exposure to the Chicago School, were crucial in developing the sociological imagination of the Black sociologists." Cayton provides an excellent case in point. He proudly acknowledged the influence of Park's ideas in his own intellectual maturation.

But, the "origin and vision" of his "sociological imagination," to use Morris' words, lay outside of white academic circles in the intellectual, political, and social traditions of his family and the black community. Cayton grew up in a home where Du Bois' ideas and works predominated. Horace followed his father's example of a strong-minded, independent, outspoken community activist who courageously protested white racism and discrimination, and who knew that African Americans' intellectual achievements equaled those of whites. During graduate studies, Horace was strongly influenced by Charles S. Johnson and E. Franklin Frazier, who considered Du Bois a mentor. Thus, while Horace absorbed the Chicago School's theories of urban sociology, his thinking represented a closer intellectual kinship with Du Bois, Frazier, and Johnson. Furthermore, Cayton influenced and was influenced by his contemporaries, particularly Richard Wright and St. Clair Drake. Cayton and Drake directly acknowledge their debt to Du Bois, as well as to the Chicago School, in *Black Metropolis*.[8]

In addition, Cayton played a vital role as an institutional leader and patron in the Chicago Renaissance. He was intimately associated with many of the most significant and influential institutions of the period—the University of Chicago, the Rosenwald Foundation, the WPA, several African American newspapers and journals (notably, the *Pittsburgh Courier* and *Chicago Defender*), the Good Shepherd Community Center and Parkway Community House. Through avenues opened by the special missions of those organizations, Horace directly and indirectly fostered, nurtured, stimulated, and contributed to a host of other individuals and organizations of the Chicago Renaissance. The Good Shepherd Center's and Parkway's cultural programs influenced the climate of the Chicago Renaissance, as well as individuals through classes, lectures, forums, theater, music, and dance. For a time, beginning in late 1946, the Hall Branch Library assumed direction of the Parkway's creative writing program, which at the time included Gwendolyn Brooks. Cayton often used the Hall Branch Library, and he supported the South Side Community Art Center, even writing the introduction to the catalog for its Second Annual Collectors Exhibit in 1948.

Furthermore, Cayton uniquely connected the WPA, the Rosebwald Foundation, and Parkway. First, Cayton received two Rosenwald fellowships (although he applied for at least four). More important, Arna Bontemps, Horace's friend and successor, supervised the WPA "Negro in Illinois" projects with Rosenwald support and from headquarters in the Rosenwald Foundation offices. Other threads are Bill and Vandi Haygood.

As the Rosenwald's director of fellowships, William (Billie) Haygood, served on the Parkway House's board of directors, and his wife Vandi, on the staff at the Fund, had worked under Cayton on the WPA research projects. Both remained close friends of Cayton's until he left Chicago. Horace cultivated relationships with major Renaissance patrons Marshall Field III, the Rosenwald Foundation's Edwin Embree, and Will Alexander. Marshall Field III, philanthropist and owner of the *Chicago Sun,* served on the board of directors for both the Rosenwald Foundation and the Parkway.

Horace's associations with leading figures of the Renaissance were of singular importance. Most prominent were his friendships with Wright, Hughes, and Bontemps, but the list is long and includes artists Charles White, Sebree, Cortor, and numerous others. These relationships also linked Chicago to the rest of the country as Wright, Bontemps, Hughes, and Paul Robeson frequented the Parkway even after leaving Chicago.

Cayton's political activism in Chicago carried the special aura of the family tradition of protest and community service, as well as his own individual dedication to "sociology-in-action." In leading protests against racism and discrimination Cayton epitomized the political drive for social reform characteristic of the period. These activities reached their most dramatic proportions for Horace at the Parkway in the 1940s.

The Parkway Forums, where University of Chicago faculty and other white intellectuals built bridges between academia and the community, became one of Horace Cayton's most striking contributions. These public lectures and panel discussions focused on a variety of topics. For the most part, each program series ran for twelve weeks, with meetings held on Thursday evenings. Parkway House also sponsored teen dances, a children's theater, free summer concerts, the Skyloft Players theatrical productions, poetry readings, and lectures. Among the young talents using Parkway's facilities and programs were James Michener, who participated in the adult writing class and literary workshops, and WPA photographer Gordon Parks, whose work was exhibited at the opening of Langston Hughes' *Sun Do Move.* Parkway also sponsored "camps" for children of all races—some were "stay-at-home" day camps, while others were two-week outings at Camp Rheinberg in Palatine, Illinois. This prompted the American Camping Association to produce a film short on inter-racial camping called "Together We Live," funded by the B'nai B'rith Foundation.[9]

During World War II, Horace directed Parkway to provide additional services "to sustain morale on the home front by helping our people take advantage of every opportunity that opens up during this war." A dormitory was created to house fifty female war workers and government employees. Horace felt especially proud of Parkway's nursery school, which enabled more women to work in war industries and at the same time helped to protect the health of the community's children. A branch of the Chicago Public Library opened at Parkway, and publisher Johnny Johnson rented office space there and produced the first issue of *Ebony* magazine, launching one of the most successful ventures in publishing history.[10]

Horace found other unprecedented ways for Parkway to serve the community. The wartime resettlement of West Coast Japanese Americans to several Midwestern cities brought hundreds of the beleaguered group to Chicago. Cayton felt compassion for their plight. He used the Parkway, and his personal network of private welfare funding sources, to make what sociologist Setsuko Nishi later called an "extraordinary contribution to Chicago Japanese Americans in their recovery from a degraded wartime identity." Beginning in 1943, he arranged forums at the Parkway for the War Relocation Authority to explain the government's resettlement program to the community. When Horace learned that Buddhists in the small Japanese American community had no place to worship, he opened up the Parkway's basement to them.[11]

During the war, Parkway Community House grew into one of the largest social service centers in the world, and the largest one serving African Americans. With up to seventeen thousand people a month using its programs and facilities, by 1945 Parkway had aided more than one hundred thousand persons. Its black, white, and Nisei staff served a diverse South Side community, ranging from what Richard Wright called the "world of the kitchenette" and people on relief, to the working and middle classes, to doctors, lawyers, dentists, and other professionals. It had become, in the words of St. Clair Drake, "an innovative and very influential institution within the Black Metropolis." The *Chicago Defender*, an ardent supporter of Parkway, noted in 1947 that it was "the warp and woof of this community." Reflecting Parkway's growth and acceptance, Cayton added prominent whites to the board of directors, including Bishop Bernard Shiel, the founder of the renowned Catholic Youth Movement; Marshall Field III; and Horace Jr.'s friend William (Billie) Haygood.[12]

Constantly needing to raise money for Parkway House, Horace often entertained members of Chicago's white elite class, such as Claire Florsheim (the widow of the well-known shoe manufacturer), socialite Katherine Kuh, and the aforementioned Marshall Field III. Madge and Susan regularly cooked for these social occasions.

Though at the top of his game, Horace eventually began souring on some of the duties required of him as director of Parkway Community House. He joked with his staff about implementing "Plan Guilt" to squeeze dollars from donors, but this process eventually caused tension and increasingly disgusted him. Susan recounted one occasion when her brother returned home after a visit to the mansion of a prominent white donor. "Horace was announced," but had to sit in a waiting room "for an hour and a half... Horace finally got the money, but he left there feeling like he was nobody to this guy, a friend he had entertained many, many times. By the time he got home, Horace was just sick."[13]

After several years of success, however, Horace's view of himself as a "race leader" and "civic activist" gradually began to change. These roles increasingly seemed a sham. As he told Richard Wright, he saw mounting evidence that Parkway was little more than a "sop thrown to the Negro community." In fact, Cayton began to see himself as part of the social machinery subjugating blacks. By late 1944, he was ready to break with "professional philanthropists," whom he considered "a corrupting influence on anyone who wants to retain any intellectual honesty about this race business." As Horace's position hardened, he came to believe that any African American in a position such as his was in danger of becoming cynical and devious. This pattern, Horace said in a letter to Wright, was an integral part of the "folklore of race relations...the mechanisms which circumvent changes and maintain the subordination of the Negro and which lead to his corruption and cynicism."[14]

Cayton and Wright for some time had viewed race issues through similar eyes. Wright's journal entry on January 12, 1945, echoed Cayton's thoughts:

> I am now more convinced than ever that we Americans have subtly evolved a magic, a folklore of race relations... They form councils, committees, etc., and then proceed to say that their hearts are in the right places, that it must be hell to be a Negro, that this and that ought to be done. And they wind up with nothing concretely done. The main problem of shunting Negroes into a separate life is not really touched.[15]

Part of Horace Jr.'s increasing distaste for the political game stemmed from a growing impatience with the lack of government response to Bronzeville's housing shortage. World War II had brought a flood of Southern black job seekers to Chicago. The housing shortage, acute even before the war, reached crisis proportions. Horace and other community leaders pressed for action from local and federal officials. Cayton was appointed to the United Committee on Emergency Housing and became chairman of its Research Committee. In January 1944, he had warned the National Housing Authority, "When you have more than three hundred thousand people bottled up and forced to live in indescribably horrible, hazardous and unhealthy quarters, piled up on top of one another, you have all the ingredients for an explosion. We cannot afford to ignore this festering sore for long." Finally, at the start of 1945, the mayor's Committee on Race Relations announced a new plan, declaring housing the city's "number one problem in race relations."[16]

With the housing problem addressed momentarily and the end of World War II imminent, the Parkway Forums took on a wider scope. The autumn 1944 forum targeted "Goals for America," while the winter 1945 series presented "A World Crisis of Race." Spring sessions discussed "Race and Color in the New World," followed by "The Common Cause of Minorities" in the summer. Another series focused on a community campaign to ban racism in motion pictures, while another traced "The Evolution of Jazz." Now called "The People's Forum," the Parkway auditorium's Thursday night meetings attracted large audiences of up to two hundred men and women, of all races and from widely differing economic, political, and cultural backgrounds.

The forums reflected Cayton's desire to use Parkway House as a focal point for civic activism. Using Myrdal's *American Dilemma* as a springboard, a forum series beginning in November 1945 addressed the importance of rallying citizens to social change, as reflected in the topics "Myrdal Report Aids Attack on Race Problem," and "Reaching Public Opinion." Horace considered the forum programs an experiment in bridging the gap between social science and community involvement, between the interchange of knowledge and action. A year later, Cayton and St. Clair Drake led a forum series based on *Black Metropolis*, urging a "social awakening for U.S. Negroes." As St. Clair Drake later noted, "We always conceived of *Black Metropolis* as a weapon in the struggle."[17]

Horace Jr.'s political activism, which reached its height while he was at Parkway House, typified the Cayton family's commitment to civic protest and community service. His efforts, too, epitomized a style of political and social reform typical for this period in American history. As Parkway director, he brought greater visibility to black artists, writers, and musicians. As a focal point in the Chicago Renaissance, the center was, in the words of one participant, "a cultural and political oasis in the brown belt."

Parkway, too, was a sounding board for the neighborhood and a place it could go to for solutions. The center frequently yielded visible—and re-warding—results.[18]

+≍≍+

Following his mother's death in the summer of 1943, Horace Jr. suffered a new wave of emotional problems. His evolving friendship with Richard Wright had become an elemental part of his life, but despite Wright's steady-ing influence, Cayton became deeply unsettled by his eroding relationship with Irma. He took a month's leave from Parkway to enter psychoanalysis, and traveled to the West Coast. From Seattle, he wrote to Richard Wright:

> Dick, I've lived so many lives that I fear even psychoanalysis won't be able to orient me to the reality which is me, if indeed such exists. I can see, with more sophisticated eyes, why I am like I am and have such trouble fitting into Negro life, thought and social activities. A Negro boy should never forget, in the United States, that he is a Negro. Being brought up in this country allowed me to forget from time to time only to be brought up sharply at other times with the fact of color and caste. Things are loose here. People on the street are genuinely proud of me as a Seattle product...This fits in with the simple success philosophy of this unsophisticated section of the country. If one does not look too deeply one would think they are reacting to me as an individual not as a Negro. That was what fooled me before.[19]

This letter reflects three central threads of Horace Jr.'s life in the mid-1940s—the growing friendship with Wright, his struggles with racism and identity, and a deepening involvement in psychoanalysis. Early in his ca-reer, he embraced sociology as a profession, as well as a means to help resolve a personal drive to find "an at-homeness." His academic interest in social stratification was rooted in the class-conscious upbringing by his parents, and was significantly influenced by the philosophy of Du Bois and his exposure to the "lower class" while working as a laborer, sailor, and policeman. But intellectual understanding, for Horace, proved insufficient. It did not alleviate his desperate need to be liked and accepted, nor the fears and resentments caused by his personal experiences with racism. In psychology and literature, especially the writings of Richard Wright, he discovered deeper perceptions of race relations and how racism conditioned personalities.[20]

Horace began visiting Dr. Helen McLean at the Institute for Psycho-analysis in Chicago. Attending several times a week, his therapy sessions continued for the next five years. He also took course work in psychology at the institute. His inner turmoil led him into numerous relationships with women, both black and white, but these were strained encounters and held no intimacy or emotional involvement for him. He also continued to be dependent on alcohol and pills (mainly Secanol, Nembutal, sleeping pills, and amphetamines), as he had since his early days in Chicago.[21]

When *Black Metropolis* appeared in 1945, almost everyone thought a brilliant future lay ahead for the forty-two-year-old author. But privately, Horace confided to Wright, "the last three years have given me hell." Behind the public and professional acclaim loomed Horace Jr.'s "dark inner landscape" of demons and "daily lynchings of the soul."[22]

Only with Wright did Horace Jr. feel he could fully be himself. This bond was evident in January 1942 when he wrote to Wright:

> I have never met anyone with whom I could talk as freely and who seemed to understand what I was trying to do as yourself. I may be altogether wrong and sometimes I suspect it, but as one human being to another we can communicate ideas. I feel even more at home with you intellectually than I do with all the sociologists with the exception of say, old Dr. Park. I am delighted, therefore, that in spite of the many differences which may exist between me and the Left, you and I will retain our friendship.[23]

Horace hardly had returned from his long vacation when he again felt the need to get away. He planned a trip to New York in November 1943, and wrote to Wright that he wanted to see him. "I am bubbling over with ideas—I am depressed beyond measure by what I see happening all around me and throughout the world. I am in desperate need of some Scotch, quiet atmosphere of my second home, and some good talk with you."[24]

Not long afterward, Cayton and Wright accepted an offer from Charles S. Johnson to visit Fisk University. The two made a memorable journey to Nashville, April 8 to 12, 1944. Upon returning, Wright spent much of the next eight months writing his autobiography, *Black Boy* (published in 1945). Cayton's experiences during this trip appeared many years later in "The Curtain: A Sojourn to the South," published by *Negro Digest,* in 1968.[25]

+≍≍+

Unlike her brother, Madge had few opportunities to travel, only taking occasional vacations, such as a trip to Washington D.C. in the spring of 1940. After her mother passed away, however, Madge had more freedom to pursue her own interests. In December 1943, she visited New York to look into finding a job and living there. Horace asked Richard Wright to help out, but nothing developed. Madge returned to Chicago and to her circle of female friends, most of them, like herself, single and employed in social work. Outside of the job, Madge devoted her time largely to attending to Horace Jr. and caring for Susan, occasionally chaperoning her at Army dances.

In mid 1944, at age forty-three, Madge unfortunately was stricken with rheumatic fever. By late June, she was "very ill," Horace Jr. told Wright. After three months in the hospital, Madge died on September 14, 1944. Late in life, Susan related a poignant story of Madge's last days:

> Lillie and I were in the hospital when Madge was dying. We were so young. We wanted to do something to fix up the room to help Madge feel better. We thought we'd bring up the paintings of her and Mom by Eldzier Cortor. When we did, Madge didn't say anything, because she wouldn't have. But her face told us it was not the thing to do, so we took them home. A few days later, Madge said, "Lillie, I want you to take my painting; that's yours. Susan, you take Mother's"...I didn't think of Lillie, I just was thinking of how hurt I was, and I said, "But, I wanted to have the picture of you." Lillie said, "It's OK, you can have whichever one you want."[26]

Decades later, as Susan recalled the incident, she mused, "I didn't see it at the time, but now I look back and see what a tender moment that was."

Revels arrived by train from Los Angeles for the funeral. For the last few years, Revels and Horace Jr. had maintained cordial relations, at least on the surface, but inwardly Revels felt a growing anger toward his older brother. Revels especially disliked Horace Jr.'s domination of Madge. "His dependence on her was a crucifying thing," he noted. With Madge's death, the differences between the brothers came to a head, and long-held resentments burst into the open. After the cremation and funeral, the two began drinking. (Revels said of Horace Jr., "He was by now a real rollin' alcoholic.") They started arguing bitterly. Horace declared he was "now head of the family" and was "going to carry out that responsibility." That was "crap," Revels pointedly told him:

> Don't carry out that responsibility as far as I'm concerned. When I put Madge in that coffin, and she was burned up, I burned you up right with her. So far as I'm concerned there is no more family, and you're not head of anything, and you're sure as hell not head of me, 'cause you're not going to do me like you did Madge.

The argument severely strained the remaining weak threads of their relationship. For many years afterward, Revels held Horace Jr. "at arm's length."[27]

Susie's death had been a passage that the family could understand and accept. She was elderly and had lived a long and good life. But Madge's death dealt a painful blow. "Nobody could accept it," said Susan, "because she hadn't even lived; she hadn't had a chance to live." They felt guilty, having constantly leaned on her, and hindered her freedom to make a life of her own. Madge had never complained and was never bitter. She acted out of love and the lifelong habit of assuming the role of caregiver.

Horace telegramed the news of Madge's death to Langston Hughes and Richard Wright, asking if they would write something about her "social idealism and life" for a memorial service. Horace included Madge's obituary in a *Pittsburgh Courier* column, publicly expressing guilt over his treatment of his elder sister:

> Because of her devotion to her family she made many sacrifices and, in a sense, our grief is mingled with a sense of guilt, for we took more from her than any of us could return… She was cheated first by us, her family, which made demands which thwarted her own ambitions and aims. She was later cheated by the cruel forces of race prejudice. Then, and finally, by circumstances.[28]

Horace's obituary emphasized Madge's place in the "great" tradition of the Cayton family, mentioned both grandfathers (a slave and a U.S. Senator), her father and mother and their accomplishments, and included a quote from the *Seattle Republican*. Horace Jr. concluded, "[W]e wish to think of her as one of the common people of the earth, who has made a small contribution to the ideals to which we are irrevocably committed." Privately, the grief and guilt that the family brought with them to the funeral led to deep wounds that took many years to heal.[29]

Madge had willed to Lillie and Susan a few savings bonds, the Revels clock, and the Cortor portraits. Horace seized these, claiming he needed them to defray funeral expenses. Although Horace had paid for Lillie to travel by train to Chicago, he sent her back to Seattle by bus. Lillie, thirty years old, carried back her only inheritance from Madge, a parcel of used clothes wrapped with string. Again, the family cast Lillie adrift.

Madge's death proved traumatic to twenty-five-year-old Susan. She had lost her mother, Ruth, when she was too young to remember. She had lost her grandmother, "Mother Susie," just a year before. Now, with Madge gone, she felt she had lost her "third mother."

Shortly after the United States had entered the war, Susan went to work for the Federal Employment Service as a switchboard operator, where she remained until 1945. After Horace and Irma separated in 1942, he had increasingly distanced himself from Susan. Horace was not warm or affectionate toward her. "Horace was cold and strict with love," she explained. Susan had only her job to keep her busy and a few friends to rely on for support.

After the war, the Federal Employment Service in Chicago reverted to State of Illinois control. The changeover left Susan and most of the other employees out of a job. Soon, she took a clerical position, this time with the Chicago Employment Security Department, where she worked for the next four years. Susan wrote to Horace in 1945, asking him to return the Cortor portrait of Susie. He refused.

+≻═≺+

Burdened with guilt over the untimely loss of Madge, Horace Jr. felt increasingly bereft of family ties. Having little in common with Susan, the only other Cayton in Chicago, he reached out more to his friend, "Dick" Wright. Through the next year, Horace spent considerable time and energy supporting Wright's effort to launch a magazine on black life called *American Pages,* which they hoped would foster racial understanding. Horace also tried to secure financial backing from benefactors Marshall Field III, Katherine Kuh, and Claire Florsheim. Disappointingly, by June 1944 Field decided that it involved too much financial risk, and the project died.[30]

In the autumn of 1944, Cayton and Wright started another literary project with the working title, "The Negro Speaks." They envisioned a sweeping collaborative effort including their friends Ralph Ellison, C.L.R. James, and Lawrence Reddick. The book would include chapters on psychiatry and its contributions to the understanding of race relations. Horace planned to author a chapter titled, "The Folklore of Race Relations." He hoped the project would "startle and convulse and shock to its moral depths white American society—and Negro society for that matter." Eventually, disagreements arose between the collaborators. Cayton, Wright, and James kept the project alive for a couple of years, but it was dropped when Wright departed for France.[31]

Meanwhile, Wright and Cayton's friendship and writing projects frequently brought them together. Wright stayed in the Parkway's guest apartment when he traveled to Chicago, and sometimes he brought his wife, Ellen, and daughter, Julia. Several times a year, Horace visited New York, often spending a few days at the Wrights, whom he now called "my secondary family." As *Black Metropolis* neared completion in 1945, Wright wrote the introduction as a special favor to his friend Horace.[32]

In early 1945—on the eve of the release of both *Black Boy* and *Black Metropolis*—Richard Wright was one of few people who knew the depth and intensity of Horace's internal struggles. It had been two years since Cayton began psychoanalysis, but he still struggled with heightened fears and "overpowering loneliness." He felt "propelled by a constant psychic pain," and the sessions increased to four times a week. Gradually, Horace gained a measure of control over his fears and mood swings, but it was, he told Wright, a "dreary, painful, tedious business."[33]

On the eve of achieving national recognition as a sociologist with *Black Metropolis*, Cayton turned to a new driving personal and professional interest—the psychology of race relations. A reading of an advance copy of Wright's *Black Boy* in January 1945 had crystallized much of Horace Jr.'s thinking about race, racism, and his own identity. The book brought out a strong emotional response, which Cayton attempted to analyze intellectually in a review titled, "Frightened Children of Frightened Parents." Cayton's twenty-five-hundred-word article, published in *Twice a Year*, emphasized that Wright had but one basic story—"how it feels to be a Negro in the United States."[34]

For years, Horace Jr. had attempted to understand and control his unsettling mood swings. After reading *Black Boy*, he concluded that the cycle of extreme emotions that he experienced was not his alone, but the heritage of every African American living under the pressures of servitude and racism. It was caused not by mere "injustice," but "*oppression*"—a way of life learned by "frightened children" from their "frightened parents." Analogous to a soldier suffering battle fatigue, this highly stressful way of living was intense and disorienting, with an "uncertainty of when, how, and where the white enemy environment will strike." Cayton knew his views would prove unpleasant to white Americans. Whites, he believed, were possessed by their own complex guilts and fears, held "a deep-seated emotional attachment to racism," and clutched tightly to the "myth that Blacks are treated fairly."[35]

After much delay, *Black Metropolis*, co-authored by St. Clair Drake, finally appeared in November 1945. It met with unanimous praise from critics as "a landmark of research and scientific achievement" and a truly significant study of social history and urbanization. It was compared to Du Bois' *The Philadelphia Negro* (1899) and Myrdal's *An American Dilemma* (1944).

Richard Wright's introduction was powerful and poetic. St. Clair Drake called it "the best essay Richard Wright ever wrote." *Black Metropolis* won the prestigious Anisfield-Wolf Award for the best book of the year in race relations. Cayton became a celebrity in circles extending far beyond Chicago. At this same time, Arna Bontemps' *We Have Tomorrow* was published, which included a profile of Horace Cayton as one of a dozen models for young people.[36]

In the summer of 1946 Horace spent a month at the prestigious New York artist's colony, Yaddo, which gave him a chance to expand "Frightened Children" into a twenty-two-page article titled "A Psychological Approach to Race Relations." This essay, published in November 1946, offered a clearer and more detailed development of the ideas first presented in the *Black Boy* review.[37]

Horace expanded his psychological analysis to whites, whose "oppressor's psychosis," he believed, resulted from their "guilt-hate-fear complex." To Horace Jr., these were hard-won and deeply personal truths wrung from his years of psychoanalysis. He devoutly felt that by understanding the operation of these psychological complexes, both blacks and whites could "achieve a maturity which is necessary to have a stable, enriching society." None of the ideas in Horace's new exposition appeared more striking than the following: "Conscious of the hate and contempt which is directed at them because of their color, feeling their own impotence and lack of manhood in the face of such aggression, this extreme in Negro character development turns their aggressions which arise out of their fear, hate, and double fear of the white man inwardly on themselves." Less than two years after publication of the article, Horace, in fact, would finally succumb to his own emotional and psychological "collapses."[38]

By October 1946, Cayton was down to two psychoanalytical sessions a week and hoped to cut the "umbilical cord" soon. "I think it'll take a year to realize whether it did much good or not," he wrote to Wright, "but I don't shake so much in the morning—that is, unless I have a hangover." The following year, however, Horace was even farther from achieving any kind of emotional resolution.[39]

‡═══‡

Three significant events in 1947 brought additional emotional trauma into Horace's life and precipitated a psychological collapse in 1948: a total breakup of his friendship with Richard Wright; his marriage to Ruby Jordan Wright; and his service as a jury foreman investigating a tragic Chicago tenement fire.

The loss of Wright's friendship came first, largely as a result of Horace's fading ability to grasp reality. It should be noted, however, that both men had a pattern of abruptly severing relationships with friends over some "betrayal." Only Horace's side of the story is recorded. He said the trouble started in late 1945 when the two men argued over a young woman, then over Wright's "attitude" toward Revels. Horace claims Wright became enamored with a "little blond girl," one of two college coeds who visited Cayton's apartment when Wright was beginning a speaking tour in the autumn of 1945. After Wright's departure, when the girl returned looking for him, Horace took her into his bedroom, undressed her, and had sex with her, an act, he told his psychiatrist Helen McLean, that was brutal, inexplicable, and deeply disturbing. Horace later revealed the next stage of this episode in some 1964 notes he wrote concerning Wright: "Later I go to New York. The Rothschilds [John and Connie] give a party for me. My brother comes. When I get there Dick is baiting Revels. I object. Then I tell him about the girl. Dick cannot forgive me."[40]

Cayton and Wright's relationship cooled sharply, assuming a professional formality. The two men saw each other briefly on Long Island in the summer of 1947, just before Wright and his family departed for Paris. Soon after, Horace lost touch with Wright for a decade. (In November 1960, when staying in a cheap hotel in Oakland, Horace read about his former friend's passing in a newspaper.)[41]

Another factor in Cayton's coming collapse was his marriage to Ruby Jordan Wright (no relation to Richard Wright). In late October 1946, Horace traveled to Portland, Oregon, to present "A Psychological Approach to Race Relations" to a Northwest Writers Conference at Reed College. Horace stayed with Steven Wright, Susan's half-brother, and his wife Ruby. When Horace returned to Chicago, Ruby followed him, and later divorced her husband. In August 1947, Horace and Ruby were married at Yaddo in New York.[42]

Susan strongly objected to the marriage. In a letter sent to her the day after the ceremony, Horace upbraided Susan for her "impudence" and he recommended psychoanalysis to help her get over her feelings. A year earlier, Susan again had contacted Horace about the Cortor portraits, but received no response. He now agreed to return the paintings, although, he snapped, it was "very ungracious" of her to have asked for them. Finally, he reasserted his position as family head, reminding Susan that she was not truly a part of the family, and she had no right to the furniture in her apartment, nor to the Cayton name. Susan, hurt and angry, fired back:

I never assumed the name Cayton, it was given to me as a child by your mother and father. I know that I am not a member of the immediate family. I have felt it and known it since I was five years old... I don't think I'm being ungracious about Mother's picture... I am more than grateful that you have consented to return the picture.[43]

Susan broke off contact with Horace for over a year.

Horace and Ruby had not been married long when old patterns re-emerged. Soon, according to several witnesses, both Horace and Ruby were having affairs. The marriage became emotionally draining, not only for Horace, but for family, friends, and others.

Another severely traumatic event for Horace occurred in October 1947, when four women and six children died in an Ohio Street tenement fire on Chicago's West Side. The *Defender* and other African American newspapers graphically reported details about the horrifying incident. City officials appointed a six-man, mixed-race coroner's jury to investigate, including Horace as foreman and his friend, Sidney Williams, the new Secretary of the Chicago Urban League. After a two-month investigation, the jury issued its report on December 12, 1947. The twenty-nine-page document charged that the deaths were "murder by arson" by person(s) unknown and declared a virtual indictment of the building department, police force, fire department, city government, and various real estate agents for negligence and inefficiency. Once again, however, city officials failed to act. Horace was distraught and consumed with "uncontrollable rage and frustration."[44]

Moreover, liberal whites now began to withdraw support from Horace and Parkway House. The Chicago Council of Social Agencies, of which Horace had been a member since February 1945, was reviewing Parkway House's status. The council's resulting report recommended that Parkway "concentrate its efforts on the immediate neighborhood." Horace's desire to act, to *do* something, was overwhelming, but he felt powerless. With no safe place to vent his extreme emotions, he turned them inward.[45]

+≥—≤+

The conclusion of World War II brought the beginning of the end to the Chicago Renaissance. Even as early as 1939, New Deal enemies in Congress had successfully engineered the closure of the Federal Theater Project, assigned the supervision of cultural programs to the generally more-conservative state level, and promoted an image that the WPA's cultural programs were infiltrated by left-wing radicals. Perhaps the year 1948 most symbolically marked the end of this period in Chicago. In December,

Cayton left for New York. Also that year, the Rosenwald Fund closed its doors. Soon, the House Un-American Activities Committee inaugurated a period of anti-Communist and anti-leftist hysteria that coincided with a backlash against the gains made by African Americans during World War II. Activists demanding "democracy at home" and the end of discrimination became objects of anti-leftist campaigns, as a narrower definition of patriotism swept across the country.

For Horace, 1948 was the year his inner world disintegrated. Remarkably, this dissolution was slow in coming, and rarely apparent until late 1947. For the most part, his family, friends, and associates saw only his successes—his work at Parkway, his civic activism, the journalistic efforts, and his other achievements, especially widely heralded *Black Metropolis*. His professional, personal, and family relationships were in chaos. Periods of manic behavior when he was "bubbling over with ideas" and thrilled by an intense consciousness of the exquisite, sublime ecstasy of life flowing through ever fiber of his being, conflicted sharply with periods of depression, when he felt haunted by the hellish spectre of absolute, hopeless despair—his "dark inner landscape." The extremes became alternately dulled and sharpened, and further complicated, by his abuse of alcohol and barbiturates. Regardless of which psychoanalytic interpretation—Freudian or other—that might be used to explain the roots of his destructive behavior, the fact remains that by autumn 1948, Horace was nearing total collapse. Learning of Cayton's dire condition, Arna Bontemps advised Langston Hughes, "Horace is not at all well and...he will take a year off—at least."[46]

Desperately, Horace clutched to the old pillars of solace—more alcohol, more pills, more psychoanalysis, and a new woman. He managed to continue contributing to the *Courier,* and wrote an occasional book review or article, urging African Americans to discard apathy and shackles, and take up the fight against segregation and discrimination, while avoiding being trapped as the tools of powerful white organizations and ideologies.

Hoping to conquer his emotional malaise, Horace tried Richard Wright's solution, i.e., writing an autobiography. Wright had emerged from the intense self-analysis recorded in *Black Boy* with a renewed sense of self and purpose. In a November 1944 *New York Post* article, Wright consented that writing the book had been "therapy...an inner adventure, akin to psychoanalysis." Horace's article, "Frightened Children of Frightened Parents," also had been an intensely personal, thinly veiled autobiographical statement. In most of his writing for the next twenty-five years, in fact, Horace explored these same themes in only slightly different forms and contexts.[47]

In 1946, Horace had written his first public autobiographical statement, "The Bitter Crop," though the piece did not appear until two years later. In August 1948, he informed Langston Hughes that he now was working on an autobiography that "would cut deeper and be much more decisive, incisive," than "The Bitter Crop." But, over a decade would elapse before he gained the emotional solace and insight he sought from his autobiographical writing. Horace Jr. struggled as director at Parkway. He applied for another Rosenwald fellowship, but was turned down. At the end of October 1948, the Parkway board unanimously approved a year's leave of absence for Horace, and soon thereafter selected Faith Jones as acting director.[48]

In December 1948, Horace and Ruby fled to New York. By August the marriage was over. In one of his last letters to Richard Wright, Horace remarked, "I guess it was a rebound from analysis." The casual simplicity of Cayton's words masked the deeply disturbing Freudian conclusions behind them. Several people close to the situation at the time claim that the relationship with Ruby utterly devastated Horace. He later wrote that the marriage was "abnormal, a sort of incestuous lust because Ruby so closely resembled Ruth, my older sister." In the wake of the turbulence and emotional wreckage, Horace slipped further into mental illness.

One day at the Parkway House, Susan discovered Madge and Susie's portraits lying face down in a dirty closet. She took the family heirlooms home, at last, for safekeeping. In New York Horace attempted to find work, but without luck. Then he tried to acquire a publishing advance, hoping to support himself in Paris for a year. By January 1949, that avenue had closed, too, and he gave up the idea. Horace dropped out of public sight, sliding into utter collapse.[49]

CHAPTER 9

A Spirit of Steadfast Determination

Revels in San Francisco and Los Angeles, 1934–1945

I N THE TENSE DAYS of the 1936-37 San Francisco maritime strike, union organizer Revels Cayton traveled everywhere with three armed body-guards as protection against a "goon" squad hired by the shipowners. The thugs were directed by opportunistic Lee Holman, the white president of the Maritime and Transportation Servicemen's Union.

One morning as Revels entered his Marine Cooks and Stewards union hall, he sensed an unusual tension in the air. He quickly learned that one of Holman's goons had been caught and was being held—and the man was black. Revels called a meeting of the strike committee to debate what to do with him. Meanwhile, the Longshoremen had gotten word of the capture and were coming to take revenge for the maiming of one of their own men by Holman's thugs the day before. Revels argued for giving the "fink" to the Marine Cooks and Stewards patrol squad—four or five tough guys who undoubtedly would beat the black goon up, but less severely than the Longshoremen would. Time was running out for Revels. "I could see that I was losing my Strike Committee," he recalled. "And then, I couldn't afford to be rejected. So, I said, 'Okay, you guys go on, do what you want. I'm out of it.'"[1]

Revels walked to the window and looked down Clay Street. The Long-shoremen were approaching, their white caps bobbing. He turned, walked out of the room, and went down the stairs. Suddenly, he remembered the horrible stories in Du Bois' *Crisis,* and it seemed as if the white-hooded clansmen in his childhood nightmares were becoming real. Revels decided this no longer was just a union matter, but, rather, "a white mob [was] gonna take a black guy out." Revels turned and ran back to the building, but he was too late. The white Longshoremen had seized the goon and "put the boots to him."

A short time later in a nearby tavern, Revels encountered one of his men who had participated in the beating. He bragged about getting in two good hits. Suddenly, he stopped and looked at Revels. "You think I hit that guy 'cause he's colored," he said. "Listen, you're the leader of a big union on this waterfront, and a lot of responsibility lies on you. I want to tell ya that you don't even know what this goddamn strike is all about."

The incident deeply disturbed Revels. How could he fight for the working class struggle when it conflicted with his race? On reflection, years later, he put it this way: "The collision between my blackness and the way I'd been trying to run my life with my working class program—it all just bubbled up, and I was an unhappy lad." He had to shrug off the issue, however, and dedicate himself to the daily exigencies of the strike.[2]

+>===<+

Revels arrived in San Francisco at a crucial time in the history of American industrial labor relations. The period from the mid 1930s to World War II witnessed the most dramatic changes in the labor movement since the 1880s. Of key importance, the New Deal's Wagner Act of 1935 dismantled "company-directed" unions and prohibited other kinds of influence by industry over labor organizations, thereby setting up a legal framework for the rise of "independent" trade unionism.

Also, in the spring of 1935, a group of leading African American unionists, intellectuals, civil rights leaders, and communists formed the National Negro Congress to address the needs of black workers and organize them into unions. Historically, the white-led American Federation of Labor, or AFL, and other unions had ignored African American workers. The AFL's selective "craft" union system had practiced overt racial discrimination; but now, change was imminent.

In the mid 1930s, black workers stood at a crossroads. To some, the new National Negro Congress held promise for effective change. At the same time, traditional white union leaders were gearing up to organize large numbers of both white and black workers in the burgeoning mass production industries, especially auto, steel, food, and rubber. In 1935, John L. Lewis and ten other union leaders formed the Committee for Industrial Organization, or CIO, within the craft-focused AFL. In two years, however, the AFL expelled these ten CIO unions. By then the CIO was organizing vast numbers of factory workers, thanks in part to the realization that black participation was crucial to any successful industry-wide unionization. By 1937, CIO membership reached 3.2 million, and a year later the association was reorganized as the Congress of Industrial Organizations with John L. Lewis as president.

The spring of 1935 also saw the start of the "popular front," whereby the Communist Party sought to make common cause with New Deal and liberal programs. At a more surreptitious level, communists hoped to exert influence by "boring from within." Consequently, the party gained considerable influence among liberal-minded intellectuals, and—key to Revels' career—in the resurgent labor movement. Party members soon assumed positions of leadership in a number of unions. (The "popular front" lasted only until 1939, when the USSR signed a non-aggression pact with Nazi Germany, setting the stage for Hitler and Stalin's invasion of Poland. Thereafter, the Communist Party's fortunes in the United States would generally plummet.)

Finally, another key development in the West Coast's dynamic labor situation took place shortly before Revels stepped onto San Francisco's docks in May 1935. That spring, the Maritime Federation of the Pacific was established, bringing together unions representing firemen, engineers, and other dockworkers and seamen. While retaining individual union autonomy within its structure, the federation was an instrument for coordinating and directing solidarity during strikes and for collective bargaining.[3]

When he came to San Francisco, Revels knew that the preceding years had been lean and hard ones for maritime workers. From his own adolescent adventure as a shipboard telephone operator, Revels could attest to the difficulties. In the days before strong independent unions were created, he recalled, "To get a job aboard ship you had to gamble, buy the rotten whiskey sold by the crimps, or pay off the janitors, who paid off the stewards." In the early years of the Depression, between one-fourth and one-third of the maritime workforce was unemployed at any one time. Hordes of destitute seamen roamed the docks, and apathy, hopelessness, and despair hung over the waterfront.

By late 1932, latent anger had produced a "mood of struggle" and the number of strikes sharply increased throughout 1933, culminating in the great West Coast maritime strike of 1934, which erupted into violence. Harry Bridges, the head of the International Longshoremen's Association (later the ILWU), led a three-day strike by convincing the teamsters and ship crews to walk off the job with his union. The bitter confrontation ended in an arbitrated settlement between the shipowners and the maritime workers, giving them a shorter work week, higher wages, and time-and-a-half pay for overtime. By now, African American seamen were joining the previously all-white Sailor's Union of the Pacific, headed by Harry Lundeberg. In addition, the Colored Marine Beneficial Association was forced to consolidate into the Marine Cooks and Stewards Union, or MCS. However, with the 1934-35 agreements between unions and shipowners due to expire at the end of 1936, the stage was set for another conflict.

＋═•═＋

When Revels arrived in San Francisco in the eventful year of 1935, he quickly became engaged in labor organizing for the Marine Cooks and Stewards Union. He was determined that the union should have a "rank and file militant policy." He also set another goal he intently pursued over the next few years—the racial integration of the MCS and, thereby, of all of the shipping lines operating on the West Coast. The problem was formidable—How to integrate the former Colored Marine Beneficial Association and other black unions into the Marine Cooks and Stewards Union (the MCS, after all, had had its own separate "colored" branch since 1908). Care was needed to prevent inflaming racial antagonism between black and white workers. Revels advocated a strategy of uniting the union based on two issues: (1) complete union hall hiring, and thus end the practice whereby shipping companies hired men straight off the docks; and (2) equal shipping rights for *all* union members. The MCS adopted the plan "in principle" during September 1935 on Revels' motion.

Revels knew that building a coalition out of the diverse groups and interests within the MCS was vital to success. He actively proclaimed that it was "anti-union" and "immoral," to "black-bait," "queen-bait," "red-bait," or "cook-bait." At this time, the Marine Cooks and Stewards Union and Harry Bridges' International Longshoremen's Association were the only maritime unions implementing these policies.[4]

During the remainder of 1935, Revels worked as the chief business agent for the union, and as a ship's delegate. As the maritime unions geared up for the big strike they knew was coming in 1936, when previous agreements expired, Revels stayed ashore, living with friends in Chinatown. He worked without pay as a port committeeman of the union's "progressive caucus," spending endless hours in discussions attempting to build unity within the MCS.

Revels steadily moved up in a leadership role at the Marine Cooks and Stewards Union. In a few months, he became the spokesman for some one thousand African American seamen who had been in the old CMBA, and now were part of the MCS. He also became the acknowledged leader of the Harry Bridges faction in the MCS. Bridges, the Longshoremen's head who was to many the hero of the 1934 strike, replaced Harry Lundeberg as president of the Maritime Federation of the Pacific at a 1936 convention.

Revels had first encountered Bridges the year before, and heard him use the expression, "nigger in the woodpile" during a meeting. Afterward, Revels approached "Brother Bridges" and politely informed him, "'Nigger' is a word of oppression, and it's a word that a man like you ought not to be using." Bridges thanked him and said it would not happen again; and he kept his word. Many years later, when Revels returned to San Francisco, he ran into Bridges at the International Longshoremen's and Warehousemen's Union (ILWU) headquarters. Bridges made a remark that revealed his still-shallow understanding of race relations. Revels recalled their short conversation:

> Bridges said, "Say, Revels, I just read an article by James Baldwin, *The Fire Next Time,* and he said the same thing you've been saying all along.
>
> I said, "Harry, you never have understood what it's all about. This guy Baldwin is against all whites. I never have been against all whites. I never fought whites in the union for being white. I raised hell against their lack of attention to blacks. I'm no black nationalist, I'm just dead set against white chauvinists."
>
> Well, Harry's got false teeth, and he clicked his teeth, and he just turned and went into his office.[5]

Revels' warmth, friendliness, integrity, sincerity, fervent idealism, political savvy, and rousing oratory soon made him a prominent figure on the waterfront and a respected lieutenant in the Bridges' ranks. He later recalled with great pride his preparation and delivery of one particular speech he made during a strike:

> When I was convalescent, I had read the history of Napoleon Bonaparte. In that book it was stressed that Napoleon said, "An army travels on its stomach."
>
> That phrase came into my mind, because I hadn't tried to sit down and write a speech. I would always just have an oblong card and make notes, sometimes just a few words. So, when I spoke, I built it up to a crescendo...ending with, "Napoleon said, as he swept over Europe, that an army travels on its stomach. And, we from the Marine Cooks and Stewards say to you wonderful fighters in this strike on the picketlines, that the great thing that we're doing is that we're going to see, come hell or high water, that this army will travel to victory on its stomach, and it'll be damn well fed by the Marine Cooks and Stewards!"
>
> Boy, if I ever saw a whole house jump to their feet and clap, clap, clap, that was it. I went back to my seat. I looked out and I thought, "Clapping white hands; and here I am raising hell."[6]

The long-anticipated 1936-37 West Coast strike lasted nearly ninety-nine days—from late October to the first week in February. At the end of the strike, the maritime unions solidified the substantial gains made in the 1934 strike, and shipowners finally accepted collective bargaining once and for all. During the strike, Revels showed an aptitude for strong leadership. At the beginning, he was elected chairman of the eleven-member MCS Strike Committee. His opponents, who led the faction of Harry Bridges' rival, Harry Lundeberg, expected that Revels would prove inept at managing union interests. They launched a rank-and-file effort to oust him, hoping to clear the way for themselves to lead the strike. Revels, however, acted pre-emptively to ensure support from his rank and file. He expanded the strike committee to fifty-five members from the original eleven, by drawing a member from every fifty-man "crew." With this secure base, Revels represented the MCS on the General Strike Committee, as well as the Coastwide Strike Committee, where he worked alongside Harry Bridges.

Revels had the strong support of African American union men, who consistently elected him patrolman. As he used a gradualist approach to integrating the major shipping lines, black MCS members slowly began shipping out on the Dollar Line, the Matson Line, and other major West Coast fleets. Revels also continued to advance in leadership roles. In 1937, he became the union's representative to the Maritime Federation of the Pacific, then with twenty-five thousand members. And in July 1937, Cayton was elected vice president of the Federation's Bay Area Council. He emphasized to the MCS membership that he would dedicate his time to visiting all federation unions in order "to promote harmony."

Revels and Secretary Gene Burke represented the Marine Cooks and Stewards Union's left-wing leadership that had emerged in 1936–37, voicing the membership's majority sentiment. Shipowners, who hoped to split the MCS as well as the Maritime Federation of the Pacific, often resorted to "red-baiting," labeling all rank and file leaders as "Communists." Generally unwilling to distinguish between unionism and communism, the shipowners viewed the MCS as a "Moscow organization," led by "Commissars" Cayton and Burke, whom they charged were directing the union for Communist Party purposes. To shipowners, "left-wing" was a term of opprobrium, but leaders like Cayton wore the label with pride; it represented black-white unity, working class unity, and industrial unionism.[7]

Although the incident regarding Holman's black goon raised the specter of some incompatibilities between his blackness and his "working class program," for Revels there seemed to be no discord in his union work on a day-to-day level. He actively recruited for the Communist Party, too, telling one gathering that he was "getting as many Negroes as he could." As a highly visible, outspoken African American waterfront radical, a variety of epithets were aimed at him, including "race agitator." But, Revels and the black rank and file who supported him made a substantial contribution to the union in these years. One observer, applauding black MCS members for their courage and devotion to the union's cause, reported, "Time and again the author has heard Negro members say: 'this union represents all that is worth fighting, dying, and living for; it's the embodiment of democracy…this union represents first class citizenship.'"[8]

In September 1939, Revels was elected secretary-treasurer of the Bay Area Council of the Maritime Federation district, a post he held until the federation's demise in 1941. One journalist recognized him as "the outstanding Negro trade union leader of the maritime industry." During a visit to Chicago three months later, the *Chicago Defender* interviewed Revels and published a long article with his photo, highlighting his contributions. Revels told the *Defender:*

> We have learned on the West Coast, as other members of our race are learning throughout the country, that the white people respect us and accept us without condescension as fellow citizens when they see us standing up for our rights. I would like to leave this parting thought— that there is no salvation for either race alone, that prejudice and discrimination threaten not only each racial group but our country as well.
>
> I believe that a united labor movement of all workers—white and colored—offers the only prospect of salvation in a world gripped by war and hate.[9]

As Revels' professional career advanced, his personal life was coming together nicely as well, at least for awhile. In mid 1939 Revels married Ethel Horowitz, whom he had known since his days at Garfield High School in Seattle. Ethel, a strikingly pretty young Jewish woman, came from a middle-class dress manufacturer's family. "Heads would turn when she walked into a room," recalled Revels. The union members quickly accepted the interracial marriage. Said Revels:

> A ship, a big liner, would come in and we'd have a party, and hell, Ethel would be right there. No one hardly ever heard of intermarriages around there at that time. There weren't any other black guys who were leaders of anything who were married to a white woman. My marriage to Ethel didn't affect anything.

In the summer of 1939, shortly after their marriage, Revels and Ethel returned to Seattle. It was apparent that his father had aged considerably. Over the following year, in fact, Horace Sr. grew more feeble and his health continued to deteriorate. In August 1940, Revels again traveled to Seattle, this time to attend his father's funeral. The passing of the torch to the younger generation brought out the intense rivalry between Horace Jr. and Revels.

Horace Jr. was "visibly eaten up with guilt," remembers Susan, over his failure to find a publisher for Horace Sr.'s autobiography. And, Horace Jr. bitterly resented the flowers, telegrams, and condolences sent by Revels' friends in the labor unions, Communist Party, and the Unemployed Councils. Horace Jr.'s friends sent nothing. He peevishly told the family that if the funeral had been in Chicago *his* friends would have done just as much.

Revels returned to San Francisco where it was becoming apparent that the CIO and Maritime Federation cooperation was nearing the end of its most useful period. Following the departure of Harry Lundeberg and the Sailor's Union of the Pacific from the Maritime Federation, and with the general structure of labor-management relations now successfully established in the maritime industries, the federation played a less and less meaningful role.

Revels still grieved over the loss of his father, and, regrettably, there was a growing rift in his marriage with Ethel. He decided in the autumn to ship out for a couple months on the S.S. *Coolidge,* travelling to the Philippines and back.

⊹═╍═⊹

A positive force in Revels' life at this time was his friend Paul Robeson. The two originally had met through Susie in Seattle, and they had seen one another on occasion in Chicago through Horace Jr.'s auspices. By this time, Robeson was an internationally acclaimed stage and screen actor, concert singer, and recording artist. Following Robeson's return to the United States in 1939, after twelve years in Europe, he devoted much of his time and energy toward increasing black membership in CIO unions. Robeson believed that the key to liberation for blacks, both in America and in Africa, was through the unity of black and white workers, and this coalition must include black leadership. These convictions grew out of Robeson's experiences, particularly during the Spanish Civil War and in the Soviet Union, and were further encouraged by his reading of Marxist literature and his association with black Communists, including Revels Cayton.

Revels and Robeson became reacquainted in San Francisco at a CIO benefit concert. They were kindred spirits, and thereafter, whenever Robeson came to town, the two men spent time together. They held much in common, not the least of which was the fact that both of their slave-born fathers had instilled in their sons great pride in black culture and heritage. Cayton and Robeson held deep compassion for the oppressed working classes in all countries, a commitment to political action to correct social ills, and an admiration for the Soviet Union. Both were intellectuals and their conversations were punctuated with a wealth of stories and anecdotes, plus an earthy sense of humor. They embraced an exuberance for life and its struggles, and shared a vision for the black race. As Robeson later eloquently stated: "The power of spirit that our people have is intangible, but it is a great force that must be unleashed in the struggles of today. A spirit of steadfast determination, exaltation in the face of trials—it is the very soul of our people that has been formed through all the long and weary years of our march toward freedom."[10]

One of their evenings together made the headlines. On November 15, 1940, after performing in a concert in San Francisco, Robeson joined Revels and other friends—some of whom were white—for a night on the town. They stopped at Vanessi's Restaurant in North Beach, then considered quite "cosmopolitan." The maitre d' allowed the first companion—who looked white—to enter, but barred Robeson and Cayton. The group politely left for the Fairmont Hotel, later joking about the incident to ease their intense infuriation. Several days later, Robeson's friends filed a suit against the restaurant, charging racial discrimination and asking over twenty-two thousand dollars in damages. A union boycott of Vanessi's was swiftly enacted, but within a matter of days, they decided to end the boycott and drop the legal proceedings. There was little hope of winning the case, and, as Revels later noted, it only would result in unfavorable publicity for Robeson, who would be smeared for trying to enter a restaurant "with a bunch of Communists." In fact, in January 1941, two months after the widely reported incident, the FBI began conducting surveillance of Robeson. By June 1941, Revels also was under FBI investigation.

Cayton and Robeson often attended CIO parties together. "All the union guys would come in," Revels recalled, and Robeson "could really get right with the guys; he was just one of us." In July 1941, both men attended the Third National Convention of the CIO-affiliated National

Maritime Union of America in Cleveland, Ohio. Robeson addressed the delegates, explaining, "I don't feel a stranger; I know Joe [Curran] and Ferdy Smith, and one of my best friends is here, Revels Cayton from out in San Francisco."[11]

Returning to San Francisco, Revels was stunned to hear rumors that he had stolen money from the federation and was having an affair with a co-worker. The situation seemed bizarre. He could not understand why his associates had not immediately challenged the charges. Revels was sure this trouble originated with Walter Stack, head of the Marine Firemen, Watertenders, Oilers, and Wipers Union. To Revels, Stack was "one of the toughest, most foul-mouthed guys" he ever met. Intolerant of rivalry, Stack ruled his union with an iron hand. This stood in sharp contrast to Revels' style with the Marine Cooks and Stewards:

> We didn't have any kind of crap like that, we wouldn't allow it. We were nice guys, democratic-minded guys. But, Walter took a real dislike to me. I think he disliked me because of the really powerful position that I had. Walter couldn't dominate me, and he couldn't dominate the Cooks and Stewards either. In connection with having power in a union, having a Party unit, we were so far ahead of the Firemen it wasn't funny. And, Stack took this as a personal thing between me and him. So, I developed, also, a dislike for Walter. I used to say, "Hell, I'll spot my pigment against Stack and still beat him." I'm sure that used to just kill him.

Cayton believed that Stack started the rumors as payback for Revels having voted against him in a council election two years earlier. At the time, Stack threatened, "I'm gonna get you for this."

Revels recalled: "I've never heard anybody say those words like that guy said them. He said it mean." As a man of high moral standards, integrity, and honesty, what bothered Revels most was that he had no opportunity to clear his name.

> You would think that in such a situation that the Party's supposed to be so great on Negro rights, and that sort of thing, that they would have done something in terms of calling a meeting—and there would have been a confrontation between Stack and myself. But, there never was. There was no chance for me, no statement by him that he did tell a lie, and there was no statement by anybody correcting that lie.

The vicious personal attack, apparently from a fellow Communist Party member, and the failure of others to defend him, caused Revels to lose some faith in the organization. Gradually, his bitterness and anger over the incident cooled. His commitment to the party remained solid, but there lingered a nagging sense of disappointment.[12]

The incident compounded other frustrations in Revels' life. His marriage to Ethel remained shaky, and he decided to ship out again on the *Coolidge*, bound for Australia. He was en route to Hawaii when the Japanese attacked Pearl Harbor on December 7, 1941. Revels spent the first few months of World War II aboard ship in the treacherous wartime waters of the Pacific. Not long after his return to San Francisco, Revels, unhappy with events in his life and desiring a change of scene, accepted a job in Los Angeles.

When America was readying for war, the dramatic increase in government spending in weapons and other military-related industries created many jobs, raising African Americans' hopes for further opportunities. By the beginning of 1941, however, when it became clear that the new jobs were going almost exclusively to whites, A. Philip Randolph called on mainstream black organizations to join in a march on Washington D.C., demanding employment in industry and opportunities in the armed forces. Many churches and other organizations, including the NAACP and the Urban League, threw their support behind the movement. The planned march was growing so massive that the Roosevelt administration relented and issued Executive Order 8802, which prohibited discrimination in the defense industries and established the Fair Employment Practices Committee (FEPC) to enforce the policy. The Communist Party had remained silent about the March on Washington Movement for five months, and only at the last moment voiced its weak support, thus putting itself and its members out of step with this significant national black protest movement.

Then, in June 1941, Nazi Germany attacked the USSR, and the American Communist Party abruptly reversed its position on the war. At the outbreak of the European conflict in 1939, the party had staunchly opposed (as did the CIO and many other labor groups) any U.S. involvement in what it called the "Second Imperialist War," and even opposed the expansion of the U.S. defense industry. But now, defeat of the fascists became the party's top priority. When the United States officially joined the Allies after December 7, 1941, the Communists' wartime policies were fully in step with the rest of the country, urging national harmony, emphasizing labor-management cooperation, and opposing strikes or other actions that would diminish the war effort against Germany. Many African Americans resented the party's change in policy, which apparently placed the interests of winning the war and saving the Soviet Union above the grievances of black workers and their struggles against workplace discrimination.

An episode at a 1942 Communist trade union meeting concisely captures the new dynamics in which Revels now operated. Revels gave a speech on "the Negro question" to the large, all-white group. In keeping with the party's position from the 1930s, Revels complained that he could not even get the white trade unions to let blacks do janitorial work in the aircraft plants. On this occasion, it was Revels' not-so-subtle tactic to spur the party into action. When he finished, there was dead silence, and the meeting adjourned quickly. Though the party leaders now had different priorities, they did not discipline nor reproach Revels, probably out of respect for his contributions to the workers' movement. Cayton remained a stalwart communist, but was becoming more independent and increasingly unwilling to parrot the party line.

In Los Angeles Revels served the national CIO as an organizer and field representative. Ethel, too, worked for the CIO. At first they lived in the Central Avenue area, but later settled in Silver Lake. They had a comfortable home, and their jobs were not too demanding. The change seemed good. It was a time of renewed hope, a time of promise. Before long, Revels was vice president of the California State CIO Council and director of the State CIO Minorities Committee. He continued to fight for more jobs for black workers, and for the integration of the large airplane and manufacturing plants that sprang up in the Los Angeles area during the war. Revels' energetic unionizing strengthened the shop union system to the point that the CIO was able to open a special office in the black community. Working with local churches, Revels formed a committee composed of prominent ministers, who lent their support to the CIO's organizing efforts.

It was during this period that his mother passed away and Revels made the long journey by train to Chicago for the funeral. Just over a year later, in the fall of 1944, when Madge died of rheumatic fever, Revels again traveled to Chicago for a funeral. The family's grief over Madge's death was intense, and Revels was quick to accuse his brother of mistreating their older sister.[13]

The *Chicago Defender* interviewed Revels before he returned to Los Angeles. Under the title, "'Race Specialists' Flayed by Coast Labor Leader," Revels emphasized the vital role that the labor movement would play in securing post-war jobs for African Americans. Turning to a tone of criticism, Revels expressed alarm at a trend towards "Negro isolationism" among a "clique of self-designated race relations specialists." These so-called "advisors," he charged, "whose sole aim seems to be to perpetuate their soft jobs by creating rather than solving race problems, are a dire danger to all the gains made by the Negro in the job field during the war period." He did not name his brother, but those who knew both men could read between the lines.[14]

Soon thereafter, Horace Jr. returned the barbs, in print. In the December 1944 *Negro Digest*, a roundtable of "race leaders" commented on the question, "Have the Communists Quit Fighting for Negro Rights?" Horace Jr. declared a strong "yes." He criticized the communists for failure to fight Jim Crow practices in industry, the armed forces, and the Red Cross. African Americans were beginning to realize, concluded Horace, that the communist position "subordinates the Negro's problem to the larger world struggle for power."[15]

⊹⇒⇐⊹

In the summer of 1945, Revels and Ethel left Los Angeles and returned to San Francisco. The end of World War II was a time of celebration, but not particularly so for Revels. Back in San Francisco, he fell into an emotional slump, dogged by melancholy and moods of defeat. His relationship with Ethel seriously deteriorated. Madge and his mother were gone. Anger—not only aimed at Horace Jr., but at Horace Sr. for favoring his namesake—ate away at Revels. San Francisco seemed completely changed. With the substantial growth of the African American population during the war years—from 4,800 in 1940 to 32,000 in 1945—race relations began deteriorating again at the end of that period. Soon, with the onset of the Cold War, the Communist Party, which had been "like a political mother" to Revels, would seem remote to him. He avoided contact with his old party associates as much as possible. It was, Revels reflected, "a very trying period, a very painful part of my life."

Revels took a truck-driving job with the Ship Scalers and Painters Union, but in the months that followed he moved on to a dispatcher's job, then to a position as vice president of the union. His life remained unsettled.

He considered joining a black church in a search for new roots and meaning, but soon decided this held no answers for him. Revels felt ready for change.

The opportunity came in mid-August 1945. He received a telegram from Max Yergan, president of the National Negro Congress in New York, offering him the position of executive secretary. By early December, Revels left for the East Coast. Ethel stayed behind in San Francisco. She told him, "I'm just not going to follow you anymore."[16]

CHAPTER 10

With the Safest Man in America

Revels and Horace Jr. in New York, 1946–1959

HARLEM WAS A FAR CRY from the city on San Francisco Bay. The area's major commercial artery, 125th Street, bustled with activity. At its intersection with Lenox Avenue stood the Schomburg Center for Research in Black Culture, a branch of the New York Public Library. At the corner of 125th and 7th avenues rose the grand Hotel Theresa, the black community's social headquarters—called by some "Harlem's Waldorf-Astoria." Seventh Avenue was a lovely boulevard with a narrow strip of grass, trees, and flowers, separating uptown from downtown. Located here was a colorful collage of nightclubs, theaters, churches, apartment buildings, doctors and attorneys' offices, and shops, from bakeries to beauty parlors, as well as a scattering of private brownstone residences.

The bright spots on the cultural landscape included The Savoy Ballroom on Lenox Avenue, featuring top bands led by the likes of Duke Ellington, Tommy Dorsey, Cab Calloway, and Lionel Hampton. Attracting crowds well into the 1950s, The Savoy was a focal point of popular culture, music, and style. On the streets walked "jitterbugs" and "hepcats" dressed in zoot suits. Malcolm Little (later Malcolm X) was there, too, a resident since 1941. Popular political figures included A. Philip Randolph, well known for his March on Washington campaigns, and Adam Clayton Powell Jr., a colorful politician and minister of the Abyssinian Baptist Church. Powell's election to the U.S. House of Representatives in 1944 made him the first African American to sit in Congress since the end of Reconstruction.

Revels Cayton's relocation to New York in January 1946 coincided with a major shift in the Communist Party line back to class struggle. Previously, General Secretary Earl Browder had led the Twelfth Party Convention in dissolving the Communist Party USA and creating the Communist Political Association in its place. Class struggle was de-emphasized as Browder pursued a policy of supporting national unity and cooperating with capitalists. After Browder's policy had been in place for a year, however, it was considered a serious mistake by a majority of communists. Consequently, the Communist Party was reconstituted at an emergency convention in June 1945, signaling public humiliation for Browder and those who had been led into "opportunism."

About this time, the National Negro Congress (NNC) began to realize it needed a man like Revels Cayton. Not only did the West Coast maritime and CIO official possess excellent leadership credentials, but he had entree to auto workers in Detroit and meatpackers in Chicago. The NNC was hoping to rebuild the organization on black trade unionist support. The Communist Party, too, approved of Cayton's appointment to the NNC leadership, signaling the party's renewed support of black workers and class struggle.

As early as 1945, Revels believed equal rights activists needed to take more aggressive action to get the kind of results they wanted. In a letter to fellow Communist Mervyn Rathborne, Revels noted, "There should be an independent, militant Negro people's movement."[1] (The kind of action Revels was calling for did come, of course, more than a decade later in the "civil rights movement" of the 1950s and 1960s.)

At the outset of his term as executive secretary of the NNC, Revels declared, "The job of the National Negro Congress has to be to rally the Negro people behind the trade union movement and the trade union movement behind the Negro people." This vision of a united black and white working class struggle for change was much the same as when he was at Seattle's League of Struggle for Negro Rights over a decade earlier. At the NNC, the time seemed ripe to vigorously pursue the struggle for black workers' rights, with African American leadership, and also to raise awareness of the broader working class struggle.

Planning began for the NNC's Tenth Anniversary Convention under the bold theme, "Death Blow to Jim Crow." The Detroit convention proved to be a highlight of Cayton's time with the NNC. Held in the spring of 1946, the four-day event included a rally that drew over three thousand people. Speakers included Paul Robeson, Benjamin (Ben) Davis Jr., one of the leading African Americans in the Communist Party and a member of the New York City Council from Harlem, and George F. Addes, secretary-Treasurer of the United Auto Workers.

Drawing the most publicity was the convention's adoption of "The First Petition to the United Nations from the Afro-American People," directed toward the recently formed world organization. Later, on June 6,

1946, Revels Cayton, accompanied by Max Yergan and NNC Vice President Charles Collins, presented the petition to the UN Human Rights Commission. They charged the Truman administration with failing "to implement Constitutional guarantees"; therefore, they declared, it was the National Negro Congress's duty to petition the United Nations on behalf of African Americans. The document requested recognition and redress of the "brutal system of oppression and discrimination" that subjected thirteen million African Americans to second-class citizenship. The UN petition received widespread publicity in both the black and white press, bolstering the NNC's organizing energy that had been generated at the convention.[2]

After the convention, Revels praised the congress's accomplishments in a "Report to West Coast Friends as to What Happened in Detroit," which he sent to many of his contacts. To Lena Horne and Lenny Hayton, friends in Hollywood, he wrote an additional note: "I'm cookin' a lot of plans for the Cultural Division of the Congress here in New York, and in Hollywood. As soon as they are finalized a little better I will send you the dope." In the report, Revels expressed hope that his friend Matt Crawford (the NNC's former northern California director and now a newly appointed vice president at the national level), would be "a real link between the movement in the East and the West Coast."[3]

Following the Detroit convention, Cayton and Paul Robeson toured major West Coast cities, conducting a series of Robeson concerts as well as union conferences to boost the development of local NNC chapters and increase membership. From Seattle to Los Angeles, and in community meeting houses, churches, and on the radio, they spoke to enthusiastic—if small—audiences, while striving "to unite the Negro peoples' liberation movement with all labor and progressive forces to establish equal opportunity for all."[4]

Revels became good friends with Ed Strong, his immediate NNC predecessor, who returned from military service in late 1946. Strong was one of the founders of the Southern Negro Youth Congress. He made an indelible impression on Revels, who described Strong as "very influential" in his life and "one of the finest men" he ever knew. A tall man with dark brown skin, Strong was extremely bright and possessed an easy-going style and gentle demeanor that charmed people. When he returned to the NNC, instead of claiming his old position and pushing Revels out—though he was pressured to do so by Max Yergan—Strong created a position for himself as "organizational secretary." Strong struck a deep chord in Revels.

"He had such idealism about the black struggle," emphasized Revels. "He had spirit, and complete dedication."

Hard times lay ahead for the NNC, however, fulfilling an earlier prophecy from former NNC president A. Philip Randolph. In 1940, Randolph had resigned from the labor congress in protest over its formal alignment with CIO unions and the Communist Party for financial support, and because of the NNC's encouragement of white participation and support, and its endorsement of the Communist Party's foreign policy positions. In Randolph's opinion, the NNC's decision-making process now "rendered it incapable of accurately reflecting the perspective of Black America." (Revels also admitted that once the NNC began accepting money from the Communist Party, it began to play "a strong role" in NNC affairs.) Eventually, too, the CIO would withdraw support from the labor congress. It became apparent only later, said Cayton, that "I had walked into something that was a corpse." By 1947, the NNC faced dwindling membership, and it never did realize a "rebirth," as Revels expected. As Randolph predicted, the NNC had little credibility as the "voice of the black masses."[5]

When coming to the National Negro Congress, Revels could not foresee the wave of anti-Left reactionism that soon swept across the nation. After the end of World War II, U.S. and Soviet foreign policies quickly came into conflict, raising international tensions in a "Cold War." A series of dramatic confrontations marked the new era—the Soviet blockade of Berlin (1948), the division of Germany (1949), the creation of NATO (1949), and the start of the Korean War (1950). Americans watched communist governments being set up in Poland and elsewhere in Eastern Europe, communist guerillas threatening Greece, and the Soviets bitterly denouncing America's far-sighted Marshall Plan that helped rebuild war-torn Western Europe.

Anti-communism at home, for the most part held in check during World War II, began to flourish as a rise in labor strikes coincided with increasing anti-labor sentiment. Racial conflict and anti-black violence was on the increase, too, as evidenced by the sharply higher numbers of Ku Klux Klan incidents. American business leaders and the House Un-American Activities Committee helped spur the rising tide. The NNC—a pro-Left, pro-labor, and pro-black organization—embodied the three primary targets of Cold War repression.

The strongest influence undercutting efforts to rebuild the National Negro Congress, however, came from the CIO. Eventually, the anti-Left leaders in the two CIO unions with the strongest NNC ties—the National

Maritime Union and the United Auto Workers—gained control of these organizations. Also, in November 1946, the head of the CIO's Industrial Union Councils, John Brophy, directed that no further financial support be given to the NNC. Although Ferdinand Smith—secretary of the National Maritime Union and for several years an NNC vice president—was elected to the CIO national executive board, his support proved insufficient to counter these developments.

Cayton also found his efforts thwarted by internal NNC conflicts. Revels gradually broke with Max Yergan, who made plans to leave the congress when it became apparent that the McCarthy anti-communist hysteria would make life difficult for him. Yergan and his supporters contended with Cayton and Ed Strong, even trying to maneuver Revels into relocating his office in Detroit. Thus, while the NNC initially had given Revels new meaning and structure in his life, his working days were increasingly fraught with contention. The bitter factional infighting began to deeply wear on him, and his personal affairs offered no relief. Shortly after arriving in New York, he had received a letter from Ethel. It was her last to him. "We held each other in weakness," she wrote. Revels knew it, too; the marriage was finished.[6]

Many nights he found solace in alcohol. Cayton's friend, Louise Berman, detected his troubled inner struggles and recommended a psychiatrist—a Dr. Rosenbaum. Revels realized he needed help and agreed. He started seeing Rosenbaum three times a week. Gradually, he was able to unravel the complicated emotional vortex of his inner life. Revels found he held deep resentment toward his brother Horace Jr. and his domineering ways. Revels still felt hurt by their father's preferential treatment of Horace Jr., holding him up as an "example." Gradually, however, Revels also came to see his brother more objectively, especially Horace's insecurities, his alcoholism, and his need to dominate. Eventually, Revels came to what he termed "a deeper understanding" of his brother. Revels continued to see the psychiatrist for two years, and found the experience immensely valuable:

> If I hadn't had this help and insight from Doc Rosenbaum, Horace would have damn near destroyed me. He [Horace Jr.] wasn't a factor in my being upset; but he was a factor in making a lot of problems for me that I had to try and understand. Dr. Rosenbaum saved my life. Really, from the time I went into that analysis, to when I came out of it, I was a different person.[7]

Revels' period of intense self-examination was not limited to the time spent with the psychiatrist. A major part of his readjustment involved developing a closer relationship with other African Americans. As a young adult, he had worked with white trade union leaders in San Francisco and Los Angeles. Now, however, he was the executive secretary of a national African American organization and living in Harlem. This gave him full reign to grapple daily with the struggles that black people faced. Ed Strong, too, spoke words that Cayton wanted and needed to hear. A new level of black consciousness developed in him, and living in a largely black community gave him a feeling of "really belonging."

And then he fell in love. At the congress offices, he had taken a liking to one of the secretaries, a quiet, strong-minded young Jewish woman named Lee Davidson, whom he had first met in Los Angeles during the war. Revels liked her sparkling eyes, slow smile, and flashing acerbic wit. Born in Brooklyn in 1916, Lee was the youngest of three girls. Her father was a milliner by trade and her mother a dressmaker. Revels and Lee were married in February 1948. After living near the Jewish ghetto for a year, they moved to the new, integrated (but largely African American) housing complex of Riverton in Harlem. A little more than a year after the marriage, Lee gave birth to a son, Michael Revels Cayton.[8]

Cayton's friendship with Paul Robeson steadily deepened until the two became "like brothers," said Revels. (Robeson's son, too, later described his father and Revels as being "like adopted brothers," and the relationship between the Caytons and Robesons was "like extended family.") Revels' mother, Susie, had been "one of those symbolic mother figures" to Robeson. The two men took numerous trips together, including the NNC-sponsored lecture series and the West Coast concerts. Robeson regularly visited the Caytons' apartment in Harlem, often staying for long hours. Revels described Robeson during this time as "lonesome," without a close relationship even with his wife, Essie, or his son. "Millions loved him, but he had few intimate friends."[9]

Revels, along with Paul Robeson and other friends, sometimes visited Café Society—the "in" night spot in Greenwich Village—where a fabulously diverse clientele gathered, including show business celebrities, politicians, jazz lovers, socialites, and labor leaders. On a given night, one might mingle with such public figures as Lena Horne, Lenny Hayton, Congressman Adam Clayton Powell Jr., Hazel Scott, Timmy Rogers, and a young Sarah Vaughn. Revels became friends with owner Barney Josephson, who called his Café Society club "a seminar with drinks and entertainment."

In October 1946, while Cayton and Robeson were visiting Los Angeles (in part to see Ferdinand Smith from the National Maritime Union), they were subpoenaed by the California Joint Fact-Finding Committee on Un-American Activities, known as "the Tenny Committee" after its chair, Senator Jack B. Tenny. The questioning of Robeson by Tenny and the committee's legal counsel, Richard Combs, proceeded with restraint and politeness for several hours. Revels later recounted the ridiculous and amusing episode:

> There was a whole flock of reporters and a commission of eight or nine people. They called on "Mr. Robeson." Paul has a knack, when he's puttin' it on, of the most gracious, most self-effacing kind of graciousness that you ever saw, and then that big smile of his flashing on and off like a neon sign.
>
> So, Combs said, "Mr. Robeson, I understand that you made a trip to loyalist Spain recently." Paul said, "Oh, yes, yes. I had the great honor to actually visit the troops in loyalist Spain, and the Lincoln Brigade in particular, a fine group of fighting men. By the way, accompanying me was Lord Atlee. We were there for about two weeks and covered the whole battle front." ["Loyalist Spain" was a socialist government in the late 1930s, and battling Spanish fascists.]
>
> Then Combs asked Paul another question, and Paul again identified himself with some English person of high title. All the time, these reporters are getting more and more giggly. Finally, the Committee turned Paul loose.
>
> So, then, much to my surprise, because there was almost no audience—the place was practically empty—they called me. So, I got up. They said, "We understand that you are here with Dr. Ferdinand Smith from the National Maritime Union."
>
> Now this is a legitimate thing—what are they doing raking me over the coals for this? I got mad right now! I said, "No, I did not come here with Dr. Ferdinand Smith."
>
> Combs' ears picked up. He said, "You mean, you didn't come here with Dr. Ferdinand Smith?"
>
> I said, "That's right."
>
> He said, "Do you know Dr. Ferdinand Smith?"
>
> I said, "No, I don't know him."
>
> Well, everything's getting quiet now, and everybody's staring at me. He started to say something else, and I said, "Now wait just a minute. Are you referring to *Mr.* Ferdinand Smith?"
>
> With that the reporters just left the room and you could hear their laughter. Everyone got the point—a racist like Combs would call a black man anything except "Mr." I don't think Combs asked me any more questions. Mr. Combs had a bad afternoon.[10]

A few days later, Cayton reported the episode to Max Yergan at the NNC, noting Robeson's "tremendous talk" to the Tenny Committee: "This red-baiting outfit took the shellacking of their life." Later that year, however, a former Marine Cooks and Stewards member testified before the Tenny Committee, naming Cayton as a communist and a "race agitator."[11]

By mid 1947, the end was at hand for the National Negro Congress. In the 1930s, the NNC had provided an institutional means to bind together the common interests of African Americans, labor, and the Left. But in the post-war years, the anti-communism backlash steadily weakened and undermined the bonds between the individual organizations in the NNC. When the congress dissolved, Revels was out of a job. Mike Quill, leader of the all-white Transport Workers Union, found him a place as a garageman, but Cayton was in for a rough ride—TWU members were noted for their virulent racism. Revels was the first African American ever hired on the Third Avenue bus line. Washing and cleaning buses from midnight to eight o'clock in the morning proved decidedly unpleasant. Cayton's co-workers, deeply prejudiced Italians and others, made the job more difficult, and on one occasion placed dried human feces in one of his buses. Revels thought to himself, "If things got this tough for the Devil, the Devil would have sat down and cried." He stuck it out for a few months, and then one day went home "sick" and never returned.[12]

The jobs that followed were hardly better. Revels took another night job with a long commute, working as a baler in a New Jersey cardboard factory. When the foreman told him that his first cardboard bale should be "put in the Smithsonian," Revels knew his time there would be short. Next, he found work in a glass factory lifting heavy pieces of glass, and passing the days under equally trying circumstances. Finally, through another friend, Bill Michaelson, Revels secured a decent position with the Retail, Wholesale, and Department Store Workers Union, Local 2, which covered Gimbel's and Sak's on 34th Street. Again, Cayton broke racial ground as the first black to integrate the union. He began as a salesman, then moved to organizer, and next to business agent. The local union was pushing to join District 65, and Cayton led the fight to get an African American into the district leadership.

In the spring of 1949, Revels signed on as one of the official "sponsors" of the short-lived Harlem Trade Union Council, formed under Ferdinand Smith's leadership. The council, urging trade unionists—both black and white—to make common cause with community leaders, began making plans to broaden African American job opportunities and defend civil rights. The HTUC, one of ten black labor councils nation-wide, participated in the "National Trade Union Conference for Negro Rights," convening in Chicago in 1950. Problems later arose when Revels led the opposition to the council's dependence on largely white left-wing union financial support. Revels had seen too many African American organizations falter because they depended on "white money" or other types of white community support. He argued successfully against Ferdinand Smith that HTUC should become a purely black independent movement.

Revels later looked back on the episode with mixed emotions. "I remember Ferdinand saying to me, 'Well, you've had your way, and now we're broke.' Perhaps it would have been better, in hind-sight, had I found a compromise." As Smith had predicted, after the HTUC voted to cut itself off from white left-wing unions, the money dried up. By then, Revels had turned his attention to other activities, and he drifted away from the HTUC.[13]

<hr />

By late summer 1949, Horace had been in New York for nine months. He was a burden to Revels and Lee, intruding upon their family life with his unpredictable, drunken behavior. He repeatedly pawned his meager possessions for cash to buy whisky and pills. The last items to go, however, always were his typewriter and the Revels clock—the Cayton family heirloom given to Senator Revels by Jefferson Davis. And, these items always were the first to come out of "hock," too, when he eventually emerged from a "bad spell." Numerous times during this period, Horace Jr. was checked into hospital recovery wards and sanitariums—either by himself, Revels, or friends—for up to three or four months at a time.[14]

Years later, in his autobiography, Horace Jr. said that his "crack up," as he called it, resulted partly from the fact that he had not found his own identity. Other reasons, he claimed, were a profound loneliness, a realization of his hatred of whites, and the discovery of "the core of the Negro[,] being a fear-hate-fear complex." Primary responsibility for his final collapse, he declared, lay in "the enemy world of race hatred," plus his own "weakness and indecision" and "failure to carry the fight to the enemy." This self-censure, however, belies the fact that Horace's emotional problems were compounded by addiction to alcohol and barbituates.[15]

Before he moved to New York, Horace had visited St. Clair and Elizabeth Drake in Greenwich Village numerous times when working on *Black Metropolis*. In the late 1940s, the village had a casual attitude—a sense of freedom and openness—that reminded Horace of Paris. For him, it was a refuge from the turmoil of Chicago, a city he had no interest in seeing again for a long time. Horace Jr. merged anonymously with the bohemian life around him as the 1940s "swing" scene segued into the "bebop" years. He mingled with New York University students and browsed bookstores. He sat in coffee houses where a new "beat" generation gave poetry readings, and visited the clubs on West 52nd Street, where the new jazz "bebop" artists, Thelonius Monk and Charlie Parker, were drawing crowds. He lived inexpensively in dilapidated housing near NYU. Cheap rent was important—he had little money and spent most of it on alcohol. Drink and distraction were easily found in the village's profusion of nightclubs, restaurants, and theaters. Horace Jr. managed to continue writing his column in the *Pittsburgh Courier,* but other jobs just came and went—with few lasting more than a few months.[16]

+⇒⇐+

In the summer of 1949 Revels was involved in the notorious Peekskill incident, marking a dramatic episode in his life. His friend Paul Robeson's pro-Russian public statements and vocal attacks against racism had earned him the enmity of various U.S. government officials. His speech at the World Peace Congress in Paris in April 1949, which the press widely—and erroneously—publicized as including a pro-Soviet statement, brought a storm of protests. Robeson reportedly said it was "unthinkable" that African Americans would fight in a war against the Soviet Union, a country that had done so much to bring full equality to its black citizens. Amid this outcry, Robeson was scheduled to give a concert on August 27, 1949, at the Peekskill picnic grounds in upstate New York. Just days before, U.S. Attorney General Thomas Clark branded the concert's sponsor, the Civil Rights Congress, a "subversive" communist-front organization and named Robeson as one of its prime supporters. A riot by white, self-styled patriots—violently prejudiced against Jews, blacks, trade unionists, and leftists—forced Robeson to give up the concert. A second concert was planned for the following week.

　　After cancellation of the first concert, Cayton assured Robeson, "You'll be the safest man in America, because with the publicity around this thing now they don't dare do anything." A week later, when Robeson performed the second concert, violence erupted. A jeering white mob ringed the concert area and lined the nearby roadways, hurling stones and sticks. The rioting spread out over an area some ten miles square. Several hundred concertgoers found themselves trapped by the anti-Robeson mob and blocked from returning to their cars and buses. An estimated one thousand state patrolmen looked on without intervening. Revels played a crucial role, rallying volunteers to form lines around Robeson's supporters and their families to protect them from the rioters. Hundreds of cars were damaged and overturned, some one hundred and fifty people were injured (including Cayton), fifty-four of whom were hospitalized, and fourteen were arrested. Revels' off-the-mark assurance to his friend later became a standing joke between the two, Robeson teasing, "Like I was the safest man in America!"[17]

While a national debate raged over Peekskill, it was dangerous for Robeson to go downtown in New York. For nearly two months, he stayed with various friends, and spent many hours at the Cayton home. Lee cooked special dinners for Revels and Paul, both of whom were large men, overweight, and trying to watch their diet. Afterwards, they talked—long political discussions, in which Revels spoke with the same, strong conviction that his mother, Susie, had in her thought-provoking conversations with Robeson many years earlier. Sometimes Revels and Robeson stayed up all night, exchanging ideas and views, and arguing till dawn. Changes in Revels' thinking prompted by his NNC work and interaction with black trade unionists, stimulated changes in Robeson's thinking. For both Cayton and Robeson, the belief in developing a distinct race consciousness and identification was accelerating.

Robeson's son, Paul Jr., recognized that Revels strongly influenced Robeson's ideological development, moving to a more pro-black position. "Revels was an important influence on my father," he emphasized in an interview, "and by the early fifties he was expressing and publicizing ideas of black independent action. Dad got a feel for the guts of the trade union movement and the black movement from Rev." Paul Jr. further noted that, when his father was blacklisted and could not rent concert halls, it was Revels Cayton who urged him to go into African American churches and build a movement, instead of relying on the NAACP or the white-controlled unions that had spurned him. Robeson followed the advice.[18]

Robeson, however, still performed most concerts before progressive and philanthropic white organizations. Revels told him he was "out of his mind," and that the white organizations were just using him, and he should be performing for and identifying himself with the black community:

> This was based on Negro identification on my part, trying to break down Paul, whose whole background had been related to white ever

since the days when he sang "Old Man River"....Paul was more and more declaring his independence from and breaking with white groups, and more and more identifying himself with the black movement. I was helping him do this by talking and agitating him.[19]

The labor movement, Revels reminded Robeson, was becoming more reactionary all the time. The AFL's anti-black policies had not changed, and, if anything, had hardened. The left-wing unions that were progressive on the "Negro question"—including Revels' own former union, the Marine Cooks and Stewards—had been expelled from the CIO. At the same time, noted Revels, blacks were beginning to be more willing to stand up and fight for better living and working conditions. He told Robeson, if a decision had to be made between the "so-called radical movement" and the black movement, his choice was clear. To believe any longer that the white working class would lead the struggle for freedom was simply being "slavishly devoted to the Left." As far as he was concerned, the Left had become "a lot of crap." Revels declared: "I'm slavishly devoted to Negroes."[20]

Robeson had come to agree with Revels—that the key to African American advancement still was through the unity of black and white workers, but with blacks leading the coalition for their cause. After 1949, Robeson suffered increasing hostility from segments of the population and U.S. government. He was boycotted from concert halls, theaters, movies, radio, television, and recording studios. In 1950 the State Department charged Robeson with pro-communist sympathies and revoked his passport. He often was ignored or discredited as a public figure.[21]

Both Robeson and Cayton had white friends who disapproved of their friendship—some considered Revels "politically irresponsible" and distanced themselves from him. A terse exchange between Cayton and white leftist writer Howard Fast at a cocktail party one night illustrates the situation. Fast said, "Paul isn't a Negro, he's a world citizen." Revels angrily shot back, "The trouble with you is you don't want him to be black, you want him to be white, and he sure can't pass for white; so now you want to make a 'world citizen' of him."[22]

Nor was the Communist Party pleased with the changes they saw in the friendship. "They hated my relationship with Paul; they thought I was a bad influence," Cayton claimed. Continuing in his own words: "The Party hated me," for not being "a captive of the dreams of the '30s." His maverick views, especially on developing black caucuses within the unions, steadily distanced him from the Communist Party leadership. It was around this time that Revels had a memorable conversation with Ben Davis Jr., one of the leading African Americans in the party. A strictly orthodox member, Davis challenged Cayton's drift away from party policies. Davis believed that the white working class would be "the vanguard," providing the leadership for all party objectives, including full justice and opportunity for blacks. Cayton answered bluntly:

> Ben, your theory…is full of shit. What's happening is that the white trade union guys are gettin' more reactionary. I think if I have to choose, I'm *not* goin' to go along with them white guys, I tell you that; I'm goin' with the blacks.

Davis, in turn, charged Revels with succumbing to "petit bourgeois weakness."

Cayton retorted, "Petit bourgeois my ass. You can stay and hope that those guys don't lynch nobody, but my decision's going to be clear, and I'm sticking with my people." Reflecting on this years later, Cayton believed this reply was entirely natural, given his past history and upbringing:

> That's what the National Negro Congress gave me, and Ed Strong. But, that's also what Reconstruction and the whole struggle of the South gave me. My mother and father's tradition came forward then.[23]

By early 1951, Revels was beginning to stand out as one of the leading militants advocating strong black caucuses in unions. In an article in the *March of Labor,* titled "Challenge to Labor," Cayton pointed out that even the most progressive unions had failed to educate their white members about the importance of the African American struggle against oppression. "The Negro liberation movement," he emphasized, "is a vital, independent force of 15 million Negroes, bearing the primary responsibility of charting the course to their full freedom." Inevitably, as black workers moved to defend the rights of their people, he warned, they would clash with "the entrenched bureaucracy of these outfits."[24]

By 1952 Revels stopped attending Communist Party meetings. He was not anti-party, and really not bitter. Revels' value system had changed and he simply drifted away. The party's priorities were not his, including the preoccupation with the Soviet Union. Nationwide in the early 1950s, many African Americans dropped out, feeling that the party had let them down.[25] In following years, Revels reflected on and emphasized the positive aspects of his relationship with the party:

> I did not leave the Communist Party because I was disillusioned. Even to imply that is to contradict the meaning of my life. If my life has any pattern, it can be described by my unswerving devotion to the interest

of the working class. And it was through the Communist Party that I first found my way to contribute to the struggle of working peoples everywhere.

That I often disagreed with the Party is true. That I grew restless at times and disappointed is also true, although such periods were often the times when I was discontented with my life in general and not alone with the Party. But, that doesn't mean that I was not at the same time deeply committed to the Party. I got a great deal out of the Party— far more than the Party ever got out of me...

...I drifted out of the Party. I didn't have any quarrel with them. I didn't disagree with their political positions on broad issues like the Marshall Plan and the Cold War. It is just that I no longer belonged. It was a little like a marriage where the parties no longer have interests in common but continue to respect each other and go on in different directions.[26]

By the late 1940s and early 1950s, Harlem's renowned cabaret nightlife was losing its glamour. Most of the artists and intellectuals who had gained wide recognition in the 1920s as leaders of the Harlem Renaissance had moved on. In early 1953, Revels, too, decided the time had come to return to California.

+⇌+

Horace Jr. stayed on in New York for six more years. Most of that time he lived in, or near, Greenwich Village. From 1952 to 1954, he served as the *Courier's* special correspondent to the United Nations. His writings on emerging African nations gradually broadened his horizons and gave him a renewed sense of purpose. In reflecting on his personal problems and those of fellow African Americans in a world context, he felt less alone and isolated. And, he began to recover from addictions and his "sickness of the soul," although he found the process agonizingly slow. For two years, Horace Jr. worked at the National Council of Churches in New York as a research associate, co-authoring the book, *Churches and Social Welfare* (1955), with Dr. Setsuko Nishi.[27]

During Horace Jr.'s eleven years in New York, he lived seven of them with Brunetta Bernstein and her husband, Sidney. Brunetta had been a friend since the Parkway Community Center days, where as a young aspiring actress she performed with the Skyloft Players. During his time with the Bernsteins, Horace Jr. took a few sociology classes at the City College of New York, and other writing and graduate-level sociology courses at NYU. There he met a lovely young woman who was to become key to his life at this time. Lore Segal was a Jewish writer who had fled Austria during World War II. The two fell in love. At this time, Lore, the Bernsteins, and Joyce Cooper Arkhurst (a friend from Seattle who had married Fred Arkhurst, Ghana's UN ambassador) provided a warm social circle for Horace Jr. They became, as he later wrote, "more of a family for me than I had known since my early childhood."[28]

Still, Horace Jr. depended on alcohol for escape, and he brooded over his alienation from himself and others. As he bounced in and out of Rockland and Bellevue hospitals throughout most of 1958, The Savoy Ballroom was torn down and replaced by an urban renewal housing project. Despite his love for Lore and the support of his circle of friends, in the following year Horace Jr. decided to leave New York. "When it came to a show down of marriage," he later admitted, "I ran to the Pacific Coast."[29]

CHAPTER 11

The Uplift

Horace Jr., Lillie, and Revels in California, 1950s to 1995

Now in his mid 50s, Horace Jr. left New York for San Francisco in 1959, taking refuge in a house for recovering alcoholics operated by the Episcopal Church. Revels and his family had moved to San Francisco several years earlier, and Horace hoped to re-establish his relationship with his only brother, and, over the next decade, he occasionally visited Revels at his home. During this period, he wrote a few articles for the *Pittsburgh Courier* and the *Chicago Defender,* but little else. Horace's erratic lifestyle put off most employers, and he usually was hired only for low-level jobs. He did, however, spend one year as a research assistant at the Langley Porter Clinic in studies on geriatric mental illness.

By 1961, Horace Jr. had ended his twenty-year association with the *Courier,* but he took up other writing projects. He completed an article, "A Picnic with Sinclair Lewis," in the spring, and over the next year contributed to an international survey conducted by the Institute for the Study of Crime and Delinquency in Berkeley. He also began writing stories about the Cayton family, which quickly developed into what was to become his autobiography, *Long Old Road.*[1]

In June 1961, when speaking at San Jose State College, Horace met Harry Branch, brother of his first wife (who now was Bonnie Branch Hansen). The chance encounter brought a renewed friendship with Harry, his wife Mary (also a writer), and Bonnie herself. For the next three years, he saw the Branches often and began a correspondence with Bonnie, mostly one-sided on Horace Jr.'s part, as he began to delve into his past. Bonnie had remarried in the early 1940s and lived in the southern Puget Sound area of Washington State. Glad for their re-established friendship, she found Horace Jr. "exciting—stimulating—and given to amazing insights into all sorts of situations, great and small." Still, as a married woman, Bonnie wished to maintain an appropriate distance from her ex-husband.[2]

The Branches offered to help support Horace Jr. financially while he worked on his autobiography. Under the arrangement, agreed upon by both parties, they would provide fifteen hundred dollars for Horace Jr.'s living expenses over the next year, and in return he and Harry would share any profits from the resulting book. The two men, both strong personalities with differing viewpoints, began to argue over how it should be written. Horace struggled with the opening chapters, and, at first, Harry tried to help. He alternately pushed and cajoled Horace Jr. through the tortuous emotional process of taking a long hard look at his life and, ultimately, facing up to himself. Branch often argued with Horace about his drinking. In the end, the writing—and the drinking—proceeded on Horace Jr.'s terms. It was a rocky road. Twice the Branches took Horace Jr. to a local hospital for sobering up, and in December 1961 another binge landed Horace Jr. in the psychiatric ward of the county hospital.[3]

While working on the autobiography, Horace lived on Monterey Bay, first near Santa Cruz, and later near Carmel. He had little to do but write, and his life proceeded slowly but rather pleasantly. He wrote in the mornings, often bicycled or went to the beach to swim in the afternoon, and spent evenings listening to music. He corresponded often with Bonnie and she became ever more important to him—not only because of their shared past, but because she was a link to his father. In the hours Bonnie spent listening to Horace Sr. tell stories about his life, she had come to know more about him than his son did. Horace Jr. recalled a long drive with Bonnie to Chicago when she related many of his father's tales; some of which he heard then for the first time.

"I am sort of living in the past," Horace Jr. confided to his ex-wife. "And, you were such a part of my past that I think of you, us, frequently." Despite their current friendship, writing about their previous relationship proved difficult for him:

> I am turning over in my mind how I will write about us. It is a happy-sad story and I want to write it honestly: two kids honestly in love against great odds who somehow managed to mess it up. I am interested in trying to understand and explain, not to blame either, who I believe wanted the best for each other. It is an important chapter, as it was perhaps the most meaningful thing in my life, although perhaps not the most eventful.[4]

Progress came slowly. In a March 1962 letter to Arna Bontemps, Cayton admitted that he was nearly out of money and the book was only one-fourth finished. He decided he wanted to meet with Bonnie before he wrote about their relationship, and he urged her to come to San Francisco. He wrote: "Emotionally, as you know, you have been the one love in my life; selfishly I want to talk to you before I finish writing about you. You with your deep psychological insight can help; but it is not alone the psychology but the remembrance of emotions." Bonnie kindly refused the invitation. It was not until 1966, a year after the book appeared in print, that Horace Jr. and Bonnie met—for the first time in nearly thirty years.[5]

Horace finished the first draft in July 1963. He also began to support himself by occasionally lecturing, and in late autumn decided to move to Berkeley. His speeches—with such titles as "America and the Racial Confrontation," and the "Psychological World of the Rejected"—were attended largely by white college students. Horace entertained the young crowds with jokes and witty digressions, stung them with incisive attacks on white racism, and inspired them with hope for a peaceful resolution of the racial conflict in America. Then, he landed a one-year position at the University of California, Berkeley, as a program coordinator, organizing workshops for the university's extension program.

The completion of the autobiography in 1964, and its publication in 1965, heralded a new period in Horace Jr.'s life. *Long Old Road* had been undertaken as "therapy," but it represented more than an exploration of one individual's troubled past. Family history was an elemental part of the Cayton tradition—Horace's father and grandfather had written personal accounts, and the relating of family history in the home had been commonplace; Horace Jr. vividly recalled his mother's stories. A three-and-a-half page autobiographical account he composed in undergraduate sociology at the University of Washington, and an eighty-six-page life history he wrote a few years later in graduate school, foreshadowed the themes he wrestled with decades later in "The Bitter Crop," and then *Long Old Road*. His autobiographical writings returned again and again to certain themes—the Cayton family's "social distinction" and stature; the realization that prospects were limited for "a colored boy"; his idealism as a young man; how his education isolated him from other African Americans; and how he felt driven by a desperate desire for attention and his "consuming vanity."[6]

Horace Jr.'s fascination with his psyche, and his ability to articulate its intricacies, imbues *Long Old Road* with a special force. The book's release prompted Arna Bontemps to write enthusiastically to his friend:

> It packs a mighty wallop, and I predict that teeth will rattle when it lands. You have done yourself proud, old man! Your special gift, I have always felt, was a capacity to live your life up to the hilt, as they say.

Obviously this has not always been without cost, but we can all rejoice that you have reached the age of reflection with literary powers still capable of transmuting the whole experience.[7]

At the same time, Horace Jr. admitted significant distortions. He variously described his efforts to Bonnie as "semi-fiction" and "fiction." He admitted, "Many facts I have forgotten and what I write will be my distillation of the truth, although the facts may not be literally true." He changed time sequences "purposely" and created fictitious people, scenes, and events for "dramatic effect." Unfortunately, this produced a book of limited value to historians.[8]

The book was disappointing to many people who knew Horace Jr. The comments of St. Clair Drake, who wanted more from him, are typical of this reaction:

I had hoped that Horace would live to tell it *all* someday in that second autobiography many of us were urging him to write—one full of his matchless ability to tell an engrossing story and suffused with the humor with which he could invest episodes that bordered on the absurd and the tragic end of which he was the central figure.[9]

Although leaving much to be desired as a historical document, *Long Old Road* is a moving testimony of the struggle to reconcile the "double vision," as Richard Wright called it, of American democratic ideals juxtaposed to the reality of oppression and second-class citizenship for blacks. The book also presented examples of the richness and diversity of the black experience. Of course, *Long Old Road* had therapeutic value—beyond its psychological importance to Horace Jr. himself—as a public expression of deeply held black rage at white presumptions of racial superiority.

Horace Jr. gained national recognition upon the book's release. He often seemed dependent on the opinions of others for his sense of self-worth, and the publication of *Long Old Road* helped bolster his ego. While his family and others who knew him well tended to dislike the book, those unacquainted with him roundly applauded it. Promotional book tours took Horace to many old familiar places, and the acclaim from civil rights groups and activists boosted his sense of accomplishment.

During this period, he began to mend the deep rift in his relationship with Susan Cayton Woodson. In the fall of 1966, he spent two weeks with Susan and her husband Harold in Chicago. Horace and Susan enjoyed long conversations, as well as Harold's gourmet cooking. One Sunday, Horace was the featured speaker at the Woodsons' church. Afterwards, in a letter to Revels, he described his September visit with Susan as "delight-ful." He exclaimed, "I am so proud of her because she is a good strong woman and is standing up to the tough times we live in, and being a good wife to Harold, who needs her support, and a good mother to Butch [Harold Jr.]." When Horace returned to Chicago in 1968 and 1969 to work on a Richard Wright biography, he rented an apartment in Harper Square near the Woodsons. Susan and Horace Jr. developed a more positive sister-brother relationship than they had enjoyed since their youth in Seattle. Susan bossed and "mothered" him, making sure he was properly dressed for the severe Chicago winter weather. He basked in the attention.[10]

Horace occasionally had exchanged letters with Lillie over the years, and his sister had visited him in California in 1964. The brief visit felt deeply nurturing to Lillie. Afterward, she wrote to tell him how happy she was to have had a chance of renewing their friendship: "It made me feel I belong and the going isn't so tough." When Horace sent a small check to help with some doctor bills, she promptly returned a long thank-you, em-phasizing, "It's not the amount, but that my brother cares; how wonderful this feels."[11]

The publication of *Long Old Road* itself, however, contributed little to improving their relationship. Horace promised to mail a copy to her, but months passed without the book arriving. Finally, Lillie's daughter, Madge, wrote and reminded Horace about this. He sheepishly replied that he had set aside a copy for Lillie at one time, but "lost" it. Lillie passed this news to Susan, sighing, "Who am I to judge." To her disappointment, when Lillie finally received *Long Old Road,* she discovered that Horace Jr. men-tioned her only once. She understood: Horace Jr. did not consider her an important part of his life or the family. She reached out to Susan, "You have been so good about keeping in touch with me on what has been going on...I had felt much left out." Still, she felt proud of her brother and continually hoped he would reciprocate more.[12]

In the spring of 1968, Horace visited Seattle to lecture at the Univer-sity of Washington and in the black community. He also went to see Lillie. She cooked him a steak and the two enjoyed a good long talk. Lillie ex-pressed a hope that Horace might move back to their hometown so they could be closer, but again he distanced himself, dismissing Seattle as a place utterly "dead" for him.[13]

Despite accolades and the improving family relationships that devel-oped following its release, *Long Old Road* did not become a magic elixir for Horace Jr.'s complex problems. In 1966, he spent over two months in

Napa State Hospital's Department of Mental Hygiene, and, in April 1967, he went in again to try to "kick" his pill and alcohol addictions. During the 1968 trip to Seattle, when he visited Lillie, he also traveled to nearby Stretch Island to see Bonnie Branch Hansen. Their reunion was friendly and pleasant, but afterwards Horace Jr. got so drunk that he had to be carried onto the airplane.[14]

In the mid 1960s, Horace began to get involved in the civil rights movement again, this time as a social analyst and teacher; he was not drawn to the type of activism he had engaged in back in the 1940s. Now an elder statesman of the movement and referring to himself as a "revolutionist," Horace occasionally taught a "Roots of Revolt" course for the UC Berkeley sociology department. He maintained an office at Berkeley's Institute of Business and Economic Research, where he had directed a federally funded project to study "Negro marketing theory." He also worked as a consultant and lecturer in the UCLA extension program, studying social and economic conditions in Watts following the 1965 riots. Horace's major interests, however, remained writing and lecturing. A 1962 reissue of *Black Metropolis* in paperback, too, had helped keep his name before the public, allowing him to continue on the lecture circuit. But as the demand for lecturing wound down, Horace began to seriously consider ideas for his next book.

He had several subjects in mind. He wanted to write a two-volume account of his parents and grandparents, and he was drawn to the idea of preparing a massive study about the predecessors of the current national civil rights movement. For this latter project, Horace planned to interview dozens of individuals who lived in the period from Booker T. Washington to Martin Luther King Jr. Another project he pondered was an anthology titled "Dark Inner Landscape: The Psychological World of the Rejected," to be edited by himself and John W. Barnes. The book would "delineate the inner emotions in the minds of the oppressed...and document the paranoid systems of the oppressor." The final section, "The Agony of Maturity," was to include Horace's essay "The Bitter Crop" and describe the means by which "a fortunate few" had escaped oppression and deprivation to achieve a life of dignity and meaning.[15]

Finally, however, Horace Jr. settled on writing a more manageable book—a biography of Richard Wright. He had known Wright, as Margaret Walker affirmed, "on levels most people didn't." Horace began the planning in early 1964, but did not actually start writing for another four years. For a long time now, he had floated along on meager cash, often with the support of friends. He knew that researching and writing required substantial funds. He was able to get a National Endowment for the Humanities grant and hired a secretary assistant, Lillian Crane, in early 1968.[16]

Horace Jr., over sixty years old and mellowing, continued making strides in repairing family relationships. For much of his life, he had pushed away family members and others who loved him. During psychoanalysis, he discovered his "inability to love"; it appears, too, that he also was unable to accept love. This now was changing. Horace corresponded with Lillie, and continued mending the relationship with Susan, while gaining a new appreciation for her and the many kindnesses she had shown him. She still thought of Horace Jr. as her brother, and he started calling her "my baby sister." Susan reciprocated with forgiveness and a willingness to forget an old wound—his marriage to Ruby.[17]

Horace also took steps to bridge the gulf separating him from Revels. He sent Revels a copy of the Sinclair Lewis article he had written in May 1961. In the accompanying letter, he wrote—with the wariness he now often exhibited when approaching his younger brother—"Please do not be alarmed, as I do not wish to push our intimacy any further than an occasional letter." Immediately after *Long Old Road* appeared in 1965, Horace Jr. heard through mutual friends that the book offended Revels. He wrote to Revels immediately. "If I did, I am devoutly sorry," Horace implored, assuring Revels that he had always respected him for his political stands. Not wanting to impose, Horace told his brother that the door was always open: "I will understand if I don't hear from you for months, but I hope sometime 'when the spirit moves you' that you will get in touch with your brother." Gradually, their relationship improved with occasional phone calls and visits in 1968 and 1969.[18]

Central to these positive changes in Horace's life was an improved relationship with himself. *Long Old Road* had been a turning point. When nearing completion of the manuscript, he mused, "I think the essence of any peace in life is not necessarily maturity but the sense of working creatively…and a belief in the values which you work toward." The book's success, and the growing family support, strengthened his self-acceptance. A paper Horace presented at the American Sociological Association conference in 1967, "Personal Experience in Race Relations," was his iteration of now familiar themes: psychology and autobiography. In summation, he told the audience, "[T]he insecurity I felt as a child—torn between what I had been taught I was and what I actually was—has now spread to all of society. While I have found an identity, to an extent, society has not."[19]

Horace Jr.'s reconstruction of his identity had been closely tied to Richard Wright, and it was gratifying at this stage in his life to devote full energy to a biography of his old friend. Horace's highly personalized vision of the book, implied by the working title "Richard Wright: Memoirs of a Friendship," was to include his own recollections of Wright, plus interviews with others who knew him, such as Ralph Ellison, Sidney Williams, Constance Webb (an earlier Wright biographer), St. Clair Drake, and the author's widow, Ellen Wright.[20]

In September 1968, Horace left Santa Cruz to spend several months conducting interviews in Chicago and New York. In Chicago, aided by sociology graduate student Carol Adams, he worked out of a small apartment in Hyde Park overlooking Harper Square, near the home of Susan and Harold Woodson. He often used the Woodson home to entertain friends, old and new, who might contribute something to the Wright story. Susan recalled that Horace Jr. liked to wear a beret and jauntily made his way over to a Hyde Park café to meet friends. In a while, he would return exhausted, exclaiming, "One more book, Lord, just one more book!" Among the more interesting vignettes in this period recalled by Susan was when Studs Terkel interviewed Horace on radio. As author of *Black Metropolis,* Terkel asked, what differences had Horace seen in the Black Belt as he rode in on the El that morning? Horace answered simply that it was all still there, just as it was twenty years before, virtually unchanged.[21]

Horace sensed time was running out. His health deteriorated steadily and doctors advised a reduction in his activities. In the summer of 1969, he wrote a will, making arrangements for the dispensation of his books, paintings, furniture, papers, and other possessions. As Horace's second year of grant support neared an end, he prepared to leave for Paris. But he first traveled to Atlanta, Georgia, where on December 7, 1969, he presented "The Search for Richard Wright," the first W.E.B. Du Bois Lecture at the Martin Luther King, Jr. Institute. Here he enjoyed a brief reunion with old friend Margaret Walker. She was delighted with Horace's plans for a book on Wright, but shocked at his appearance: "He was not the same man; he was so broken." It was Horace Cayton Jr.'s final public appearance in the United States.[22]

Three days before Christmas 1969, Horace headed for Paris. He planned to interview scholar Michel Fabre, then in the midst of his own research of an extensive Wright biography. Horace also hoped to see Wright's widow, Ellen, and gain her support, as well as access to Wright's papers. The prospects were not encouraging. Two years earlier, Horace had requested her support, enclosing an outline of his National Endowment for the Humanities proposal. She responded with surprise, having suddenly heard from him after no contact in nearly two decades. In the project description, Horace claimed he had known Wright "intimately" for over "thirty years," a serious overstatement that she pointedly ridiculed. In fact, it had been seven years at most. Ellen expressed unhappiness with Horace's preoccupation over her late husband's lack of formal education, and she accused Horace of harboring a frivolous and insensitive attitude toward him, both as a person and writer. Her limited time, Ellen concluded, would be reserved for the Fabre work then in progress, which would be objective and definitive.[23]

Horace did not see Ellen Wright in Paris, but he did spend time with Michel Fabre, participating in one of his seminars at the Sorbonne. "Horace was visibly tired, physically," Fabre later recalled, "but he was full of humour and repartée." It proved to be Horace's last presentation. Barely a month after arriving in Paris, the book on Wright unfinished, he died alone in a room at the Hotel Residence Montparnasse. On the cold morning of January 22, a maid bringing breakfast found Horace's body on the floor. A doctor who had attended him several times in the preceding weeks issued the death certificate, indicating that "natural causes" ended his life. A death notice and his hotel bill were sent to the American Embassy, which contacted Revels. Horace Jr.'s body was cremated in Paris and the ashes returned to a funeral home in Chicago. At the Chicago memorial service, St. Clair Drake's eulogy placed his friend's passing in a positive light:

> Those of us who were close to Horace…are glad that when he reached the end of what he called the *Long Old Road* in the title of his autobiography, he was where he most wanted to be—Paris, and was doing what he most wanted to be doing—working on a biography of Richard Wright. Life had not always been kind to Horace Cayton, but it was smiling upon him just before the end.[24]

Following Horace Jr.'s death, there were numerous expressions indicating the extent of his personal impact and professional contribution. Memorial services were held in Chicago and Santa Cruz. Obituaries appeared in New York, Chicago, San Francisco, Santa Cruz, and Seattle newspapers. The University of Washington Press, already planning to reprint *Long Old Road* in paperback, advertised its release for the spring of 1970. Lore Segal, Horace's intimate companion from his New York years, already had included him in her first book, *Other People's Houses* (1964). She would long remember Horace. Segal's 1985 novel, *Her First American,* would feature a fictionalized but identifiable Horace Jr. with the name of Carter Bayoux, "a middle-aged, hard-drinking intellectual."[25]

In the latter half of his life, Horace only sporadically was able to draw stability from the Cayton family and its legacy. Perhaps, Horace's most glaring break from the Cayton traditions was his inability to establish his own family. Although married to three different spouses, and having relationships with dozens of female companions, he chose not to have offspring. He once told Richard Wright, "I don't much like children." Yet, he was proud of the children's programs he developed at the Parkway Community Center. He enjoyed the company of adolescents, and often worked with teen groups at the Parkway center, too. Perhaps, Horace's childlessness was related in part to the fact that he seemed unable to sustain a marriage—Irma once said of the man she married not once, but twice, "He was brilliant, but he had trouble completing things." One of his friends, Ruth Williams, said that Horace "didn't want the responsibility" of having children. Horace once wrote to Bonnie Branch Hansen, saying, "not having children for fear or finance has colored my life."[26]

Only by reliving his own past did Horace achieve a significant level of control over his "unruly emotions," as he called them. In the numerous versions of his autobiography, he recreated again and again his family history and thereby his sense of self and continuity. Like the other Caytons, he made individual and worthwhile contributions to the wider community and to the struggle for freedom, for the dream of an America where the ideals of democracy matched the reality. At the memorial service for Horace in Chicago, St. Clair Drake eulogized his friend for traits Horace had admired in his father, "pride and courage in the face of repeated adversities." His courage failed him many times, but in the latter years of his life, after he worked through his own history, with perseverance his courage grew.

✦

Most often Horace is remembered for *Black Metropolis, Black Workers and the New Unions,* and *Long Old Road.* In particular, *Black Metropolis* represented a major achievement in urban history and in the sociological understanding of the processes and impacts of urbanization and racism on a minority group in one of the country's major cities. The book has been characterized as "an unequalled masterpiece, written with verve and profound understanding." Sociologist Aldon Morris calls *Black Metropolis* a "classic," citing the superb scholarship, historical perspective, holistic descriptions of subtle and complex social relationships, critical analyses, and sophisticated insights that produced an authoritative work of enduring value. The hundreds of bibliographic citations of Cayton's writings in social science monographs are a testament to their continuing value. Horace's studies of Chicago and black workers led him to urge fellow African Americans to fight racism and discrimination in alliance with whites, yet to rely principally on building and maintaining their own organizations. Later, in a broader context as a correspondent to the United Nations, he delivered the same message. He believed the problems of black people were much the same the world over, and only mutual support—black solidarity—could bring real progress.

Horace's interest in the psychology of race relations produced some of the early and significant contributions to our understanding of the effects of racism on mental health. In the process of discovering his own particular "oppression psychosis" and the complex of hatreds and fears that tormented him, he saw his own reflection in the kindred experiences of other African Americans. Horace used insights gained during his analysis to bring the psychoanalytical point of view to the study of racial dynamics. At the same time, his analyst, Dr. Helen McLean, profited from the association with Cayton and Richard Wright. Her articles, "Racial Prejudice" (1944), "Psychodynamics of Race Relations" (1946), and "The Emotional Health of Negroes" (1949) represented some of the first professional literature on the subject.

Horace Cayton Jr. had a profound and lasting personal influence on a great many people. In the end, he left behind a number of friends who genuinely loved him, who were, in effect, an artificial extended family. Bonnie Branch Hansen recalled Horace's "vulnerability and caring, compassionate sensitivity," his "laser-beam humor" and sense of the absurd, and "his genius for sizing people up, for grasping what they were in essence." Horace Jr.'s long-time friend, Brunetta Bernstein, in beautiful expression, summarized his life: "It is a wonder not to be explained—a life lived to bring untold enrichments to some, like me, and pain to others, those who could not know what was there—it was their loss."[27]

+——◆——+

Four years after Horace Jr. died, Lillie moved to California to be near her daughter, Sue. Lillie would live only for another year and a half after her arrival in San Diego. Her other daughter, Madge, remembered one special day in August 1976 when she went to visit her mother in the hospital.

"She gave me the strangest look," Madge recalled, "a look of, 'I'm done; the kids are grown, they've got their own families. I don't have to do any more.'" The next morning, another sunny summer day, Lillie's heart stopped.[28]

In February 1943, Lillie had married Percy Lee Martin, her third husband. With wartime employment surging, she found well paying, but physically demanding, work as a scaler and laborer at the local Puget Sound shipyards. Lillie and Martin had two daughters: Madge born in October 1946, and Susan (Sue) born in November 1947. Lillie continued to drink heavily and her life remained chaotic and unsettled. She went through another divorce, and then married again, her fourth, to Leroy Rice. They had two sons, Leroy (Cayton) born in July 1950, and Richard (Rice) born in June 1952.[29]

Only Susan had tried to keep in contact with Lillie after Madge Cayton's funeral in Chicago in 1943. Susan occasionally received news from Lillie and responded by sending a card or calling by phone. In the 1950s, Susan made regular trips to Seattle to visit friends and relatives, including her actual father, Floyd Wright. She sometimes saw Lillie, too, but the visits were brief and unpleasant. One time Susan arrived at Lillie's residence when she was gone, finding the house "a pigpen," with dirty clothes scattered about, Lillie's three oldest children nowhere to be found, and the baby lying in a pile of blankets and clothing. When visiting, Susan usually did some housecleaning and tried to be supportive, but there seemed to be little she could do for Lillie and her family. "I saw her when she was down and out," Susan later said, "but I was too vain, and I didn't really see it."

By the early 1960s, Lillie was without a husband again. Her alcoholism ravaged her health and devastatingly impacted the children and household. Lillie's mothering was so insufficient that the state's social services agency initiated proceedings to remove the children from her custody. Lillie had attended her first Alcoholics Anonymous meeting in 1953, but it was the fear of losing her children that finally drove her to make a firm commitment to AA. She had hit rock bottom before, but this was the worst. In all, it would take Lillie almost ten years to struggle out of alcoholism, which she often said was coming up "from under the rocks."

Susan saw a changed Lillie during a 1965 visit to Seattle, when they attended an AA meeting. Many years later, Susan looked back on this memorable occasion when Lillie spoke before the gathering:

She said, "My name is Lillie Cayton Fisher, and I'm an alcoholic" (the "Cayton" was put in for me). It just seemed like the whole room closed off, like the curtains came down. I saw nobody. Lillie was looking at me; I was looking at her. There was no one in the room but two sisters talking. I heard no coughs. I heard nothing [but her]. Lillie said, "Susan," and started a story, about how she dug down to the bottom, the rocks, and then after she hit the rocks, she dug a little deeper. She couldn't go any deeper. She must have shook hands with the devil. Then, she started telling how she came up.

...Lillie came back just glowing, just like she'd seen the Lord. I didn't know how to accept the glow, it was so beautiful. She sat down, and the meeting went on. She was still glowing, but, honey, she didn't outglow me! "Oh, God," I was just saying in my heart, "Mama, Madge, where are ya? You've got to hear it! You've got to see it!"[30]

Struggling through her trials, Lillie developed an inner strength enabling her to be serene in the worst of circumstances. Drawn to help other people, Lillie became an AA activist. Soon she was "twelve-stepping" others, helping them through AA's dozen steps toward freedom from alcoholism. Sometimes she took recovering alcoholics into her home, especially women who were victims of spousal abuse. She understood what kind of "hell" these women were living. For many years, her pattern had been to attract men, particularly younger ones, who were abusive and violent. "Her main problem was men," said her daughter, Madge. "She always picked the wrong one." When she slipped back to the wine bottle, it often was tied to her relationships with men. Madge said, "She fought love within the family. But, she put her love into men, and she put her love into helping people."[31]

Just a year after joining AA, the difference in Lillie was dramatic. Her entire appearance, way of dressing, and behavior had changed radically for the better. She attended regular AA meetings and early morning breakfasts, often taking along one or two of her kids. Within a few years, she began working in AA programs in institutions around the greater Seattle area, visiting penitentiaries at Monroe, Shelton, McNeil Island, and Walla Walla. Soon she was running the AA program for the Seattle-King County Jail. There was a big change in her home life, too. The household was well organized and Lillie kept it immaculate. The children now had a mother who—although often not warm and affectionate—was loving, strict, watchful of their friends, and mindful of how they spent their time.

By June 1964, Lillie was divorced from Leroy Rice. A year later she married Robert Fisher, who attended trade school to learn tailoring while working part-time. Lillie did day work in the home of the white president of Bethlehem Steel and his family, who "loved" Lillie. The roof of Lillie's house deteriorated until it could no longer keep out Seattle's ever-present moisture and became too dilapidated to live in. Lillie was forced to move her family back to "the Projects," the Rainier Vista housing complex in south central Seattle. Lillie, like her mother and Horace Jr., became diabetic and suffered various health problems, including a 1966 accident that injured several spinal vertebrae. Dismayed but not beaten, she wrote to Susan, "I can say with the trials I am now going through…if I did not have God and AA close by I don't believe I could make it."[32]

Meanwhile, Lillie's children were growing up and struggling to create lives for themselves. At times it seemed that her daughter, Sue, was making the same mistakes Lillie had when she was young. Lillie confided to Susan, "I worry about her and pray about her. There is nothing I can do to help her but lay her in God's hands. How she reminds me of the Caytons. Specially Horace." But Lillie remained devoted to her child, and to helping others. In 1965 she took in a seven-year-old neighbor girl after her mother had a stroke.[33]

By 1970 life was better for Lillie. The youngest child, Richard Rice, now was eighteen years old. Lillie had taken better care of her health and was involved in community activities, such as volunteering at the Neighborhood House Mothers' Club in the High Point area. Her marriage to Robert Fisher regrettably had ended in divorce. After she put him through vocational training, Fisher fell for another woman—adding insult to injury, the other woman was a friend of Lillie's. Nevertheless, Lillie was managing well enough to write to Susan, "Still working with drunks and getting along without a man and learning to live with myself pretty damn well." Lillie eventually remarried one last time, to Alan Houston.[34]

Late in 1970, Lillie was hired as a special consultant with the Outreach Program during the construction of Interstate 90 in Seattle. The new highway corridor would cut a broad swath through a largely African American residential neighborhood. Helping families to relocate to new homes gave Lillie a new opportunity to use her people skills. Serving the Seattle black community in a role apart from AA work pleased her very much. In a profile of herself that she prepared for the project directors, Lillie stated:

> Lillie Fisher, the youngest in the family, carries on with…the family tradition. She continues to lift people up and is a great encouragement and tribute to her family…Lillie is a down-to-earth person and she likes people; she is concerned over their common welfare, helping to

relieve the pressures of worried people and trying to make them comfortable with the changes is her bag. [She is] always looking and hoping to help somewhere, somehow, and to put a little happiness where happiness may be lost and a person needs a friend.[35]

Lillie's innate desire to help other people, however, made it hard for her to understand when others—especially family members—sometimes did not respond to her offers of help. On several occasions over the next few years, she asked her siblings for money. She wrote to Revels when she needed cash for closing costs on a small house she was trying to buy, but a year passed without an answer. Revels finally did write, offering some money, but nine months later Lillie still had not received it. On one occasion, Lillie did not want to write him because she did not have "the courage to ask him." She wrote another time when she owed back taxes to the IRS. Susan sent money to help out, but again, Revels did not respond to Lillie's request for help. Disappointed, she complained to Susan, "That's the way it is and why is it I won't get it in my thick head that his back is turned on us."[36]

In Lillie's last years, she reached out more to Susan. "It felt wonderful," Lillie told her, when family members "by love and faith" hold on to each other. She thanked God and AA, telling Susan, "I guess that is one thing so wonderful about this program AA, it teaches you to let everybody be a human being in their own peculiar way." The appreciation was mutual. Susan wrote letters glowing with sisterly love and support:

> Remember this: You are a beautiful Black woman, made up of conditions of early Seattle, a good mother, good to and good for working people, regardless of their color. You relate to all poor people. I saw this on my trip to Seattle. First time I have seen this since mother, when she was working with the Open Forum. Don't underestimate yourself, my dear…Very few could have even made it just half way down the road you have come all the way down.[37]

Lillie joined the Lutheran Church in 1971, because "They don't stick God down your throat and I like it better that way." But, her main activities were with the AA. Lillie became a speaker in wide demand on the West Coast, from Washington to California. Even when illness prevented her from appearing in person, she would send a tape recording of one of her speeches. In 1972 Lillie traveled to San Diego for her daughter Sue's graduation from San Diego City College. While there, Lillie spoke to a large AA gathering at Balboa Park. For an hour, Lillie told of her long road to sobriety that had required her to take a hard look at herself:

And, I took an inventory of myself. And, you know, I found out I didn't know who Lillie was. I didn't know who she really was. And, until I could live with Lillie, I wasn't going to be able to live with anybody else. Until I could like her, and live with her, and could love her, I couldn't love anybody else.[38]

Lillie had to struggle to accept herself, just as Horace Jr. did in the last years of his life. Now, having learned to live with herself, Lillie continued to reach out to Revels, despite his having rebuffed her requests for money. When he sent a Mother's Day card in 1974, she responded with a long, newsy letter, telling him, "I appreciate the lines that you wrote; made me feel in your humble way you love your sister." Lillie was then living alone in a low-rent neighborhood, where burglaries were frequent. One day she was assaulted by a man she had befriended; he held a knife at her throat for three-and-a-half hours. Toward the end of the year, experiencing health problems and fed up with her job, Lillie decided to move to San Diego to be with her daughter, Sue, and her family.[39]

In San Diego, despite health problems, Lillie continued to attend AA functions whenever possible. She volunteered at a nearby senior citizens center and halfway house for women, and brought in a small income selling Avon products. Lillie talked of writing her autobiography. As spring moved into summer, her health continued to decline, until cancer and diabetes ended her life at sixty-two.

Family and friends attended a memorial service, then gathered at Sue's home. A recording of Lillie's 1972 AA speech was played. Revels appeared to sleep at times and later confessed, "The little bit I heard was horrible." Susan Cayton Woodson occupied herself by attending to guests and heard only parts of the speech. But Lillie's children listened intently. One of them said to Susan, "We never get tired of hearing Mother's messages; we can hear them all day long." More than just children's love for their mother, they appreciated Lillie in ways her other family members had difficulty understanding, with the exception of Susan. AA Members understood very well. They put up a large banner at the memorial in San Diego that read, "LILLIE, AA LOVES YOU." AA members in Seattle also held special services in her honor.[40]

From the gathering at Lillie's memorial, it was apparent that she had assisted many people. One young man approached Susan to tell her how Lillie helped him three years earlier. His story reveals the depth of Lillie's compassion, the firmness of her faith that a better life is possible for anyone, and her vision of the inner beauty and dignity inherent in each individual. The young man had called Alcoholics Anonymous before, but always backed out. He hit rock bottom and called AA again. They sent Lillie. He wanted help, and then he did not want help. He let Lillie in, but to show his resentment he started drinking. She sat down, read the newspaper, watched television, and pretended to ignore him. He became completely drunk, and then, watching Lillie, urinated on himself and lay down on the floor in the puddle. Lillie looked at him and said, "When you want help, let me know, 'cause I'm here waiting for you." He became abusive, using vulgar language. She calmly repeated that she was there to help him, all he had to do was hold out his hand. He vomited all over himself, then finally, exhausted emotionally and physically, he held up his hand. Lillie went to him, and they held each other and wept for a long time. Then, Lillie cleaned him up, mopped up the mess on the floor, and got him into AA.

Lillie helped many people directly in this way, whereas others were helped by her example. Hearing her tell her own story inspired them. As she wrote in her self-profile:

> Where fate and destiny forced me to lose many years, I have been able to recover and share my success and encouragement with people. Being this kind of person I have been able to give people a lift...Lillie, who has gained her dignity...is in a position to help some who might have lost some of theirs...She never meets a stranger. With all of the struggles, it's good to be alive in this universe.[41]

In the end, even Lillie's siblings, who had often judged her harshly in the past, came to appreciate her. She proved herself a Cayton. Revels, late in life, concluded, "Maybe in her way she was the greatest of all of us." Susan put it thus: "Lillie was the strongest one. She made it. She died sittin' down."[42]

A few months after Lillie's memorial service, two of her children, Madge and Leroy, scattered Lillie's ashes on Puget Sound as she had requested, so she could be with her mother Susie.

In early 1953, Revels had decided to leave New York for San Francisco. During the preceding summer, he had lost a bitter fight to be elected business agent for District 65 of the Department Store Workers Union. This was followed by a period of unemployment and nagging health problems, including a back condition and asthma. In May 1953, when Revels and sixty-five others were named as "communists" by Dorothy Funn, a former associate from the National Negro Congress, Revels already was in San Francisco. Like many identified as communists before the House Un-American Activities Committee, Cayton was never indicted. For the most part, the committee was interested in only those who could provide damning testimony against Paul Robeson.[43]

San Francisco in the 1950s was a markedly different place from New York, as well as from what it had been when Revels departed in 1945. Trade unionism was in decline and working class leaders wielded less clout in city politics. The urban skyline began sprouting tall steel and glass office buildings, obscuring much of the original, quaint turn-of-the century architecture. City officials took up urban renewal, led by the San Francisco Redevelopment Agency, aggressively clearing decaying properties in the downtown areas. The first freeway networks were boosted by the 1956 Federal Highway Act. San Francisco, known for its maritime culture, rugged openness, and enterprising population was transforming itself into a commercial, financial, and corporate center as well. The North Beach and Fillmore districts attracted counterestablishment "beatniks" and other social rebels, then alienated white youths in increasing numbers. When the 1950s gave way to the 1960s, hippies moved into the low-rent Haight and Ashbury areas, while across the bay, rebellious, idealistic Berkeley students actively took up civil rights issues and other social causes.

Also new to Revels was the significant deterioration in race relations in the Bay Area. During the war, African Americans seeking jobs in the shipyards and factories poured into the region, transforming the populations of San Francisco, Oakland, Berkeley, and Richmond. Between 1940 and 1950, the region's black population soared from 17,000 to 117,000. But, as the post-war economic boom faded, their vision of upward mobility proved largely illusory. By the mid-1950s, non-whites faced increasing racial barriers and found themselves locked out more—politically, economically, and socially. A large majority of blacks experienced increased discrimination in education and employment, and lived in deteriorating and segregated neighborhoods, with rising crime.

A few months after Revels returned to San Francisco, his wife Lee and son Michael (later Revels Jr.) joined him. Revels' health problems prevented him from working as a longshoreman, as he had hoped. Finally, he got a job at a United Grocers warehouse. The work was hard for Revels, who was quite overweight. Although the crew dubbed him "Cable Car" because he was "big, fat, and moved slow," they elected him union representative for the shipping floor.

After the United Grocers warehouse closed, Revels went to work at the Hills Brothers coffee plant from 1956 to 1960. As a result of pushing to get blacks into leadership positions in ILWU locals, he was labeled a "black nationalist," but his reputation began to spread. He watched and took inspiration from African American labor activities in other parts of the country, and from the general activist ferment of the growing civil rights movement. The physical demands of the job at Hills Brothers caused worsening lower back problems, until he could no longer do the work. At age fifty-three, the physical breakdown made him feel like he had been thrown "on the scrap heap of labor." He found some consolation in his home life. Lee was steady and supportive, and there was great satisfaction in watching his son Michael—now a bright and energetic eleven year old—growing up.

Revels joined the working class Macedonia Baptist Church for political, not religious, reasons. He believed African American churches could be a force for positive social change. His effort to radicalize the church failed, but it provided the personal contacts for later assembling a major coalition of church and labor leaders in San Francisco. Despite Revels' frustrations with the church, he became the leading layman in the Baptist Ministerial Alliance, working toward a church-labor coalition. "I continued striving," he observed, "for 'the uplift,' as my Mother said." He recalled her advice: "Son, you must always strive for the uplift; try to do good, try to do what uplifts humanity."

In 1961, during his period of unemployment, Revels was approached with a job offer. His friend Hal Donleavy, an employee of the ILWU and the Pacific Maritime Employers Association, explained that they had no idea how to tackle the problem of integrating a new non-profit housing development. The 299-unit Saint Francis Square was to be "experimental, inter-racial," said Donleavy, and "I've told everybody you're the guy to do it." Thus, Revels began as a consultant at the Saint Francis Square project, at wages of about one hundred dollars a week.[44]

The initial problems confronting Cayton looked formidable: How could the mutual fears of various ethnic groups be overcome to get the right "mix" of people for a genuinely integrated, moderate-income housing development? Revels cleverly managed this by convincing leading African American ministers and the black press—with assistance from activist Dick Gregory—to exercise patience while whites were accepted first into the completed units. Then, African Americans and other minorities were interviewed and accepted. The plan worked. Saint Francis Square became genuinely integrated, building by building, in approximate proportion to the city's population as a whole—40 percent white, 25 percent Asian, 25 percent African American.

In April 1963, Revels was named the first manager of Saint Francis Square, a position he held for over four years despite frequent attacks by "white chauvinists." At the dedication ceremonies in August, Revels shared his feelings about the significance of the new community: "We are responsible to all, and each person is responsible to each other," he declared. "Here, the very best people of the city are going to live good lives, dedicated to the proposition that we will all play our parts to show the country that Saint Francis Square knows how."[45]

Under Revels' leadership, Saint Francis Square earned a national reputation as a model of integrated urban housing development. Revels gave credit to his mentors in the unions who had given him the right leadership skills to make a success of Saint Francis Square.

> How do you become a good manager while under constant attack? I've been doing this all my life. Some guy said, "You know, it's a miracle how St. Francis Square became touted across the country, because Revels doesn't know a goddamn thing about being a manager."
>
> This other guy said, "Yeah, but he knows a hell of a lot about how to put something together and keep it together."
>
> The Marine Cooks and Stewards taught me, how to take a group of three hundred families and give them a common purpose, love for their cooperative, and love for Saint Francis Square, rallying the best of them to become really fanatical in trying to build that place…It's the same way you build a union. It's the same way you build anything—you build it with people, understanding and really loving people yourself. You can't fake it.[46]

In the meantime, Revels turned his attention more and more to his lifelong passion, politics. In August 1960, he attended a "California Conference of Negro Leaders," sponsored by Stanford University's political science department. The three-day conference brought together leaders from a variety of fields, from business and labor to religion, education, and the arts. The following year the leadership conference convened in Sacramento. Cayton was one of fifty delegates who met with Governor Edmund Brown to press for action on the worsening unemployment situation for blacks. These efforts produced no apparent progress at the time, but in the long run they prepared the way for one of Revels Cayton's most significant contributions to the Bay Area—the founding of the Church-Labor Conference in San Francisco.

The Church-Labor Conference was predicated on the idea that African American church leaders and trade unionists both had been left out of the local political arena; yet they had many common interests and could wield power by joining forces. The idea caught on. At the time, black activists in San Francisco and across the country were beginning to rise up, declaring that the time had come for their equal share of political power and demanding long denied civil rights. Revels had been meeting with other black labor leaders, notably the ILWU's Leroy King, and with church leaders, including Reverend Bedford of the Macedonia Baptist Church. The mechanism existed for exercising a voice in city affairs; all they needed was the right issue.

It was not long in coming. The year 1963 brought a host of civil rights incidents and issues. In January Revels was part of an eight-man delegation of black San Francisco community leaders who met with Governor Brown, presenting a six-point program to "make California first in human rights." The state, they bluntly advised Brown, had "a long way to go." Three months later, demonstrations broke out in many parts of the nation. On April 3, 1963, in Birmingham, Alabama, Martin Luther King Jr. led a demonstration calling for the desegregation of schools and public facilities, and demanding equal employment opportunities. A month later, the Birmingham police assaulted demonstrators with fire hoses and dogs, and the protesters responded by throwing rocks and bottles. In the next two weeks, demonstrations showing support were staged in some fifty cities, ten of them in the North. Revels' long-time friend, Matt Crawford, came to him, saying it was his responsibility to get things going. "San Francisco could move, and you're the guy to move it," said Crawford. "You've got to see what you can do about shaking up some kind of demonstration in this city." Revels met with the newly formed Church-Labor Conference and told them of Crawford's challenge. They supported the idea and asked Revels to be coordinator.[47]

Revels began by using an organizing principle—a rock thrown into a smooth pond creates a ripple effect. Sound trucks, one of them carrying Revels' fourteen-year-old son, Michael, canvassed San Francisco neighborhoods and across the bay in Berkeley. Mayor John Shelley endorsed the demonstration, as did Governor Brown. Word spread and excitement grew until the result, ten days later, was San Francisco's "Human Rights Day," on May 31, 1963. A crowd of twenty thousand marched up Market Street.

A giant banner proclaimed the theme of the mass rally—"We March in Unity for Freedom in Birmingham and Equality in San Francisco." It was a dramatic and remarkable day; in the words of an observer, "one of the greatest civil rights demonstrations in the nation's history."[48]

The following year—during the 1964 presidential election when San Francisco hosted the Republican National Convention—the church-labor machinery went to work again. This time, the rally drew a crowd of sixty thousand demonstrators. They thunderously disapproved of the convention's nomination of archconservative Barry Goldwater for president, and decried a string of racist incidents and civil rights abuses occurring over the preceding months, including the shooting of Medgar Evers and the bombing of a Birmingham church that killed four schoolgirls in the South. These two successful civil rights demonstrations left Revels with a deep sense of exhilaration and accomplishment. In later years, he looked on them as among his finest achievements.

In September 1964, Mayor Shelley appointed Revels to a one-year term on San Francisco's first Human Rights Commission. Revels represented both African American and union interests. Although playing a low-key role, his performance enhanced his standing in city political circles. Another door opened for Revels two years later when he became deputy director of the San Francisco Public Housing Authority. At Saint Francis Square on a sunny afternoon in June, a crowd of two thousand people turned out for a "Community Day Picnic" in honor of Revels Cayton. He said good-bye to the many friends who came to wish him well on his venture into the city's bureaucracy. In his farewell speech, Revels congratulated the residents for being "a powerful force for good throughout the city" and for showing that "three hundred families can capture a dream and inspire a multitude." The ILWU *Dispatcher* hailed Cayton for his contributions to Saint Francis Square, while describing the event in glowing terms: "It was a gathering in the spirit of St. Francis—a meeting of people, a crossing of all racial, religious, cultural and ethnic lines, to break bread together. In this way lies the road to peace."[49]

Cayton's transition to city government was not easy. His reputation as a radical had preceded him. Eneas Kane, executive director of the Housing Authority, was approached by a man who claimed that Revels was unfit for a government position because he was known to have been a communist. Kane, a well-known supporter and member of Alcoholics Anonymous, responded that he himself had once been an alcoholic, but not anymore, and he knew Cayton had been a communist, but not anymore. That ended the matter.[50]

During two years with the housing authority, Revels learned to walk a fine line between the staff, who were bound by bureaucratic inertia and could be insensitive to tenants' concerns, and the tenants themselves, many of whom were second- and third-generation recipients of government relief, living in public housing conditions that Revels described as "horrifying." Because of Revels' reputation as a radical, and his refusal to side with the housing authority when he believed it was wrong, he gradually earned the respect of many tenants. He worked to gain trust by using a "team spirit" approach he had learned from his union mentors, holding regular meetings with the residents of each unit.

When Joseph Alioto, a highly successful and talented lawyer with wide popular appeal, became the Democratic candidate for mayor of San Francisco in 1967, he approached the city's leading black trade unionists for their support. At a meeting including Cayton, Bill Chester, Dave Jenkins, and Leroy King, Alioto agreed to a list of demands in exchange for their support in the election. Among the requirements, Alioto would appoint an African American to his cabinet. The morning after Alioto's election as mayor, he called the same group to his house to discuss their concerns and his plans. Revels recalled that he had to made a distinct impression on the mayor-elect:

> He raised some questions, and I disagreed with him and told him, "No, no." I finally said to him, "Look, I've been black a whole lot longer than you. I think that my life as a black man should count for something in this argument." In other words, I was telling him, "Look, don't be trying to tell me about my own life." So, it was said nicely, but I was putting him in his place.[51]

Alioto decided Cayton was his choice as deputy for social programs. Revels hesitated; to him, the position seemed like "a good place to get killed," either by politics or a heart attack. After the two men discussed a wide range of issues—including Cayton's former membership in the Communist Party—Alioto restated the offer, and Revels accepted. This opportunity was much more in line with Cayton's interests and personal style than dealing with the housing authority bureaucracy. Revels later said, "I just couldn't see sitting there...doing that kind of organizing, systematizing and all the rest of it." Furthermore, tenant relations at Saint Francis had stabilized, and Revels was looking for another challenge. In later years as he looked back on this period, Revels observed, "It seems like I have always sought out situations where there was sharp struggle. That's what I thrived on."[52]

Cayton worked under Alioto throughout his first term as mayor (Alioto eventually served from 1968 to 1976). Revels and his staff dealt with the city's racial problems and developed special programs for the aged and emotionally disturbed children, but they focused most of their efforts on the problems of young people, implementing a range of social services to assist unemployed and underprivileged youth. Donald Canter, columnist for the *San Francisco Examiner,* recognized Cayton for trying "to make the training programs for the underprivileged something more than make-work schemes and the summer job programs for school kids into more than keep-them-off-the-street schemes." Revels took pride in the massive summer jobs program for youth, under which his office established seven neighborhood youth councils to distribute jobs financed by federal funds and California State gas taxes.[53]

In 1972 Revels reached sixty-five—the mandatory retirement age for San Francisco public officials. In retrospect, his solid accomplishments in the mayor's office stand up well in the face of charges that Cayton had been "a mere token" who allowed himself to be used by "the establishment." At the time of his retirement, he addressed this issue: "When I went to City Hall, that didn't mean I went to the other side of the barricades...I found you can do some good when you're part of 'the establishment.'"[54]

During Revels' term in the San Francisco mayor's office, his brother Horace Jr. passed away. The two had seen little of one another since Revels left New York, although they had visited occasionally after Horace Jr. moved to California in 1959. A considerable emotional distance had yet separated them. Horace Jr. still had tried to dominate their relationship, but, unlike in earlier years, this had little effect on Revels. Horace Jr.'s addiction to alcohol and sleeping pills interfered with attempts to improve relations with Revels.

Horace Jr.'s death in Paris in January 1970, like his life, brought mixed reactions from his brother. Revels wrote to Susan in Chicago, saying he now might miss his brother more than he had thought at first. "Horace like all of us was a man of many parts," he noted objectively. "Sometimes we see only the part closest to us." Over time, Revels had matured in his relationship with his brother, but he still struggled to resist passing judgment on Horace:

Anything I say about Horace comes out of my perception of why he went to pieces. All the rest of it is just a series of indiscretions that he made. It's just like telling dirty jokes on some guy, you know. So what? He was a desperate alcoholic, and so insecure, never finding a place, really, where he was comfortable, never.[55]

Revels continued to be active in community affairs after retirement from the mayor's office. In 1972 he became Director of Community Development in the Economic Opportunity Council of San Francisco, and he established a consulting business in housing and social programs. He was designated administrative assistant to Superior Court Judge Joseph Kennedy, serving from 1976 to 1980, and also was appointed to the San Francisco City-County Juvenile Justice Commission in 1977, a position he held for the next ten years. Among the honors that came to Revels in his later years was the naming of a street for him in Amancio Ergina Village, a new seventy-two-unit housing development modeled on Saint Francis Square.

A veteran of over forty years in the labor movement, Revels Cayton had witnessed many changes. In the classic union struggles of the 1930s, he served prominently as a high-level organizer in key West Coast maritime labor organizations. He had been one of the founders of the trade union council movement. He was the first African American to take a job on the Third Avenue bus line in New York City, and the first to work as a salesman in a city department store.

He had been a maverick, too, clashing with white union leaders, from the late 1940s into the 1960s, over implementing black caucuses in the ILWU and other unions. Harry Bridges and Lou Goldblatt of the ILWU for years disapproved of his activities, but, in time, grudgingly accepted his efforts. It was the ILWU that honored Revels Cayton by naming a street after him—Amancio Ergina Village was built with seed money from the ILWU and PMA pension funds.

Revels was one of the few prominent public figures able to bridge the gap between the labor struggles of the 1930s and the civil rights movement of the 1960s—and he served in many significant roles throughout that vast period. Revels Cayton and Paul Robeson were among the earliest voices calling for "black power," the independent exercise of social, cultural, and economic influence by an independent coalition.

Robeson was branded a "Communist" by the House Un-American Activities Committee and a fomenter of black revolution. As Revels put it,

"So he got double trouble." Robeson had never been a member of the Communist Party, and Cayton dismissed the matter as meaningless anyway. "Paul was really an advanced Marxist," he explained. "There is no question about his revolutionary understanding." Revels was disdainful of attempts in later years to "whitewash" Robeson's political views. It was *not*, he emphasized, "just a simple question of getting caught up because he had been discriminated against."[56]

Unlike Robeson, Revels *was* a member of the Communist Party for a considerable part of his career, and he basically followed the party line on the "Negro question." Clearly, the Communist Party "used" Revels in ways, and he was aware of this. In turn, he "used" the party, gaining among other things, leadership skills and political power. Moreover, his response to being "used" by the party was akin to that of his friend Robeson: "The Communists use the Negro, and we only wish more people would want to use us this way."[57]

Revels held a profound, lifelong commitment to the working class struggle, for black and whites, that came to him as a youth when convalescing from sleeping sickness. He remained positive and appreciative toward the Communist Party even late in life:

> I hear people today bashing the Party for all its mistakes, and I understand them because the Party made plenty of mistakes. But I'm not one of them. I am proud today when I look back on those early years in the Party, when I remember that the Party was in the forefront, fighting for the right to organize unions, for paid vacations and sick leave, seniority rights, and all the other working conditions we take for granted today as legal rights. In the 1930s, the Party was the first to rally against fascism, and the positions it took on issues in those years stand up very well today.[58]

Revels' voice urging equal rights and justice for African Americans never weakened. In fact, like his grandfather Hiram Revels and his father Horace Sr., Revels seemed to seek out situations where he became the physical and symbolic representative of his people. Revels followed his father's example, too, in rarely shying away from controversy in his professional and public activities. Like his mother Susie, Revels felt a need to perform public service and he held genuine affection for all people—a human quality that made him a warm, personable, and persuasive union and civic leader for both blacks and whites. Susie had also given him a grounded sense of his racial and social identity that sustained him in difficult times.

Alone among his siblings, Revels had a reasonably stable personal life and a long distinguished professional career—marked by the Cayton "spirit of steadfast determination" and a devotion to community activity that benefited people of all colors whose lives he touched.

Revels Cayton died at his home in San Francisco on November 4, 1995, at age eighty-eight.

The Legacy Endures

Susan Cayton Woodson

I N SEPTEMBER 1949, Susan married a bright young chemist, Harold Woodson. Born in Texas in 1914, Woodson had migrated to Chicago with his family just after World War I. He had been a successful and distinguished student at the University of Illinois, Chicago, as a Rosenwald Fellow in chemistry in 1945, and received an M.S. degree. Within a year after their marriage, the birth of a son, Harold Jr. ("Butch"), ended Susan's job at Chicago Employment Security, and afterward her attention focused on home life.[1]

Through the 1950s, Susan devoted herself to her family and worked part-time out of the home in the Rosenwald building, selling dresses under the business name, "Sue's Shopping Service." A clientele of doctors' wives and other middle class women brought in enough extra income for her to buy a used car and put aside a little money. These were hectic, fulfilling, happy years. To have the choice of working or not, afforded by her husband's steadily advancing career, seemed to Susan "better than if he'd put a mink coat around my shoulders." From the mid-1950s to mid-1960s, Harold held positions with the Laboratories of the Illinois Department of Agriculture. In 1965 he moved to the State Department of Public Health, where he worked until retirement twenty years later.[2]

In the early 1960s, when Susan's son began high school, she rejoined the labor force, taking a clerical job with the Amalgamated Clothing and Textile Workers Union, where she remained for the next twenty years. Susan took the initiative in having her family join a church. Her choice, All Souls First Universalist Society, a branch of the Unitarian Church, could be called a "typically Cayton" one—she wanted her son to be exposed to white people. "I didn't want him to be lost in a totally black world; I wanted him to know about people other than blacks." She found the church and its multi-ethnic congregation appealing in other ways—it resembled an open forum. The coffee hour following Sunday service reminded Susan of the Cayton family dinner table, years before in Seattle, where "they tore the speaker up!" In Cayton style, she did more than just join, she became actively involved, serving on the church board and traveling to nearby communities for church-sponsored seminars.[3]

Like the other Cayton women, Susan found her opportunities in the labor force sharply circumscribed by discrimination. But, marriage to a scientist and the establishment of a new home and a middle class family lifestyle helped provide some insulation from the social forces that generally exploited Madge, Lillie, and black women in the post-war years. Susan retired in 1985 from her job at the Amalgamated Clothing and Textile Workers Union, but remained busy with a variety of community activities.

Susan readily attributes her civic work to being raised in the Cayton home. Since the mid-1970s, Susan has been a member of the board of directors of the South Side Community Art Center in Chicago. Among other community activities, she serves on the board of the Vivian G. Harsh Research Collection of Afro-American History and Literature. From her comfortable apartment overlooking Washington Park, she manages the Susan Woodson Gallery, one of the nation's best small collections of African American art. For Susan, it is more than a personal interest. "It's important that African Americans begin collecting black art," she says. "White people are buying our history out."[4]

Throughout Susan's adult life, but especially in later years, she has felt great pride in, and devotion to, the Cayton family. This led her to become, in effect, the family archivist, saving for posterity many of the family's letters, books, and memorabilia. Horace noted this, and in August 1969 had willed his personal effects and papers to Susan just prior to departing for Paris. After Horace's death a few months later, she wrote to Lillie, "I do want your children to have a feeling of belonging to your own family."

+====+

The next generation of Caytons has matured and carried forward the Cayton legacy with their own unique expressions, as did their parents. The children of Revels, Lillie, and Susan have become both middle-aged parents and grandparents, who remember and respect their family heritage—some more, some less. They are deeply devoted to their immediate and extended families, although only a few of them carry a special sense of being a "Cayton." Some have proudly continued the tradition of using "Cayton" and "Revels" as middle names for their children. They tend to be strong-minded, politically astute, and ready to express an opinion. Also prominent is their interest in community involvement, higher education, history, politics, and even autobiography. And, for the most part, they have stayed in the same geographic areas as their parents, mainly the greater Seattle and San Francisco metropolitan areas.

Susan, now in her 80s, looks back on the decades of her life and reflects on the changes in the family and American society. She views the new generation with pride, but also concern. To her, some of them are "Caytons," some are not. "It's a different world," she says. "They can live in a wealthy neighborhood around white people if they want, and some do. I don't see as much striving to improve the race, but they're doing their own thing, getting themselves together." She thinks of her son, nieces, and nephews, and smiles, adding, "I'm so happy they're in this new world."

ABOUT THE AUTHOR

Photo by Lynette Safari Dickson

Richard Hobbs lives with his wife on Whidbey Island in Washington's Puget Sound region, where they enjoy raising and riding horses. He holds a Ph.D. in history from the University of Washington and is a consultant with over twenty years experience in historical-related services, including writing, research, archives and records management. He has worked with a variety of private and governmental organizations, and lived for three years in the Middle East where he was an advisor to the Government of Bahrain.

ENDNOTES

Abbreviations

ARC   Amistad Research Center
BLYU   Beinecke Rare Book and Manuscript Library, Yale University
CHS   Chicago Historical Society
CPL   Chicago Public Library
ILWU   International Longshoremen's and Warehousemen's Union
MFP   Maritime Federation of the Pacific
NAACP   National Association for the Advancement of Colored People
NNC   National Negro Congress
NUMCS   National Union of Marine Cooks and Stewards
SCNY   Schomburg Center for Research in Black Culture, New York Public Library
SFSU   San Francisco State University
SSD   Seattle School District
UCB   University of California, Berkeley
UC   University of Chicago Library
VGHRC   Vivian G. Harsh Research Collection of Afro-American History and
         Literature (Chicago Public Library)
UW   University of Washington Libraries
WSA   Washington State Archives

Chapter 1 Notes
Of a Senator and Slaves

1. The ceremony was held at the home of A.J.T. Edwards and was performed by Reverend William Shanklin, pastor of the First Methodist Episcopal Church (*Seattle Post-Intelligencer*, July 13, 1896).
2. Revels Cayton, interview by the author. Cayton was interviewed on numerous occasions, all in San Francisco: September 21–22, 1975; May 27–29, 1978; August 19–20, 1978; October 23–26, 1979; September 6, 1981; July 25–30, 1985; June 16–18, 1986; August 12–14, 1986; July 30–August 2, 1987; and September 10, 1988 (telephone interview).
3. Horace R. Cayton [Jr.], *Long Old Road* (New York: Trident, 1965), p. 3.
4. On the Caytons' marriage certificate, Horace's mother's name is given as "Mary Middleton."
5. U.S. *Eighth Census, 1860*, Mississippi, Claiborne County.
6. *Cayton's Weekly*, August 23, 1919; Bonnie Branch Hansen, interview by the author. Hansen (Horace Cayton Jr.'s first wife) was interviewed on several occasions: June 7, 1975, Grapeview, Washington; and June 24–28, 1998, Chicago. It is interesting to note that in 1919, Horace Sr. published an account in which he referred to a white man, "Mistah Bob (my father)," the son of a plantation owner whom he called "Cap'n Big Gun," and his wife, "Ol' Miss Liza." In this story Cayton indicated that his mother, Mandy, was a "beautiful mulatto" slave girl on the plantation. Other relatives in these stories are "Miss May (my sister)"—that is, Horace's white half-sister—and another sister named "Nancy Jane," a "beautiful octoroon young woman" who, like Horace, was the offspring of Mistah Bob and Mandy (*Cayton's Weekly*, August 23, 1919).

7. *Long Old Road*, p. 3; Arna Bontemps and Jack Conroy, *Anyplace But Here* (New York: Hill and Wang, 1966), p. 260.

8. U.S. *Ninth Census, 1870*, Mississippi, Claiborne County, Roll 726.

9. *Long Old Road*, p. 3; *Catalogue of the Officers and Students of Alcorn University*, 1871–72 (Jackson: Kimball and Raymond, 1873).

10. "The Leary Family," *Negro History Bulletin*, v. 10, no. 2 (November 1946), pp. 27–31; Julius Eric Thompson, "Hiram R. Revels, 1827–1901: A Biography" (Ph.D. dissertation, Princeton University, 1973), pp. 6–8. Joseph H. Borome, ed., "The Autobiography of Hiram Rhoades Revels Together with Some Letters by and about Him," *Midwest Journal*, v. 5, no. 1 (Winter 1952–53), p. 80; "Leaders in North Carolina," v. 5, no. 5 (February 1942), p. 103; Jean Libby, Hannah Geffert and Jimica Kenyatta, "Hiram Revels Related to Men in John Brown's Army," www.alliesforfreedom.org. Revels' birth date occasionally appears as 1822, but most authorities cite the year 1827 (Thompson, "Revels," pp. 6–7). Unfortunately, the U.S. Censuses of 1830 and 1840 list only the names of heads of households. The 1830 Census for Cumberland County, North Carolina, lists two households that may have been that of Hiram Revels: one headed by Nancy Revels, a free black, age 36–55; and another headed by Patty Revels, a free black, age 36–55 (U.S. *Fifth Census, 1830*, North Carolina, Cumberland County, Roll 120).

11. Revels quoted in Borome, "Autobiography of Hiram Rhoades Revels, p. 80. Except for a brief period in the 1850s, Revels remained a Methodist, first in the African Methodist Episcopal Church and then in the Methodist Episcopal Church North. Hiram Revels may have had a second brother. See Thompson, "Revels," pp. 6–8; also Maurine Christopher, *America's Black Congressmen* (New York: Crowell, 1971), p. 1.

12. See note 11 above.

13. Gerald E. Wheeler, "Hiram R. Revels: Negro Educator and Statesman" (Master's thesis, University of California, Berkeley, 1949), pp. 6–7; Thompson, "Revels," p. 30. Phoebe sometimes appears as "Phoeba."

14. Borome, "Autobiography," p. 90; Revels' speech before the Senate Committee on the District of Columbia, February 8, 1871, in which he made a plea for desegregated schools and argued generally against discrimination, is reprinted in Philip S. Foner, ed., *The Voice of Black America: Major Speeches by Negroes in the United States* (New York: Simon and Schuster, 1972), pp. 371–76.

15. Elizabeth Lawson, *The Gentleman from Mississippi: Our First Negro Senator* (New York: privately printed, 1960), pp. 3, 16; Warmoth T. Gibbs, "Hiram R. Revels and His Times," *Quarterly Review of Higher Education among Negroes*, v. 8 (April 1940), pp. 64–91; Thompson, "Revels," pp. 78–111; George A. Sewell, *Mississippi Black History Makers* (Jackson: University Press of Mississippi, 1977), pp. 25–26.

16. Revels quoted in a five-page biography of Revels [probably by daughter, Susie Revels Cayton], n.d., "Hiram Revels" file, Horace R. Cayton Papers, Vivian G. Harsh Research Collection of Afro-American History and Literature, Chicago Public Library (hereafter, Cayton Papers, VGHRC); Susie Revels Cayton, "A Brief Sketch of Hyram R. Revels," n.d. [ca. 1937?], item 188, Hiram R. Revels Papers, Schomburg Center for Research in Black Culture, New York Public Library (hereafter, Revels Papers), SCNY; Thompson, "Revels," pp. 180–94; Wheeler, "Hiram R. Revels," p. 69.

17. *Catalog of Rust College, 1895–1896*, Rust College Library; typewritten obituary, "Susie Revels Cayton" file, Cayton Papers, VGHRC. The school changed its name to Shaw University in 1870, to Rust University in 1882, and finally back to Rust College in 1915. See Webster B. Baker, *History of Rust College* (Greensboro: North Carolina, 1924). Hiram later served as presiding elder of the Methodist Episcopal Church for the Upper Mississippi Conference.

18. Susan Cayton Woodson, interview by the author. Woodson was interviewed on numerous occasions, all in Chicago: September 2–5, 1978; November 21–25, 1979; August 7,

1980; December 10–16, 1983; July 28–30, 1987; December 13–15, 1988; February 18–23, 1993; November 19–21, 1997; and June 20, 1998.

19. Hiram Revels to Phoebe Revels, October 4, October 21, November 16, 1870, Revels Papers, SCNY; Howard quoted in Lawson, *Gentleman,* p. 11.

20. See Mary F. Berry and John W. Blassingame, *Long Memory: The Black Experience in America* (New York: Oxford University Press, 1982), pp.76–77. See also Jean Noble, *Beautiful Also Are the Souls of My Black Sisters* (Englewood Cliffs, N.J.: Prentice-Hall, 1978).

21. Susie Cayton, "Licker" [unpublished, three-page typewritten short story], 1880 [?], and "The Storm," n.d., "Susie Revels Cayton" file, Cayton Papers, VGHRC; Susie Cayton, "A Brief Sketch of Hyram Revels," Revels Papers, SCNY; typewritten obituary, "Susie Revels Cayton" file, Cayton Papers, VGHRC; Thompson, "Revels," p. 195; Susie's Rust graduation program in Revels Papers, SCNY.

22. Wheeler, "Hiram R. Revels," pp. 67-68; Dunham, *Centennial History,* p. 11; Ida B. Wells, *Crusade for Justice: The Autobiography of Ida B. Wells,* ed. Alfreda M. Duster (Chicago: University of Chicago Press, 1970), pp. xiv-xv. Lawson, *Gentleman,* p. 55. Maggie and Perry Howard had no children. Years later, Howard became an attorney in Washington, D.C. and a member of the Republican National Committee. In 1951, Howard became the defense attorney for W.E.B. Du Bois when the latter was arrested for his peace activism.

23. Profiles of Redmond and Howard are in Berry and Blassingame, *Long Memory,* pp. 39-41, 49-52.

Chapter 2 Notes
Way Out West

1. *Long Old Road,* p. 3; Clell G. Ward, "An Investigation of the Founding and Development of Alcorn A.&M. College, 1871–1900" (Master's thesis, Tennessee A.&I. University, 1962), p. 26. On the history of Alcorn University, see also *Officers and Students of Alcorn A.&M. College,* Melerson G. Dunham, *Centennial History of Alcorn A.&M. College* (Hattiesburg: University and College Press of Mississippi, 1971); W. Milan Davis, *Pushing Forward: A History of Alcorn A.&M. College and Portraits of Some of Its Successful Graduates* (Okolona: Okolona Industrial School, 1938); and Julius E. Thompson, "The Size and Composition of Alcorn A&M College Alumni, 1871–1930," *Journal of Mississippi History,* v. 51, no. 3 (1989), pp. 219–31.

2. Thompson, "Revels," pp. 128–35; Harry Branch, interview by the author, Grapeview, Washington, June 7, 1975; Revels Cayton and Donnie Hancock, interview by the author, San Francisco, October 26, 1979.

3. Bontemps and Conroy, *Anyplace,* p. 260; *Cayton's Weekly,* January 18, 1919, April 17, 1920; Vernon Lane Wharton, *The Negro in Mississippi, 1865–1890* (Chapel Hill: University of North Carolina Press, 1947), p. 254.

4. *Cayton's Weekly,* January 4, 1919. Cayton described his skin color at about age twenty as "between a mulatto and a quadroon" (*Cayton's Weekly,* August 2, 1919).

5. Ibid.

6. Thompson, "Alcorn A&M College Alumni, 1871–1930," pp. 219–31; Thompson, "Revels," pp. 131–74. *Cayton's Weekly,* July 11, 1919. Horace Cayton Jr. may have attended other years; however, only the catalogues for 1872–73 and 1880–81 exist from Alcorn's early years.

7. John Hope Franklin, *From Slavery to Freedom* (New York: Knopf, 1967), pp. 398ff; H.G. Hawkins, "History of Port Gibson, Mississippi," *Publications of the Mississippi Historical Society,* v. 10 (1909), p. 294.

8. Nell Irvin Painter, *Exodusters: Black Migration to Kansas after Reconstruction* (New York: Knopf, 1977), pp. 149–59; Robert G. Athearn, *In Search of Canaan: Black Migration to Kansas, 1879–80* (Lawrence: Regents Press of Kansas, 1978), p. 239.

9. *Long Old Road*, p. 3; *Cayton's Weekly*, August 23, 1919.

10. Painter, *Exodusters*, pp. 149–50.

11. *Western Cyclone* [Nicodemus, Kansas], August 12, July 29, 1887.

12. *Rooks County Record* [Stockton, Kansas], August 5, 1887.

13. *Western Cyclone*, August 12, 1887.

14. *Rooks County Record*, August 19, 1887.

15. *Western Cyclone*, August 26, 1887.

16. King County Superior Court Civil Case File #89476, H.R. Cayton *vs.* H.L. Wilson, *et al.* (August 17, 1912–November 4, 1913) at Puget Sound Regional Archives branch, Washington State Archives; Kansas State Penitentiary, Indexes, 1888, Kansas State Historical Society.

17. *Cayton's Weekly*, January 4, 1919.

18. Typewritten obituary, no author, n.d., "Horace R. Cayton" file, Cayton Papers, VGHRC; *Cayton's Weekly*, January 11, 1919.

19. Ibid.

20. Ibid., January 18, 1919.

21. Ibid., March 13, 1920.

22. Ibid., January 4, 1919.

23. Ibid., January 11, 1919.

24. Esther Hall Mumford, *Seattle's Black Victorians, 1852–1901* (Seattle: Ananse Press, 1980), pp. 85–86.

25. *Seattle Post-Intelligencer*, May 27, 1893.

26. Warren J. Brier, "A History of Newspapers in the Pacific Northwest" (Ph.D. dissertation, State University of Iowa, 1957), p. 739; Mumford, *Seattle's Black Victorians*, pp. 85–87. In 1895 Oxendine was publishing another paper, the *Amusement Herald*, but it failed, and he moved with his family to Portland and later to San Francisco.

27. *Seattle Post-Intelligencer*, May 24, 1894; *Helena Colored Citizen*, September 3, 1894.

28. *Seattle Republican*, January 4, 1896, p. 16.

29. Ibid.; Revels Cayton, interview; Bonnie Branch Hansen, interview.

30. Revels Cayton, interview; Bonnie Branch Hansen, interview.

31. Phoebe and "Doll" Revels to Susie Revels Cayton, July 21, 1896, Revels Papers, SCNY.

Chapter 3 Notes
The Queen City

1. *Seattle Republican*, September 7, 1906, p. 6; Harry Branch, interview.

2. *Daily Intelligencer*, May 28, 1879.

3. *Seattle Republican*, August 31, 1906, April 5, 1907. See Mumford, *Seattle's Black Victorians*, pp. 17–18.

4. *Long Old Road*, pp. 18–20.

5. *Seattle Republican*, August 5, 1898.

6. Ibid., August 9, 1901.

7. *Seattle Post-Intelligencer*, November 22, 1895; *Seattle Republican*, July 26, 1901.

8. Hoge, in partnership with his brother-in-law, purchased the *Post-Intelligencer* from L.S.J. Hunt and directed the paper until 1897. He served on the Republican State Central Committee, holding posts as chairman and treasurer.

9. *Cayton's Weekly*, November 29, 1919, September 1, 1917; Seattle *Argus*, February 8, 1896.

10. *Seattle Daily Republican,* March 2, 1896; Horace R. Cayton [Sr.], *Cayton's Yearbook; Seattle's Colored Citizens, 1923* (Seattle: H. R. Cayton & Son, 1923), p. 12.
11. *Seattle Republican,* August 16, 1895.
12. Mumford, *Seattle's Black Victorians,* p. 81. Other businesses remained in operation under slightly different names, including the First National Bank of Seattle (later Seattle-First National Bank), and Bonney & Stewart Undertakers (later Bonney-Watson).
13. *Seattle Post-Intelligencer,* August 26, 1894. See also Robert A. Campbell, "Blacks and the Coal Mines of Western Washington, 1888–1896," *Pacific Northwest Quarterly,* v. 73, no. 4 (October 1982), pp. 146–55; Quintard Taylor, *The Forging of a Black Community: Seattle's Central District from 1870 through the Civil Rights Era* (Seattle: University of Washington Press, 1994), p. 25.
14. *Seattle Republican,* July 5, 1901.
15. *Seattle Post-Intelligencer,* January 10, 1895; Cayton quoted in Mumford, *Seattle's Black Victorians,* p. 83.
16. Spokane *Spokesman-Review,* September 6, September 19, 1894; Bontemps, *Anyplace,* pp. 261–62. Watson Squire was Washington territorial governor from 1884 to 1887, and a U.S. senator from 1889 to 1897.
17. Quoted in Bontemps and Conroy, *Anyplace,* p. 262. Bontemps and Conroy may have been quoting from Horace Cayton Sr.'s manuscript autobiography, possibly acquired ca. 1940 from Horace Cayton Jr. The manuscript has since been lost. (See chapter 11.) The same fragment appears at the end of an eighty-six-page life history that Cayton Jr. prepared about 1930–31 for Professor Robert Park at the University of Chicago. (Horace Cayton, "Life History of Horace Cayton," Cayton File, Robert Ezra Park Papers, Special Collections, University of Chicago Library [hereafter, Park Papers].) The "colonel" mentioned may have been Colonel Crockett, a transplanted Southerner prominent in Seattle business and Republican politics in the early 1890s.
18. Mumford, *Seattle's Black Victorians,* p. 89; W.E.B. Du Bois, ed. *Efforts for Social Betterment among Negro Americans,* Atlanta University Publications, No. 14. (Atlanta: Atlanta University Press, 1909). In 1900 John and Ella Ryan produced several issues of the *Washington Exponent* before relocating to Tacoma, where they published the *Forum* successfully from 1903 to 1920.
19. *Seattle Post Intelligencer; Seattle Republican,* August 13, 1894.
20. *Spokesman-Review,* September 21, 1894.
21. *Post-Intelligencer,* September 11, 1895. Historian Esther Mumford cites one Burdette letter as "one of the most blatant examples of tomming" of the time (Mumford, *Seattle's Black Victorians,* p. 25).
22. Hiram Revels to Susie Revels Cayton, January 19, 1897, Revels Papers.
23. Notebook of Susie Revels Cayton, Cayton Papers; Susie Cayton, interview by Washington Pioneers Project (WPA), July 7, 1936, Washington State Library; Susie Cayton, "Sallie the Egg-Woman," *Post-Intelligencer,* June 3, 1900. Also reprinted with a brief and excellent profile of Susie in Jean M. Ward and Elaine A. Maveety, eds., *Pacific Northwest Women, 1815–1925: Lives, Memories and Writings* (Corvallis: Oregon State University Press, 1995), pp. 173–79. The Caytons first lived downtown at 5th and Seneca Streets, then rented a wood frame house at 1223 7th Avenue from 1896 to 1903.
24. *Seattle Republican,* February 15, 1901.
25. Ibid, July 6, 1900.
26. Hiram Revels to Susie Revels Cayton, September 10, 1900, Revels Papers, SCNY.
27. Holly Springs newspaper quoted in Thompson, "Hiram R. Revels," p. 189; *Seattle Republican,* February 8, 1901, p. 1.
28. Inventory and Administration of the Estate of Hiram Revels, #2661, 1902, Revels Papers. His financial support of Emma's education is discussed in Hiram's letter to Susie Revels Cayton, September 10, 1900, Revels Papers, SCNY. Emma married Clifford C. Hancock in Seattle on November 23, 1907 (*Seattle Republican,* November 29, 1907).

They later had two boys, Farnsworth, born September 1908, and Donald, called "Donnie," born September 1909. Donnie, the Cayton cousin closest to Revels Cayton, died in September 1987.

29. *Post-Intelligencer,* September 19, September 20, 1895.

30. Ibid., March 25, 1901. Cayton's report of the arrest appears in the *Seattle Republican,* March 29, April 5, 1901. See also *Seattle Star,* March 25, 1901, p. 1. This scene became a part of the Cayton family oral legacy. Nearly seventy-five years after the event, Revels Cayton used similar terms to tell the story when interviewed for this study.

31. *Seattle Republican,* March 29, 1901.

32. See *Post-Intelligencer,* April 21, May 21, 1901; *Seattle Republican,* March 29, 1901; *Seattle Star,* March 29–April 2, 1901.

33. On Horace Cayton Sr.'s arrest, see *Post-Intelligencer,* various issues, March 26–May 24, 1901; *Seattle Star,* various issues, March 30–May 24, 1901; *Seattle Republican,* April 5, April 12, May 24, 1901; *Seattle Times,* March 26, 1901; Murray Morgan, *Skid Road: An Informal Portrait of Seattle, rev. ed.* (Seattle: University of Washington Press, 1982), pp. 135–37.

34. *Post-Intelligencer,* May 21, 1901. On the Cayton trial, see *Seattle Star,* May 21–28, 1901; *Post-Intelligencer,* May 22–25, 1901; *Seattle Republican,* May 31, 1901; and *State of Washington v. H.R. Cayton,* criminal cases # 10778 and #2015, Clerk's records, King County.

35. Milo Root later became a member of the Washington State Supreme Court, 1904–08. Winsor retired from legal practice in September 1907.

36. *Post-Intelligencer,* May 24, 1901.

37. Ibid., May 25, 1901; *Argus,* June 1, 1901; *Seattle Republican,* May 31, 1901.

38. *Seattle Star,* May 28, 1901.

39. *Cayton's Weekly,* November 8, 1919.

40. Ibid., July 28, 1917, January 11, 1919; *Seattle Republican,* September 7, 1906; June 19, 1908.

41. Ryan quoted in *Seattle Republican,* June 14, 1907.

42. *Long Old Road,* p. 3

43. *Seattle Republican,* "Northwest Negro Prosperity Number," June [?], 1907; Mumford, *Seattle's Black Victorians,* pp. 94–98.

44. *Seattle Republican,* March 2, October 19, 1906.

45. Ibid., July 13, 1906.

46. Ibid., November 22, November 29, 1907. See *Seattle Republican,* various issues, January to June 1908; *Seattle Star,* various issues, November to December 1908.

47. *Seattle Republican,* January 4, 1907, January 3, December 25, 1908.

48. *Seattle Times,* July 23, 1909.

49. *Seattle Republican,* June 25, 1909. The Cayton House was a joint venture with Mrs. M.A. Teister. In *Long Old Road* (pp. 17–21), Horace Jr. incorrectly states that Booker T. Washington attended the Exposition. He was invited but was unable to come. Washington's wife and son attended, but there is no evidence that they stayed at the Cayton rooming house or with the Caytons.

50. *Seattle Republican,* October 15, 1909, March 14, 1913, December 28, 1906.

51. Ibid., August 5, 1898.

52. See *Long Old Road,* p. 24; Bontemps, *We Have Tomorrow,* pp. 26–33; Ayer, *American Newspaper Annual,* 1902–1913.

53. *Seattle Republican,* July 26, 1901.

54. *Seattle Star,* June 5–7, 1906; *Seattle Republican,* December 3, 1909.

55. An African American was not added to the Seattle Police Department until 1906. (Ibid., April 20, 1906)

56. *Seattle Republican,* January 26, 1906.

57. Cayton quoted in *Post-Intelligencer,* August 6, 1899. See also Seattle *Argus,* March 30, 1901; *Seattle Republican,* October 5, 1906.

58. Seattle *Argus,* August 12, 1899; *Seattle Patriarch*, October 8, 1910; *Seattle Republican*, May 15, 1908, March 4, 1910.
59. See *Seattle Republican*, November 30, 1906. The black community's petition concerning the 1906 Brownsville riot was drafted by Susie Cayton. The petition, which requested reinstatement of the dishonorably discharged soldiers, was dismissed by President Roosevelt because it did not include the names of the soldiers found guilty of rioting.
60. *Seattle Republican,* November 27, December 11, 1908; April 9, September 3, 1909.
61. A similar suit was filed later in 1909 against a Mount Baker family (Ibid., November 12, 1909). Earlier, Attorney J. Edward Hawkins had encountered similar difficulties. In 1905, when he purchased a house on Capitol Hill, his white neighbors attempted to prevent Hawkins from moving in, but their efforts were unsuccessful (Esther Mumford, "Seattle's Black Victorians—Revising a City's History," *Portage,* v. 2, no. 1 [Fall/Winter 1980–81], pp. 16–17).
62. King County Superior Court Civil Case File #89476, H.R. Cayton *vs.* H.L. Wilson, *et al.* (August 17, 1912–November 4, 1913), at Puget Sound Regional Archives branch, Washington State Archives; *Crisis,* v. 6, no. 2 (June 1913), p. 69. Cayton's attorney was his old friend, Milo Root. Cayton appealed the ruling, but a few months later in November 1913 withdrew the request and the case ended. The author is indebted to Esther Hall Mumford for information on the wider impact of the Cayton case.
63. *Cayton's Weekly,* June 19, 1920.
64. *Seattle Republican*, March 7, 1913.

Chapter 4 Notes
Life on the Horns

1. Ralph Ellison, *Shadow and Act* (New York: Random House, 1964), pp. 315–16.
2. The Laurel Apartments (originally called the Caytonian Court), were located at 303 22nd Avenue South. During World War I, the apartment house was filled with renters, so the Caytons lived at 9030 Rainier Avenue South (January–August 1915), and 1804 22nd Avenue South (September 1915–January 1917).
3. *Cayton's Weekly,* January 5, 1918.
4. Ibid.
5. *Cayton's Weekly,* July 14, 1917. The date of the first issue may have been August 18, 1916. The earliest surviving issue is July 14, 1917.
6. Ibid., March 23, 1918.
7. Ibid., July 28, 1917; January 5, 1918.
8. Ibid, August 25, 1917.
9. *Cayton's Yearbook,* 1923, p. 22.
10. *Cayton's Weekly,* August 25, 1917, p. 6. Executive committee members included D.L. Cardwell as chairman, B. Frank Tutt, the barbershop owner who Cayton called "the father" of the Seattle chapter, Harry Legg, the proprietor of the Alhambra Cash Grocery, Frank Smith, and attorney Andrew R. Black. The other charter members who filled the league's leading posts were Z.L. Woodson, president, Will Chandler, vice president, and Dr. Felix Cooper, secretary.
11. Ibid., September 8, September 1, September 12, 1917.
12. *Cayton's Weekly,* September 29, 1917; July 28,1917.
13. Calvin F. Schmid and Wayne W. McVey Jr., *Growth and Distribution of Minority Races in Seattle, Washington* (Seattle: Seattle Public Schools, 1964), pp. 3–6.
14. *Crisis,* v. 20, no. 4 (August 1920), pp. 180–81; ibid, v. 17, no. 6 (April 1919), p. 284; *Cayton's Weekly,* July 21, 1917; Reports of the Seattle Branch of the N.A.A.C.P., 1914, 1915, 1926–28, National Association for the Advancement of Colored People (NAACP)

Records, Seattle Branch Files, Manuscripts Division, Library of Congress; *Crisis,* v. 9, no. 6 (April 1915), p. 306.

15. *Cayton's Weekly,* September 8, September 15, 1917, August 31, September 6, 1918.
16. Ibid., December 8, 1917.
17. Ibid., July 28, August 4, 1917; January 5, 1918.
18. Ibid, August 31, 1918.
19. Wesley Jones to H. Cayton Sr., September 22, 1917; Cayton to Jones, August 10, 1914; Wesley Jones to J. Silas Harris, August 19, 1919; Wesley Jones to Thomas J. Calloway, February 12, 1920, Wesley L. Jones Papers, University of Washington Libraries (hereafter, UW).
20. *Seattle Times,* September 11, 1918.
21. *Cayton's Weekly,* May 10, 1919. For Horace's reminiscences in *Cayton's Weekly,* see January 4, January 11, January 18, 1919. These and others are collected in Richard S. Hobbs, ed., *Autobiographical Writings of Horace R. Cayton, Sr. Published in Cayton's Weekly, 1917–1920* (Manama: Delmon Press, 1987).
22. Ruth Cayton to Susie Cayton, July 18, August 1, August 19, 1919, Cayton Papers; Susan Cayton Woodson, interview; Revels Cayton, interview. The Caytons were living in a six-room house at 317 22nd Avenue South, just two doors down from the Laurel Apartments. At various times, it served as the Cayton family residence, an undertaker's establishment, and the ILD District 12 headquarters office. In 1931, when the Caytons were forced to turn over the Laurel Apartments to the bank, they were able to keep the house on 22nd Avenue.
23. Susan Cayton Woodson, interview; *Cayton's Weekly,* November 1, November 8, 1919.
24. Ibid., November 27, 1920.
25. *Cayton's Weekly,* February [n.d.] 1920; ibid., August 4, 1917.
26. *Cayton's Weekly,* May 22, February 7, 1920, June 19, 1920; *Cayton's Monthly,* February 1921; Revels Cayton, interview. Emma Houston, who had lived with the Caytons from the age of twelve until her marriage to Clifford Hancock, returned when he deserted the family, bringing with her to the Laurel Apartments her two sons, Farnsworth and Donald. They lived with the Caytons for several years, moving into their own home sometime after WWI.
27. Edward Pitter, interview by the author, Seattle, August 19, 1975; Revels Cayton and Donnie Hancock, interview; Revels Cayton, interview. John Gayton and Horace Cayton both came to Seattle from the same area of Mississippi at about the same time. Apparently, they were acquainted before their arrival in Seattle (*Long Old Road,* p. 95).
28. *Lincoln Industrial Fair Association* (Seattle: Horace R. Cayton, 1925, 1926, 1927), in Fred Patterson Woodson Papers, UW.
29. Horace R. Cayton [Sr.], *Cayton's Yearbook; New Year 1930* (Seattle: Horace R. Cayton and Son, 1930), pp. 7, 17, 26, 29.
30. *Cayton's Weekly,* July 21, 1917.
31. Revels Cayton, interview; Susan Cayton Woodson, interview, Chicago; Susie Cayton to Madge Cayton, n.d. [ca. spring 1938], Cayton Papers, VGHRC.
32. Revels Cayton, interview.

Chapter 5 Notes
Go Out and Achieve

1. Quotes from Revels Cayton, interview, and Susan Cayton Woodson, interview.
2. *Long Old Road,* p. 3.
3. Ibid., pp. 12–14.
4. Madge attended Walla Walla Grammar School, then Emerson before entering Franklin High School in 1915.

5. *Long Old Road,* pp. 28–29.
6. Revels attended Rainier, Brighton, Coleman, and Washington schools.
7. *Long Old Road,* p. 159.
8. Susan Cayton Woodson, interview.
9. Revels Cayton and Donnie Hancock, interview; *Cayton's Weekly,* December 21, 1918.
10. Revels Cayton and Donnie Hancock, interview.
11. Revels Cayton, interview; Marguerite Jamison Isaac, interview, Seattle, July 26, 1987.
12. *Long Old Road,* pp. 6–8; Revels Cayton, BBC interview.
13. *Long Old Road,* pp. 4–6.
14. On Horace Cayton Sr.'s views, see *Cayton's Weekly,* October 25, 1919, concerning social equality and "cotton field philosophy."
15. Revels Cayton, interview; Revels Cayton, BBC interview; Susan Cayton Woodson, interview; Susie Cayton, Washington Pioneers interview. Apparently, the children only heard their mother refer to the man she almost married as "my Jo-Jo."
16. Revels Cayton, interview. On Horace Cayton Sr.'s views on amalgamation of the races, see also, *Cayton's Weekly,* July 21, October 6, 1917, August 2, August 23, 1919, and earlier in *Seattle Republican,* August 27, 1909.
17. *Cayton's Weekly,* May 11, May 25, June 1, 1918, January 4, 1919.
18. *Long Old Road,* pp. 25–28; Revels Cayton, interview; Susan Cayton Woodson, interview.
19. *Long Old Road,* p. 13.
20. Ibid., p. 14; Revels Cayton, interview.
21. Revels Cayton, BBC interview.
22. *Long Old Road,* pp. 28–36, 40–74; Horace Cayton, "Life History," Park Papers, UC. Horace's records at Franklin and then Broadway High School indicate he had problems in school in late 1918 and all of 1919 (Student Records, SSD Archives).
23. *Long Old Road,* pp. 77–80; *Cayton's Weekly,* January 24, January 31, 1920; Horace Cayton, Juvenile Case #6418, Clerk's records, King County. It is also worth noting that Susie's niece, Marguerite Jamison Isaac, said Horace Sr. had the attitude that "his kids could do no wrong" (interview). A similar comment was made by family acquaintance Edward Pitter (interview by the author, Seattle, August 19, 1975).
24. *Long Old Road,* pp. 81–82; Revels Cayton and Donnie Hancock, interview.
25. *Cayton's Weekly,* January 24, 1920; Irma Jackson Cayton Wertz, interview by the author (Wertz was interviewed on three occasions, all in Chicago: December 15, 1983; February 20, 1993 [with Susan Cayton Woodson]; and June 29, 1998); *Long Old Road,* pp. 82–95; Bonnie Branch Hansen to Susan Cayton Woodson, February 12, 1993, Cayton Papers, VGHRC. Revels said that his brother spent only one or two weeks in Chehalis. Horace Jr. wrote in his autobiography that it was nearly six months (Revels Cayton, interview; *Long Old Road,* pp. 93–95).
26. *Long Old Road,* pp. 95–126; Horace Cayton, "Life History," Park Papers, UC.
27. *Long Old Road,* pp. 25–28.
28. Ibid., pp. 124–26.
29. Bonnie Branch Hansen to Susan Cayton Woodson, February 12, 1993, Cayton Papers; *Long Old Road,* pp. 161–62.
30. Bonnie Branch Hansen, interview; *Long Old Road,* pp. 163.
31. *Encephalitis lethargis* (or, *lethargica*), commonly called "sleeping sickness," is to be distinguished from African sleeping sickness. The name means "inflammation of the brain that causes lethargy," or sleepiness. Epidemics of the disease occurred in both Europe and the United States around the time of WW I and continued for a period of about ten years. An influenza virus has been suspected as the cause of the epidemics, which occurred at roughly the same time as the great influenza epidemics that circled the globe. At the time Revels Cayton came down with the disease, about one-third of *encephalitis lethargis* cases were fatal.
32. Revels Cayton, interviews, and BBC interview.

Chapter 6 Notes
The Torch is Passed

1. Susan Cayton Woodson, interview; John B. Kirby, *Black Americans in the Roosevelt Era: Liberalism and Race* (Knoxville: University of Tennessee Press, 1980), pp. 13–29.
2. Revels Cayton, interview.
3. In 1935, the International Labor Defense (ILD) combined efforts with the NAACP and other legal organizations to form the Scottsboro Defense Committee. Two years later, in 1937, the Supreme Court reversed the convictions of four of the Scottsboro Boys; the last was freed in 1950.
4. Richard B. Moore had been a member of the Communist Party since the early 1920s. A West Indian living in Harlem, Moore was a gifted and passionate public speaker, and he served for a number of years in various positions for the ILD and the League of Struggle for Negro Rights (LSNR). In the first half of 1934 the Harlem Communist Party sent Moore on a series of speaking tours for the ILD. He was accompanied by Revels Cayton and "Mother Wright."
5. Revels Cayton, letter to the author, June 13, 1989.
6. Revels Cayton, interview; "Hunger March File, 1933," Mayor's Records, City of Olympia, WSA; letter from Maurice Thompson to Clarence D. Martin (Governor), November 18, 1932, Box 35, Washington Emergency Relief Administration Records, WSA; *Vanguard* (Seattle), January-March 1932, and January-March 1933; John A. Hogan, "The Decline of Self-Help and Growth of Radicalism among Seattle's Organized Unemployed" (M.A. thesis, University of Washington, 1934), pp. 77–80; Richard C. Berner, *Seattle, 1921–1940: From Boom to Bust;* v. 2 of *Seattle in the 20th Century* (Seattle: Charles Press, 1992), pp. 291–294; Arthur Hillman, "The Unemployed Citzens League of Seattle," *University of Washington Publications in the Social Sciences,* v. 5, no. 3 (February 1934), pp. 181–270.
7. *Voice of Action,* February 5, 1934; February 12, 1934; February 27, 1934; Revels Cayton, "Declaration of Candidacy," January 6, 1934, Seattle City Clerk's Records; Revels Cayton, interview.
8. E.M. Hugh-Jones, "A Little Nest of Fascists," *New Republic,* v. 79 (May 30, 1934), pp. 68–69; Revels Cayton, "ILD Head Tells of Visit to Roslyn Strike Field," *Voice of Action,* April 17, 1934, p. 3; May 8, 1934, p. 4; Revels Cayton, interview. At the time, State Patrol Chief William Cole was making concerted efforts to use the WSP's broadened authority to arrest "agitators," particularly communists, socialists, Wobblies, and other radicals. The arrest of Cayton and the English couple is mentioned in a letter from Cole to Governor Martin, on May 4, 1934 (Washington State Patrol Records, Box 8, "Cle Elum Strike, 1934," WSA).
9. *Voice of Action,* August 3, 1934. The LSNR was formed by the Communist Party in November 1930 and affiliated with the ILD. It superseded the American Negro Labor Congress, established in 1925.
10. Ibid., September 14, September 21, November 23, 1934.
11. Revels Cayton, "Herndon Called Fearless Leader," *Voice of Action,* December 7, December 21, 1934. After serving five years, Herndon was released in 1937 following a Supreme Court decision reversing his conviction.
12. Revels Cayton, "Anti Intermarriage Bill is Attempt to Smash Unity," *Voice of Action,* February 15, March 29, 1935.
13. Revels Cayton, BBC interview; quote from William F. Dunne, *The Great San Francisco General Strike* (New York: Workers Library, 1934), p. 58. The Marine Workers Industrial Union (MWIU) was formed by a convention of radical seamen and union leaders on April 26, 1930, in New York. Inspired by the Communist Party and heavily influenced by

former IWW members, the MWIU announced itself as the "New Red Union of Marine Workers." At the end of the 1934 strike, with ship owners officially recognizing the International Seamen's Union, leaders of the MWIU dissolved their organization in February 1935, directing members, in accord with the new "popular front" Party line, to merge with the ISU from below.

14. Revels Cayton, interview; Sue Martin and Madge Thompson, interview, Seattle, April 23, 1999; Revels Cayton and Donnie Hancock, interview; Susan Cayton Woodson, interview; Student Records, SSD Archives Susan Cayton [Woodson] to "Hun" [Madge Cayton], March 31, 1938; Susie Cayton to Madge, n.d. [ca. spring 1939]; Susie Cayton to Madge Cayton, May 5, 1940, Cayton Papers, VGHRC.

15. "Revels Data To Library," newspaper clipping, n.d., Cayton Papers, VGHRC; Borome, "Autobiography," pp. 79–92; Horace Cayton Sr. to Herman Meulder, May 22, 1937, Revels Papers, SCNY. Some fifteen years would elapse before the Revels autobiography would be published in the obscure *Midwest Journal*.

16. Horace Cayton Sr. to Du Bois, September 14, 1935, *The Correspondence of W.E.B. Du Bois,* ed. Herbert Aptheker, 3 vols. (Amherst: University of Massachusetts Press, 1973–1978), 2: pp. 111–12. Aptheker erroneously attributes the letter to Horace Cayton Jr. The letter originated in Seattle (Horace Jr. was in Chicago in 1935); also the language and style is unquestionably that of Cayton Sr.

17. Susie quoted in Revels Cayton interview.

18. Virginia Gayton, interview, Seattle, June 18, 1975; Arnold Rampersad, *I, Too, Sing America,* vol. 1 (1902–1941) of *The Life of Langston Hughes* (New York: Oxford University Press, 1986), p. 240; Cayton quoted in *Long Old Road,* p. 307. Rampersad states that Hughes also met Horace Cayton Jr., "a young policeman"; however, in 1932, Horace Jr. was in Chicago.

19. Horace Cayton Sr. to Hughes, March 8, 1939; Hughes [by James Derry] to Horace Cayton Sr., March 25, 1939, Langston Hughes Papers, Beinecke Library, Yale University (hereafter, BLYU); Susan Cayton Woodson, interview. Cayton's manuscript was typed by Floy Collins (now Ruffings).

20. Susan Cayton [Woodson] to "Hun" [Madge Cayton], March 31, 1938; Horace Cayton Sr. to Madge Cayton, March 20, 1940; Susan Cayton [Woodson] to "Hun" [Madge Cayton], February 13, 1940; Susie Cayton to Madge Cayton, May 5, 1940, Cayton Papers.

21. Susan Cayton Woodson, interview. Susie's payment of the $144 bill to the Angelus Mortuary took a full year (note, n.d. [Susie Cayton's handwriting; headed "The Angelus"]).

22. *Northwest Enterprise,* August 23, 1940; *Post-Intelligencer,* August 18, 1940.

23. Lillie Cayton to Susan Cayton [Woodson], n.d. [ca. autumn 1940]; Susie Cayton to Susan Cayton [Woodson], October 21, 1940, Cayton Papers, VGHRC.

24. Susie Cayton to Madge Cayton, n.d. [December 1936], Cayton Papers, VGHRC.

25. Susie Cayton to Susan Cayton [Woodson], October 21, 1940, Cayton Papers, VGHRC.

26. Susie Cayton to Susan Cayton [Woodson], February 16, 1942, Cayton Papers, VGHRC.

27. Byrd Kelso to Madge Cayton, August 23, 1943, Cayton Papers, VGHRC.

28. Madge Terriye Thompson, interview, Seattle, July 31, 1986, and April 23, 1999 (with Sue Martin); Susan Cayton Woodson, interview.

Chapter 7 Notes
A Black Metropolis

1. St. Clair Drake and Horace R. Cayton [Jr.], *Black Metropolis: A Study of Negro Life in a Northern City* (New York: Harcourt, Brace, 1945), pp. 379–80.

2. In 1940, Bronzeville was bounded on the north by 28th Street, on the south by 63rd Street, on the west by State Street and on the east by Cottage Grove Street.

3. Horace Cayton [Jr.], "Personal Experience in Race Relations" (paper read at American Sociological Association Annual Conference, San Francisco, August 29, 1967), p. 7, Cayton Papers, VGHRC.

4. Bonnie Branch Hansen to Susan Cayton Woodson, February 13, 1993, Cayton Papers, VGHRC.

5. *Long Old Road,* pp. 185–207.

6. Cayton's other advisors on the project were Edwin Embree, author of *Brown America: The Story of a New Race* (1931), and Will Alexander, head of the Farm Security Administration. Alexander and Embree were both with the Rosenwald Foundation (Embree was head of the foundation), which Horace Jr. would later work closely with as director of the Parkway Community Center.

7. Cayton to Louis Wirth, July 8, 1934; Wirth to Cayton, July 13, 1934, Louis Wirth Papers, UC. Of the twenty-two chapters in *Black Workers and the New Unions,* Cayton wrote eighteen and Mitchell four.

8. Bonnie Branch Hansen, interview. There is only one reference to this period in Horace Jr.'s autobiography: "When she [Bonnie] expressed a willingness to try to make a go of it again I was tempted, for I still cared for her, but I was unable to reach a decision and this resulted in a deep depression, almost a crack-up" (*Long Old Road,* p. 208).

9. Charles S. Johnson to Cayton, Sept. 25, 1934; Cayton to Wirth, October 1, 1934, Wirth Papers, UC.

10. Cayton to Wirth, July 2, September 6, 1935, Wirth Papers, UC.

11. Cayton to Wirth, August 17, 1935 [postcard], September 6, 1935, Wirth Papers, UC; *Long Old Road,* pp. 228–30. The meeting between Cayton and Myrdal planted the seed for a collaborative book project, which they were to pursue several years later.

12. After Horace met Irma, he went back to Chicago and ended the relationship with Elizabeth Johns; he was able to secure the return of his mother's ring, which he had given to Johns. The following year Johns went to work as a research assistant on WPA projects under Cayton. There she met St. Clair Drake and the two later married. The early years of Irma and Horace Jr.'s marriage are discussed in Wertz, letter to the author, April 17, 1998; Wertz, "A First WAC"; Wertz, "First Black WACS Overseas," *Dawn Magazine,* July 1979, pp. 20, 27; and *Long Old Road,* pp. 174–254, various pages.

13. Cayton to Wirth, March 31, 1936.

14. Cayton to Wirth, April 14, 1936; Fred H. Matthews, *Quest for an American Sociology: Robert E. Park and the Chicago School* (Montreal: McGill-Queen's University Press, 1977), pp. 102, 176–77. See Cayton's tribute to Park in the *Pittsburgh Courier,* February 26, 1944.

15. See note 13 above.

16. Drake and Cayton, *Black Metropolis,* pp. xii–xiv; W. Lloyd Warner, "Methodological Note," in ibid., p. 776.

17. James Edward Ellefson, "The Works Progress Administration and the Negro in Chicago, 1935 to 1943" (Master's thesis, Western Illinois University, 1973), pp. 34–38; Cayton to Richard Wright, June 24, 1943, Richard Wright Papers, BLYU. The projects received sponsorship from the Institute of Juvenile Research, the Cook County Bureau of Public Welfare, and the Illinois State Employment Service, plus individual sponsorship and assistance from various University of Chicago faculty, principally Louis Wirth and Earl Johnson.

18. Articles on the Cayton-Warner WPA projects appeared in the *Chicago Defender,* October 1937–January 1939, various dates, and May 20, 1940. See also *Long Old Road,* pp. 236–39; Cayton to Wirth, March 28, 1937 and May 24, 1939, Wirth Papers, UC; Drake and Cayton, *Black Metropolis,* pp. xii–xiv.

19. Mary Elaine Ogden, "The Chicago Negro Community, a Statistical Description" (Works Progress Administration, December 1939, mimeographed), p. viii.

20. St. Clair Drake, "To Horace Cayton from St. Clair Drake, January 1970," speech (Horace Cayton Jr.'s memorial service, Chicago, Illinois, February 14, 1970), box 22, St. Clair Drake Papers, SCNY (hereafter, Drake, "To Horace").

21. *Pittsburgh Courier*, May 1, 1937; see Wirth's recommendation for Cayton, March 16, 1937; Cayton to Wirth, February 8, 1937, Wirth Papers, UC. Horace's Rosenwald Fellowship was renewed in May 1938 for 1938–39 (*Chicago Defender*, May 7, 1938; "Fellowships," box 400, folder 8, Julius Rosenwald Fund Archives, Amistad Research Center, microfilm [hereafter, Rosenwald Archives, ARC]).

22. Wertz, letter to the author, April 17, 1998.

23. Cayton, "Negroes Live in Chicago," *Opportunity*, v. 15 (December 1937), pp. 366–69; and *Beacon* (Chicago), December 1937.

24. Cayton, "No Friendly Voice," part 2 of "Negroes Live in Chicago," *Opportunity*, v. 16 (January 1938), pp. 12–14; and *Beacon* (Chicago), January 1938; Horace Cayton and Estelle Scott, "At Least 225 Race Families Should be in Jane Addams Homes, Statistics Show," *Chicago Defender*, January 29, 1938.

25. *Chicago Defender*, February–July 1938, various dates; ibid., October 26, 1940; Wirth to *Chicago Defender*, May 18, 1938, Wirth Papers, UC.

26. "Bulletin of the Society for Social Research" [and related Society records], Special Collections, UC; statement by Horace Cayton [21 pages] to the U.S. Congressional Committee on Interstate Migration, Chicago hearing, August 1940, box 34, folder 8, Ralph Bunche Papers, SCNY. The following graduate degree papers used Cayton-Warner research materials:

   Baur, Edward Jackson. "Delinquency Among Mexican Boys in South Chicago." M.A., University of Chicago, 1938.

   Daniel, Vattel Elbert. "Ritual Stratification in Chicago's South Side Churches for Negroes." Ph.D., University of Chicago, 1940. (Summarized in a published aticle, "Ritual Stratification in Chicago Negro Churches," *American Sociological Review*, v. 7, no. 3 (1942), pp. 352–361).

   Davis, Ralph Nelson. "The Negro Newspaper in Chicago." M.A., University of Chicago, 1939.

   Dorey, Frank D. "Community Turnover on the South Side of Chicago; A Study of the Expansion of the Negro Communities and Their Effects upon the White Protestant Churches." B.D., Chicago Theological Seminary, 1942.

   Henderson, Elmer William. "A Study of the Basic Factors Involved in the Change in the Party Alignment of Negroes in Chicago." M.A., University of Chicago, 1939.

   Hutton, Oscar Douglas. "The Negro Worker and the Labor Unions in Chicago." M.A., University of Chicago, 1939.

   Maddox, Jessie. "Attitudes of the Negro of the Lake Street Area of Chicago Toward the Institutional Life of the Community." M.A., Chicago Theological Seminary, 1940.

   Nierman, Bernys Surkin. "A Study of Unmarried Negro Men and Women Twenty-one Through Thirty-five Years of Age Receiving Assistance as One-Person Cases from the Chicago Relief Administration (District Office Number One), with Reference to Their Independent Economic Adjustment," M.A., Northwestern University, 1941.

   Roberts, Robert. "Negro-White Inter-Marriage." M.A., University of Chicago, 1940.

   Strong, Samuel M. "Social Types in the Negro Community of Chicago: An Example of the Social Type Method." Ph.D., University of Chicago, 1940. (Also published article, "Social Types in a Minority Group Formulation of a Method," *American Journal of Sociology*, v. 48, no. 5 (1943), pp. 563-573.)

27. *Chicago Defender*, January 7, January 14, 1939.

28. Cayton to W. Lloyd Warner, n.d. [ca. March 1939], Wirth Papers, UC.

29. Horace Cayton, "Projects Now in Progress" and "General Study of the Negro Community in Chicago," memoranda, WPA, Chicago, May 1939, Wirth Papers, UC; Bontemps correspondence with WPA, Rosenwald Fund, and University of Chicago (Apr. 1938–Dec. 1943) in Arna Wendell Bontemps Papers, Special Collections, Syracuse University Library (hereafter, SUL); correspondence files "WPA" and "Negro in Illinois," box 154, folders 6–8, Rosenwald Archives, ARC. Three projects remained in process: "Indexing of the Negro Press," "A Study of Language and Communication in the Negro Community," and "Bibliography by and About the Negro." Horace Jr. planned to (and later did) oversee these projects as sponsor and general director, a position comparable to Warner's previously. The continuing WPA projects proceeded under auspices of the Federal Writers Project for Illinois, supervised by Arna Bontemps. The bibliographic study, directly supervised by Elizabeth Wimp from 1938 to 1940, became the "Chicago Afro-American Union Analytic Catalog," containing 75,000 index entries from the Chicago libraries. These projects were merged with information gathered by the Illinois Writers Project into what became known as "The Negro in Illinois" study. This planned book never saw publication; however, some of the essays were summarized in the 95-page booklet *Cavalcade of the American Negro,* published for the 1940 American Negro Exposition. More notably, Arna Bontemps and Jack Conroy used much of the material to write *They Seek a City,* published in 1945 and again in 1966 under the title *Anyplace But Here.*

The surviving records of the Cayton-Warner Research and the "Negro in Illinois" study are scattered among the following six institutions: Harsh Collection, Chicago Public Library; Newberry Library (Jack Conroy Papers); Illinois State Historical Library; Schomburg Center, NYPL (St. Clair Drake Papers); Manuscript Division, Library of Congress; National Archives and Records Administration.

30. Horace Cayton Sr. to Madge Cayton, July 4, 1939, Cayton Papers.
31. *Chicago Defender,* October 21, 1939.
32. J. Copeland, "The History of Good Shepherd Community Church," June 18, 1941, box 45, NIL, VGHRC.
33. "Former Nomad Heads Largest Negro Center," *Chicago Tribune,* April 5, 1942.
34. Cayton to Myrdal, February 26, 1940; Cayton to Wirth, March 4, 1940, Wirth Papers, UC.
35. Cayton to Myrdal, April 8, 1940, Wirth Papers, UC. See also Gunnar Myrdal, *An American Dilemma* (New York: Carnegie Corporation, 1944), pp. 863, 1126. The principal WPA resources used by Myrdal were Drake's study (which he termed an "unpublished manuscript prepared for this study"), and what he vaguely referred to as "a collection of unpublished interviews with old residents (in possession of the Social Science Research Committee of the University of Chicago)."
36. Cayton to Richard Wright, January 23, 1942, Wright Papers, BLYU; Cayton, "The Problem, Program and Facilities of the Good Shepherd Community Center" [pamphlet, 25 pp.], June 26, 1940,); report, June 19, 1941, minute book, pp. 159, 199 [on Cayton's appointment as director], Parkway Community House Records, box 1, Chicago Historical Society (hereafter, Parkway Records, CHS). The few surviving records of the Good Shepherd Community Center and Parkway Community House are mainly financial records (1939–49, 1953–55) and some meeting minutes of the Board of Directors (1939–45). These are in the Parkway Records, CHS.
37. Rampersad, *Life of Langston Hughes,* pp. 32–33; Irma Jackson Cayton Wertz quoted in ibid., p. 37. Hughes lectured on "Poetry and the War." See also *Chicago Daily News,* November 13, 1943; Videotape Oral History of Parkway Community House, November 21, 1997 (hereafter, Parkway Oral History, VGHRC). Participants in the videotaped oral history of the Parkway included: Sidney Jones, Helen Cooley, Magdalene Crawford Webb, Dorothy Rogers Livingston, Susan Cayton Woodson, Frances Reese Johnson, Rosina Tyler McLemore, and Harsh Collection staff. Official announcement of the name change from

GSCC to Parkway is in Wirth Papers, UC. On Langston Hughes and the Skyloft Players, see *Chicago Defender,* April 4, 1942; September 30, December 30, 1944.

38. Cayton to Wright, July 24, October 7, 1942, Wright Papers, BLYU; *Chicago Defender,* October 12, 1940. Nembutal and Secanol (Secobarbitol) are short acting, habit-forming sedatives. Prolonged use at high dosages, as in Cayton's case, leads to increased tolerance and physical and psychological dependence…The principal symptoms of intoxication include slurred speech, irritability, insomnia, poor judgement, confusion, and unsteady gait…Withdrawal symptoms are severe and may be fatal (Denise Boudreau, R.Ph., letter to the author, October 15, 1998). In an interview by the author, Irma stated that Horace would send her to different drug stores to purchase Secanol for him (before a prescription was required). When he was in one of his "periods," he would take a handful of the pills with a glass of whiskey.

39. Susie Cayton to Susan Cayton [Woodson], "Xmas 1941"; Susie Cayton to "Cousin Nellie," April 15, 1943, Cayton Papers, VGHRC.

40. Susie Cayton to Langston Hughes, n.d. [December 25, 1942], Hughes Papers, BLYU. The tone of this letter is so positive, supportive, and intentionally uplifting that it appears to have been prompted by a mood of depression (or distress over feelings of failure and lack of money) that Susie detected in Hughes. At the close of the letter she wrote, "Should this Xmas morn have dawned without your presence not only 'our people' but the entire universe would have sustained a loss—I call that success. I am very proud of you." Hughes inscribed the poem, "Written at Parkway Community House, April 23, 1943." The original is in the home of Susan Cayton Woodson in Chicago.

41. Horace Cayton, "My Encounter with Richard Wright," p. 2,4, Cayton Papers, VGHRC. The significance and sheer volume of the bibliographic and statistical data being gathered by the WPA project led Cayton to envision an "Institute for the Study of the Negro in the United States," which would serve as a data depository and a center for black research. Warner assisted in developing a plan for the institute, while Burgess, Wirth, and others supported the idea. Horace continued to push for what he called "my pet hobby" for several years, but by the mid-1940s it was apparent that the problem of funding the institute was insurmountable. See Cayton to Wirth, May 28, 1937, "A Plan for the Organization of an Institute for the Study of the Negro in the United States," Wirth Papers, UC; and Cayton to Wright, June 24, 1943, Wright Papers, BLYU.

42. Cayton, "My Encounter with Richard Wright," p. 7.; Cayton, "The Search for Richard Wright," speech (First W.E.B. Du Bois Lecture, Institute of the Black World, Atlanta, Georgia, December 7, 1969), Cayton Papers, VGHRC. On Cayton and Wright, see Cayton, *Long Old Road,* pp. 247–63; Richard Wright Subgroup, Cayton Papers, VGHRC; the Cayton-Wright correspondence in Wright Papers, BLYU [188 letters, 1940–50]; Hazel Rowley, *Richard Wright: The Life and Times* (New York: Henry Holt, 2001), pp. 189–90, 249–50, 277–79, 297–301, 319–22, 354, 364; Michele Fabre, *The Unfinished Quest of Richard Wright* (New York: William Morrow & Co., 1973), pp. 201, 206, 229, 232–34, 248–50, 260–61, 268–71, 281–82, 287, 293–94, 339, 363, 422, 504, 509, 512, 562–63, 571–72, 577, 579–81, 585, 588, 591; Constance Webb, *Richard Wright: A Biography* (New York: Putnam, 1968), pp. 107–108, 210–14).

43. Wright, "Introduction," Drake and Cayton, *Black Metropolis,* pp. xvii–xviii.

44. Richard Wright, *12 Million Black Voices* (New York: Viking Press, 1941), p. 6. Cayton's review appeared in his column "Wright's New Book More Than a Study of Social Status," *Pittsburgh Courier,* November 15, 1941.

45. The Parkway pamphlet is in Cayton Papers, VGHRC.

46. Cayton to Wright, July 24, October 7, 1942, Wright Papers, BLYU. See also Wertz's "A First WAC" and "First Black WACS Overseas."

47. "Horace R. Cayton, Internal Security," Bureau File 100–18434, Federal Bureau of Investigation Records, Washington, D.C. See also *Long Old Road,* pp. 251–52; Cayton, "Negro Morale" (paper presented to 21st annual Institute of the Society for Social Research,

August 14–15, 1942); Everett C. Hughes to Horace Cayton, June 11, 1942, box 4, Society for Social Research Records, UC; Patrick S. Washburn, "The *Pittsburgh Courier* and Black Workers in 1942," *Western Journal of Black Studies,* v. 10, no. 3 (1986), pp. 109–18; Richard M. Dalfiume, "The Forgotten Years of the Negro Revolution," *Journal of American History,* v. 55 (June 1968), pp. 90–106. The FBI investigated Horace also in 1950 and 1951. The 1950–51 investigation, prompted by reports that Cayton had been "active in connection with Communist dominated or infiltrated organizations in the Chicago area," was closed for lack of evidence. He was investigated again in 1959 and 1960 in San Francisco, presumably because of his renewed relationship with his brother, Revels, who previously had been affiliated with the Communist Party. See "Horace R. Cayton, Internal Security," Bureau Files 100–32189, and 47–25366, Federal Bureau of Investigation Records, Washington, D.C.

48. Cayton, "Fighting for White Folks," *Nation,* v. 155 (September 26, 1942), pp. 267–70; Arna Bontemps to Langston Hughes, November 4, 1942; Nichols, *Bontemps-Hughes Letters,* p. 121.

49. Cayton to Wright, October 7, 1942, Wright Papers, BLYU. On the Caytons' divorce (Tucson, Arizona), see *Chicago Defender,* October 14, 1944. Irma married Lt. William ("Jack") Wertz in December 1944. They settled in Detroit in 1954, where Dr. Jack Wertz practiced psychiatry prior to his death in 1975. Irma played an active role in Detroit civic affairs and continued to do so after she was widowed. In 1997 she received recognition from the Detroit Civic Theater, which has named their meritorious service award in her honor.

50. For a time, Cayton expected to co-author his proposed "Study of the Negro in Chicago" with W. Lloyd Warner, but no formal plan fell into place; Warner moved ahead, instead, with his book, *Color and Human Nature.*

51. Madge's obituary of Susie Cayton is in Cayton Papers, VGHRC. On Susie's death see Nichols, *Bontemps-Hughes Letters,* pp. 134–35.

52. "Mary Francis" [Susie Cayton] to Irma Cayton, October 12, 1942 [photocopy], Cayton Papers, VGHRC.

53. Revels Cayton, interview; Irma Cayton Wertz, interview; Susan Cayton Woodson, interview; *Long Old Road,* pp. 287, 289, 313. Lore Segal recalled Horace's account of his last conversation with Susie as follows: "Horace said, 'Are you proud of what I've done?' and she answered, 'What do I care what you've done. I'm dying.'" (Letter, Lore Segal to the author, September 1, 1988.)

Chapter 8 Notes
Dark Mirror of Our Lives

1. Langston Hughes, "A Character," *Pittsburgh Courier,* June 12, 1948; Margaret Walker, interview by the author (Walker was interviewed on two occasions, both in Chicago: December 11, 1983, and February 21, 1993); "Former Nomad Heads Largest Negro Center," *Chicago Tribune,* April 5, 1942; "An American Family," *Headlines and Pictures,* July 1945, p. 32.

2. Hughes, "A Character"; Sidney Williams (with Harold and Susan Cayton Woodson, Enoch Waters, Cyrus Colter, and Fern Gayden), interview by the author, Chicago, September 3, 1978; Ruth Williams, interview by the author, Chicago, November 22, 1997.

3. Margaret Walker, interview.

4. *Chicago Defender,* January 26, 1970.

5. Cyrus Colter (with Harold and Susan Cayton Woodson, Enoch Waters, Sidney Williams, and Fern Gayden), interview by the author, Chicago, September 3, 1978.

6. Interestingly, Horace Jr.'s years in Chicago (1931–1948), coincide closely with the period typically cited for the Renaissance (1935–1950). On the arts in the Chicago Renaissance, see the following: Samuel Floyd, *The Power of Black Music* (New York: Oxford University Press, 1995), pp. 100–135; Alain Locke, "Chicago's New Southside Art Center," *American Magazine of Art*, v. 34 (1941), pp. 370–74; Willard Motley, "Negro Art in Chicago," *Opportunity* (January 1940), pp. 19–22, 28–31; Joyce Russell-Robinson, "Renaissance Manque: Black WPA Artists in Chicago," *Western Journal of Black Studies*, v. 18, no. 1 (1994), pp. 36–43; Craig Werner, "Leon Forrest, the AACM and the Legacy of the Chicago Renaissance," *Black Scholar*, v. 23, no. 3–4 (1993) pp. 10–16.

7. Robert Bone, "Richard Wright and the Chicago Renaissance," *Calloo*, v. 9 (1986), p. 454. On literature in the Chicago Renaissance, see the following: "A Golden Spot for Literature," *Chicago Defender*, February 21, 1993; Bone, "Richard Wright and the Chicago Renaissance," pp. 446–68; Arna Bontemps, "Famous WPA Authors," *Negro Digest*, June 1950, pp. 43–47; Jack Conroy, "Memories of Arna Bontemps, Friend and Collaborator," *American Libraries*, v. 5, no. 11 (December 1974), pp. 602–6; Margaret Walker, "New Poets," *Phylon*, v. 11 (1950), pp. 345–54.

8. Aldon Morris, "The Sociological Imagination and the Chicago Renaissance," speech for "Chicago Renaissance" symposium, sponsored by the Harsh Research Collection, Chicago, October 3, 1998, copy loaned to the author. On Cayton and Du Bois, see Cayton, *Long Old Road*, pp. 20–21; *Black Metropolis*, pp. 787–88; and David Levering Lewis, *W.E.B. Du Bois: Biography of a Race 1868–1919* (New York: Henry Holt, 1993), p. 207. On Cayton and Frazier and Johnson (especially Cayton's views on slavery and the African American family) see Cayton, "E. Franklin Frazier: A Tribute and Review," *Review of Religious Research*, v. 5, no. 3 (Spring 1964), pp. 137–42; also Cayton, "Dark Inner Landscape," (October 1964), unpublished manuscript, Cayton Papers, VGHRC.

9. On the Parkway Forums, see *Chicago Defender*, October 1942 to October 1943, various issues; Parkway Oral History, VGHRC; *Chicago Daily News*, November 13, 1943. On Langston Hughes and the Skyloft Players see *Chicago Defender*, April 4, 1942; September 30, December 30, 1944.

10. *Chicago Daily News*, November 13, 1943.

11. Setsuko Nishi, interview by the author, Brooklyn, New York, April 15, 1981; Nishi, "Negro-Nisei Identifications: Some Observations from Wartime and Postwar Chicago," paper (presented at "Chicago Symposium in Memory of Horace R. Cayton," Chicago, February 14, 1970); Cayton to Arna Bontemps, March 23, 1943, Bontemps Papers, SUL; Parkway Oral History, VGHRC. Regarding his sensitivity to prejudice against other ethnic groups, Horace Jr. was much like his father. In the March 30, 1900, issue of the *Seattle Republican*, Horace Sr. blasted white locals who opposed the acquisition of land by recent Chinese immigrants in the area. Cayton declared that since the Chinese had been permitted into the United States, they had a "God-given right to make a living, wherever they so desire." He continued: "The lands of this section are not being developed very rapidly by the Americans, and if the Chinamen will develop them, they are deserving of much personal praise instead of personal abuse and violent intimidations for so doing. Any man, woman or child permitted to land on American soil should be protected both in the spirit and the letter of the law, and the ones first and foremost to seeing that such is done should be the native white men, who claim to stand for all that's good in the shape of freedom of mankind."

12. Parkway Oral History, VGHRC; *Chicago Defender*, April 5, 1947; Drake, "To Horace," Drake Papers, NYPL.

13. Financial records, Parkway Records, CHS; Parkway Oral History, VGHRC; Susan Cayton Woodson, interview.

14. Cayton, *Long Old Road*, pp. 259, 309–22; Cayton to Richard Wright, October 22, October 30, November 10, 1944; January 22, 1945, Wright Papers, BLYU.

15. Wright quoted in Fabre, *Unfinished Quest*, pp. 581–82.

16. *Chicago Defender*, January 6, January 13, January 20, 1945. See also Horace's column in the *Pittsburgh Courier*, December 9, 1944, on "Interracial Commissions," which ended with Horace advising his readers, "The one method of insuring the committee will function effectively is for citizens to maintain a consistent militant pressure on it."

17. *Chicago Defender*, November 3, November 10, November 17, November 24, December 12, 1945; Annual Report 1944–45, "News in the Making at Parkway Community House," Cayton Papers, VGHRC; "To Horace," Drake Papers, NYPL. The program for the fall 1945 series, "An American Dilemma: The Negro and Democracy," is in Box 389, Welfare Council of Metropolitan Chicago Records, CHS.

18. Doris Saunders, interview.

19. Cayton to Wright, August 13, 1943, Wright Papers, BLYU.

20. Cayton, "Personal Experience in Race Relations," Cayton Papers, VGHRC.

21. Cayton to Wright, August 13, 1943 and October 11, 1946, Wright Papers, BLYU; Nichols, *Bontemps-Hughes Letters*, p. 219; Revels Cayton, interview; Susan Cayton Woodson, interview; Irma Cayton Wertz, interview, 15; *Long Old Road*, pp. 255–91. Dr. Helen Vincent McLean (1896–1983) was co-founder of the Institute for Psychoanalysis in Chicago, established in 1932. Horace's interest in psychology and psychiatry came to light very early. In Professor Norman Hayner's sociology class in 1928, when the term "psychiatrist" came up for discussion, Horace was the only one who knew its meaning, and so the class promptly dubbed him the "psychiatrist" (Notes, "Horace Cayton," Box 4 [Criminology], Hayner Papers, UW).

22. Cayton to Wright, May 5, 1945, Wright Papers, BLYU.

23. Cayton to Wright, January 23, 1942, Wright Papers, BLYU.

24. Cayton to Wright, October 15, 1943, Wright Papers, BLYU.

25. Cayton, "The Curtain: A Sojourn to the South," *Negro Digest*, v. 18, no. 2 (1968), pp. 11–15.

26. Susan Cayton Woodson, interview.

27. Revels Cayton, interview. Regarding the argument between Revels and Horace Jr. after Madge's funeral, see also chapter 9.

28. Telegram, Cayton to Langston Hughes, September 16, 1944, Hughes Papers, BLYU; Cayton to Wright, December 15, 1943, Wright Papers, BLYU; Cayton, "An Obituary [Madge Cayton]" *Pittsburgh Courier*, September 30, 1944.

29. Cayton, "An Obituary."

30. See Fabre, *Unfinished Quest*, pp. 270–71, 581. See also Cayton to Wright, March to April 1943, and March to June 1944, various dates, Wright Papers, BLYU; and Cayton to Susan Cayton [Woodson], August 1947, Cayton Papers, VGHRC.

31. Cayton to Wright, October 22, 1944, Wright Papers, BLYU. See also Fabre, *Unfinished Quest*, pp. 268, 580–81.

32. *Long Old Road*, pp. 259, 309–322.

33. Cayton to Wright, February 1, February 17, 1945, Wright Papers, BLYU.

34. "Frightened Children of Frightened Parents" appeared late in the autumn of 1945 in the double issue of *Twice a Year*, edited by Dorothy Norman of the *New York Post*. Horace Jr. sent a copy of "Frightened Children" to Wright, who responded enthusiastically, noting in his journal both admiration for Horace's intelligence and courage, and appreciation for the similarities in their thinking on race relations. See Wright's journal, February 19, 1945, Wright Papers, BLYU.

35. Horace credits Helen McLean for the first exposition in scientific or literary literature of the "fear-hate-fear complex." See Cayton's letter to Wright, February 1, 1945, Wright Papers, BLYU; and Cayton, "A Psychological Approach to Race Relations," p. 16. In this article Cayton also cites McLean, "Frightened People," unpublished paper read at Fisk University, July 2, 1945.

36. Anna Rothe, ed., *Current Biography: Who's News and Why, 1946* (New York: Wilson, 1946), pp. 103–106; "An American Family," *Headlines and Pictures*, July 1945, pp. 29–32; St.

Clair Drake, "To Horace," St. Clair Drake Papers, SCNY; "Strangers and Friends: Horace R. Cayton," in Arna Bontemps, *We Have Tomorrow*, pp. 26–33; *Long Old Road*, pp. 257–91, 309–27; Cayton to Bontemps, September 12, 1945, Bontemps Papers, SUL. St. Clair Drake authored roughly two-thirds of *Black Metropolis*, according to Horace Jr., who felt it appropriate that Drake's name appear first. (Cayton to Lloyd Warner, January 10, 1944, Box 5, Drake Papers, SCNY.) St. Clair Drake told the story of "How We Wrote Black Metropolis" in October 1981 at a conference hosted by the Chicago Center for Afro American Studies and Research (Box 38, Drake Papers, SCNY).

37. Cayton, "A Psychological Approach to Race Relations," *Reed College Bulletin*, v. 25, no. 1 (November 1946).
38. Ibid., pp. 5–27.
39. Cayton to Wright, October 11, 1946, Wright Papers, BLYU.
40. Cayton, "My Encounter with Richard Wright," p. 6; *Long Old Road,* pp. 262–63.
41. *Long Old Road*, pp. 269–91; Cayton to Bonnie Branch Hansen, November 3, 1961, Cayton Papers, VGHRC.
42. Cayton to Carl Van Vechten, September 9, 1947, Carl van Vechten Papers, BLYU; Nichols, *Bontemps-Hughes Letters*, p. 218. In his letter to Hughes on March 11, 1947, Bontemps described Ruby as Horace's "very delightful intended."
43. Cayton to Susan Cayton Woodson, August 1947; Woodson to Cayton, September 1947, Cayton Papers, VGHRC.
44. "Inquest on the Bodies of Ruth Griggs, et al.," File No. 206039, Records of the Cook County Medical Examiner, Chicago (photocopy in Cayton Papers); *Long Old Road*, pp. 322–27; Ruth Williams, interview; *Chicago Defender*, October 18 to December 20, 1947, various issues. Ironically, an article by Horace only recently had been published in *Negro Digest* listing Chicago as one of "America's 10 Best Cities for Negroes."
45. Horace Cayton [Jr.], "America's 10 Best Cities for Negroes," *Negro Digest*, v. 5, no. 2 (October 1947), pp. 4–10; "Parkway Community House: A Review of the Program" August 9, 1948, Box 389, WCMS, CHS.
46. Bontemps to Hughes, October 17, 1948, Nichols, *Bontemps-Hughes Letters*, p. 239.
47. Fabre, *Unfinished Quest*, pp. 252–53.
48. Cayton to Hughes, March 16, 1949, Hughes Papers, BLYU; Horace and Ruby Cayton files, "Fellowships—Turndowns, 1948," Box 476, folders 28, 29, Rosenwald Archives, ARC.
49. Cayton to Wright, June 17, August 9, 1949, January 22, 1950, Wright Papers, BLYU; *Long Old Road*, pp. 348–54. Ruby (Jordan) Wright Martin, a resident of Tacoma, Washington, refused to be interviewed for this study.

Chapter 9 Notes
A Spirit of Steadfast Determination

1. Revels Cayton, BBC interview.
2. Ibid.
3. The Federation was comprised of the Sailor's Union of the Pacific (SUP), the Marine Cooks and Stewards (MCS), the Marine Firemen, Watertenders, Oilers, and Wipers (MFWOW) [all affiliated with the International Seamen's Union (ISU)], the International Longshoremen's Association (ILA), the Marine Engineers' Beneficial Association, the Masters, Mates, and Pilots, and the American Radio Telegraphists' Association. Records of the Maritime Federation are at the Labor Archives and Research Center, San Francisco State University (hereafter MFP Records, SFSU).

4. Revels Cayton, BBC interview; *Voice of the Federation*, September 26, 1935; Albert Morris Bendich, "The History of the Marine Cooks and Stewards" (Master's thesis, UC, Berkeley, 1953), pp. 26, 29–30.

5. Reference is to James Baldwin, *The Fire Next Time* (New York: Dial Press, 1964).

6. Revels Cayton, interview.

7. Revels Cayton, interview; Bendich, "History of Marine Cooks and Stewards," pp. 47–48, 80–81; Joseph Bruce Nelson, "Maritime Unionism and Working Class Consciousness in the 1930s" (Ph.D. dissertation, University of California, Berkeley, 1982), pp. 328–75; Minutes of Regular Headquarters Meetings, July 22–October 17, 1938, Carton 15, NUCMS Records, Bancroft, UCB.

8. Bendich, "History of Marine Cooks and Stewards," p. 233.

9. *Chicago Defender*, November 18, 1939.

10. Paul Robeson, *Here I Stand* (Boston: Beacon Press, 1958), p. 100.

11. On Cayton and Robeson's relationship, see Martin Bauml Duberman, *Paul Robeson* (New York: Knopf, 1988), pp. 309–11, 675.

12. Revels Cayton, interview; Jay Sauers to Mervyn Rathborne, et al., June 23, 1941, MFP Records, SFSU. A possible and unexplored factor in the incident is some kind of FBI involvement. One is tempted to speculate that FBI informants or sympathizers willingly spread the rumor to damage Cayton's reputation and to create a rift between him and the Communist Party. In 1941 the "Communist threat" that bureau director J. Edgar Hoover saw as sweeping the country prompted a significant increase in FBI activity. At the same time that Revels was under investigation (June 1941), the FBI also was investigating his brother Horace Jr. in Chicago. A file also was opened on Lillie Cayton during WW II when she took a job at a Seattle shipyard. The FBI files on the National Negro Congress contain over three thousand documents. As head of the NNC from 1945 to 1947 and an avowed communist, Revels Cayton was a "person of interest" to the bureau; although FBI investigation files on Revels Cayton were not available when this study was prepared, it is safe to assume that the bureau continued to have an interest in his activities following his involvement with the NNC. The bureau continued to track Robeson's activities until his death thirty-five years later.

13. Regarding the argument between Revels and Horace Jr. after Madge's funeral, in a letter to the author, June 13, 1989, Revels Cayton re-stated the argument with his brother: "It is not true that I hit him on the chin [see *Long Old Road*, p. 318]. What is true is that we fought—verbally—and I am sure our body language was threatening, but I did not hit him. I made no mention of Dad or my hating the two of them. I did not blame Horace for Madge's death. I made one simple statement: that he was not head of any family and to get it clear in his head that when they put Madge in that coffin, they 'put you and the whole damn family in it too.'" Susan Cayton Woodson described a similar version of the scene in an earlier interview by the author.

14. *Chicago Defender*, September 23, 1944.

15. Horace Cayton, "Roundtable: Have Communists Quit Fighting for Negro Rights?—Yes," *Negro Digest*, v. 3, no. 2 (December 1944), pp. 66–68.

16. Revels Cayton, interview.

Chapter 10 Notes
With the Safest Man in America

1. Revels Cayton to Mervyn Rathborne, December 21, 1945, Box 48, National Negro Congress Records (hereafter, NNC), SCNY.

2. Streater, "National Negro Congress," pp. 329–36; *New York Times*, June 7, 1946; a photocopy of the UN petition is in National Negro Congress Subject File, ILWU Archives, Anne Rand Research Library, San Francisco (hereafter, ILWU Archives).

3. Revels Cayton, "A Report to West Coast Friends as to What Happened in Detroit," [n.d.], Carton 8, SFCIO, Bancroft, UCB; Revels Cayton to Lenny and Lena, June 24, 1946, Box 72, NNC, SCNY.

4. Revels Cayton and Paul Robeson to "Dear Friend," October 1, 1946, Carton 8, SFCIO, Bancroft, UCB. NNC records of the convention and its immediate aftermath are in Box 62, NNC, SCNY.

5. Revels Cayton to Phil Weightman, January 3, 1946; Revels Cayton to Gus Hawkins, January 3, 1946; Revels Cayton to Mervyn Rathborne, December 21, December 26, 1945, Box 6, NNC, SCNY.

6. Ethel (Horowitz) Cayton quoted in Revels Cayton, interview.

7. Revels Cayton, interview.

8. Revels Cayton, interview; Lee Davidson Cayton, interview, San Francisco, July 30, 1985.

9. Paul Robeson Jr., interview; see Martin Bauml Duberman, *Paul Robeson* (New York: Knopf, 1988), pp. 309–10, 675, 701. Duberman relates the following story about Cayton and Robeson as "an example of the closeness" of their relationship: "Robeson talked to Cayton (and to few others) about his relationship with Lena Horne, telling Cayton that she broke up with him when he refused to marry her" (*Robeson*, p. 701).

10. Ibid. Robeson's testimony before the Tenny Committee on October 7, 1946, is reprinted in Foner, *Paul Robeson Speaks*, pp. 178–81. See also Duberman, *Paul Robeson*, pp. 308–9.

11. "Affidavit of William P.M. Brandhove," December 9, 1946, California Legislature, *Un-American Activities in California*, Third Report, 1947, p. 163; see also "Affidavit of William D. Handelsman," pp. 283–90.

12. Revels Cayton, interview. For more on Mike Quill and racism in the TWU, see: August Meir and Elliot Rudwick, "Communist Unions and the Black Community: The Case of the Transport Workers Union, 1933–1944," *Labor History*, v. 23, no. 2 (Spring 1982), pp. 165–197; and James J. McGinley, *Labor Relations in the New York Rapid Transit System, 1901–1944* (New York: King's Crown Press, 1949).

13. One of the last public activities of the HTUC was a rally of three hundred people called in September 1950 to protest the State Department's revocation of Paul Robeson's passport. The speakers included Robeson and Ben Davis Jr. (*New York Times*, September 10, 1950).

14. Revels Cayton, interview; Susan Cayton Woodson, interview; Setsuko Nishi, interview; Brunetta Barnett Bernstein, interview.

15. *Long Old Road*, pp. 264–65, 341, 355.

16. Ibid., 350–56. In 1950–51, Horace Jr. worked some months for the American Jewish Committee as a research assistant to Samuel Flowerman in a study of the Jewish family ("Curriculum Vita," Cayton Papers, VGHRC).

17. Revels Cayton, interview; Paul Robeson Jr., interview; Duberman, *Paul Robeson*, pp. 364–70, 701; Howard Fast, *Peekskill, U.S.A.: A Personal Experience* (New York: Civil Rights Congress, 1951); Gilliam, *Paul Robeson*, pp. 145–54. Newspaper accounts, like those by the *New York Times*, spoke mostly of "anti-Communists" and "Communists and Communist sympathizers," but a majority of the pro-Robeson group were, in fact, not communists. The *New York Times* accounts appear from August 27 to September 7, 1949.

18. Paul Robeson Jr., interview; Duberman, *Paul Robeson*, pp. 310–420; Foner, *Paul Robeson Speaks*, pp. 15–22; Ramdin, *Paul Robeson*, pp. 134–86.

19. Revels Cayton, interview; Paul Robeson Jr., interview; Duberman, *Paul Robeson*, pp. 249–50, 310.

20. Record, "Rise and Fall of a Maritime Union," pp. 81–92; Philip S. Foner, *Organized Labor and the Black Worker, 1619–1981* (New York: International Publishers, 1982), pp. 282–83; Revels Cayton, interview.

21. Duberman, *Paul Robeson*, pp. 336–403; Foner, *Paul Robeson Speaks*, pp. 4, 7; Ramdin, *Paul Robeson*, pp. 164–200. On the revocation of Robeson's passport, see Robeson, *Here I Stand*, p. 47.

22. Fast quoted in Revels Cayton, interview.

23. Ben Davis Jr. was the original attorney for the celebrated case of Angelo Herndon. Davis rose in party ranks, and in 1950 he and eleven other top leaders were indicted and convicted under the Smith Act for being members of the Communist party. Davis was sentenced to five years in prison. The Supreme Court upheld the conviction in 1951. For more on Davis, see his autobiography (published posthumously), *Communist Councilman from Harlem* (New York: International Publishers, 1969), pp. 7–16.

24. Revels Cayton, "Challenge to Labor," *March of Labor*, March 1951, pp. 14–15, 28.

25. In 1953 the Communist party nationally suffered a sharp drop in African American membership. See Glazer, *Social Basis*, pp. 174–79.

26. Revels Cayton, letter to the author, June 13, 1989.

27. *Long Old Road*, pp. 264–65, 341, 355, 373–76; Setsuko Nishi, interview. Horace's early drafts of *Long Old Road* for the chapters on this period he titled "Mending a Soul is Tedious" (Part Six). See Horace Cayton to Arna Bontemps, March 20, 1962, Bontemps Papers, SUL.

28. Lore Segal and Susan Cayton Woodson, interview, Chicago, November 23, 1979; Lore Segal to the author, September 1, 1988; *Long Old Road*, pp. 374–99.

29. Nichols, *Bontemps-Hughes Letters*, pp. 373-74. Quote in Horace Cayton to Bonnie Branch Hansen, "1962," Cayton Papers, VGHRC.

Chapter 11 Notes
The Uplift

1. Horace Cayton [Jr.], "A Picnic with Sinclair Lewis," in *Soon One Morning: New Writings by American Negroes, 1940–1962*, ed. Herbert Hill (New York: Knopf, 1962), pp. 22–35 (also published as chapter 13 of *Long Old Road*).

2. Bonnie Branch Hansen to Susan Cayton Woodson, February 13, 1993, Cayton Papers, VGHRC.

3. Cayton to Hansen, May 4, 1962; Harry Branch to Hansen, February 25, 1962, Cayton Papers, VGHRC.

4. Cayton to Hansen, October 10, 1961, January 9, 1962, Cayton Papers, VGHRC.

5. Cayton to Arna Bontemps, March 20, 1962, Bontemps Papers, SUL; Cayton to Hansen, February 8, 1962, Cayton Papers, VGHRC.

6. Drake, "To Horace," Drake Papers, SCNY; *Long Old Road*, pp. 400–402; Cayton to Bontemps, January 5, 1964, Bontemps Papers, SUL. Horace Jr.'s "Life History," written for Park's class, is in Cayton File, Park Papers, UC. His "Autobiography for Prof. Hayner, U. of Wash., SOC I," typed manuscript, is in Cayton Papers, VGHRC. Apparently Hayner sent a copy to Cayton in 1966 or 1967. Cayton incorporated the text into his speech, "Personal Experience in Race Relations," to the American Sociological Association Conference in 1967. Horace's original title for the autobiography was "From Which No Traveler Returns." Later, in final negotiations with Buck Moon of Trident Press, Horace wanted the title "No Pity Wanted," but Moon and Horace's literary agent, Henry Volkening, preferred "Long Old Road." In an early book outline that Cayton sent to Arna Bontemps, it is interesting to note his title for chapter 23: "Families Don't Follow Blood Lines: Still They Do." The original 601-page manuscript for *Long Old Road* is in the Twentieth Century Archives, Special Collections, Boston University.

7. Bontemps to Cayton, February 21, 1965, Bontemps Papers, SUL.

8. Cayton to Hansen, February 27, 1962, Cayton Papers, VGHRC.

9. Drake, "To Horace," Drake Papers, SCNY.

10. Horace Cayton Jr. to Revels Cayton, August 12, September 22, 1966, Cayton Papers, VGHRC.

11. Lillie Cayton to Horace Cayton Jr., July 20, August 22, October 21, 1964, Cayton Papers, VGHRC.

12. Madge Terriye Thompson, interview; Lillie Cayton to Susan Cayton Woodson, August 3, 1965, May 29, 1970, Cayton Papers, VGHRC.

13. Lillie Cayton to Horace Cayton Jr., August 20, 1968, Cayton Papers, VGHRC.

14. Cayton to Gordon Curtis, December 3, 1965, Cayton Collection, Bancroft, UCB; Cayton to Stan Stevens, April 21, 1967, Cayton Papers, VGHRC; Richard Berner, interview by the author, Seattle, July 29, 1980. Dr. McLean wrote to Susan Cayton Woodson, "I know, however, how uncertain such periods of seeming normality can be with Horace. Either the manic or depressive state of his illness recurs with lightning speed" (November 28, 1966, Cayton Papers, VGHRC).

15. Cayton to Bonnie Branch Hansen, July 1, 1962, July 22, August 12, 1963, January 4, 1966; Cayton to Susan Cayton Woodson, December 28, 1965; "A Proposal for the Collection of Historical and Social Data about the American Negro for the Period 1900 to the Present," n.d. [ca. 1964–65], Cayton Papers, VGHRC; Cayton to Bontemps, January 5, 1964, Bontemps Papers, SUL. The manuscript for "Dark Inner Landscape" is in Cayton Papers, VGHRC.

16. Margaret Walker, interview; Cayton to Hansen, March 2, 1964, Cayton Papers, VGHRC. Mary Branch, telephone interview by the author, August 16, 1978.

17. Horace Cayton Jr. to Revels Cayton, August 12, September 22, 1966; Horace Cayton Jr. to Susan Cayton Woodson, July 15, December 28, 1965; August 31, 1968, Cayton Papers, VGHRC.

18. Horace Cayton Jr. to Revels Cayton, May 13, 1961, September 22, 1966, Cayton Papers, VGHRC.

19. Horace Cayton Jr. to Bonnie Branch Hansen, September 26, 1963; Cayton, "Personal Experience in Race Relations," Cayton Papers, VGHRC.

20. Cayton, "My Encounter with Richard Wright," Cayton Papers, VGHRC. Cayton's taped interviews are in the Wright Subgroup, Cayton Papers, VGHRC. His interview with Sidney Williams (August 1967) was published as "Reminiscences," in David Ray and Robert M. Farnsworth, eds. *Richard Wright: Impressions and Perspectives* (Ann Arbor: University of Michigan Press, 1993), pp. 151–57. Apparently, a significant group of papers relating to Horace Cayton Jr. and Richard Wright disappeared. Cayton wrote to Wright scholar Kenneth Kinnamon, "I had a voluminous correspondence with Wright, and the entire collection was lost along with many other records by a storage company several years ago" (Cayton to Kinnamon, September 28, 1964, Cayton Papers, VGHRC). Earlier, he had written to Bontemps, "I lost most of my papers, pictures, documents, scrapbooks, etc. when I moved out here" (Cayton to Bontemps, November 5, 1963, Bontemps Papers, SUL).

21. Studs Terkel, telephone interview, February 24, 1993; Terkel, *Hard Times*, p. 434.

22. Horace Cayton Jr. to Revels Cayton, August 15, August 21, 1969, Cayton Papers, VGHRC; Margaret Walker, interview. A photocopy of the Atlanta speech is in Cayton Papers, VGHRC.

23. Ellen Wright to Cayton, December 18, 1967, Cayton Papers, VGHRC. Ellen Wright was also reacting to Cayton's discussion of Richard at the 1964 Asilomar Conference, published in Herbert Hill, ed., *Anger and Beyond*. Michel Fabre's work resulted in *The Unfinished Quest of Richard Wright* (1973).

24. Fabre, "Report from Paris: The Last Quest of Horace Cayton," *Black World*, v. 19 (May 1970), p. 45; letter, U.S. Embassy, Paris, France, to Revels Cayton, February 9, 1970, Cayton Papers, VGHRC; Fabre, "*Mort du sociologue noir* Horace Cayton," *Le Monde*, 29

January 1970, clipping in "Obituaries" file, Cayton Papers, VGHRC; Drake, "To Horace," Drake Papers, SCNY. A cassette tape recording of Fabre's seminar is in Cayton Papers, VGHRC. Horace Jr.'s death at the relatively young age of sixty-six probably can be attributed to what, according to Fabre, was his "'usual' troubles: diabetes and a weak heart" ("Report from Paris," p. 45).

25. Charles A. Davis, "Black Greatness from the Past," *Chicago Defender* (December 22, 1983), p. 17; Lore Segal, *Other People's Houses* (New York: Harcourt Brace, 1964); and *Her First American* (New York: Knopf, 1985); Margaret Walker, interview. See also Myrdal, *American Dilemma*, pp. 863, 1004, 1007–1008, 1438, 1439; John H. Bracey, Jr., August Meier, and Elliot Rudwick, "The Black Sociologists, The First Half Century," in *The Death of White Sociology*, ed. by Joyce Ladner (New York: Random House, 1973), p. 21; Drake, "To Horace," Drake Papers, SCNY. See also, Aldon Morris, "Reflections on a Classic: *Black Metropolis*," speech for symposium "Life and Legacy of Horace Cayton," February 20, 1993, sponsored by the Harsh Research Collection, copy loaned to the author.

26. Brunetta Bernstein, letter to the author, March 9, 1993; Ruth Williams, interview; Bernstein to Susan Cayton Woodson, September 8, 1988; Bonnie Branch Hansen to Woodson, February 13, 1993, Cayton Papers, VGHRC. Horace's dislike of children was also remarked upon in interviews with Lore Segal (interview by the author, Chicago, November 23, 1979) and Revels Cayton.

27. Brunetta Bernstein to Susan Cayton Woodson, September 8, 1988; Bonnie Branch Hansen to Woodson, February 13, 1993, Cayton Papers, VGHRC.

28. Madge Terriye Thompson, interview.

29. The FBI opened a file on Lillie in 1944, probably at the time she applied for work at the shipyards. "Lillie Revels Martin," File No. 100-15271 (dated 4-29-44), Federal Bureau of Investigation Records, Washington, D.C. The file contains only six pages, one of which was withheld.

30. Susan Cayton Woodson, interview.

31. Madge Terriye Thompson, interview.

32. Lillie Cayton to Woodson, April 18, 1966, Cayton Papers, VGHRC.

33. Lillie Cayton to Woodson, n.d., June 13, 1964, June 1, 1965, Cayton Papers, VGHRC.

34. "Neighborhood House Mother's Club," clipping; Lillie Cayton to Woodson, September 17, 1970, Cayton Papers, VGHRC.

35. [Lillie Cayton Fisher, profile, four-page typed manuscript], and "Community Consultant I-90 Project," newsletter, February 1971 [front page with photo of Lillie], Cayton Papers, VGHRC.

36. Madge Terriye Thompson, interview; Lillie Cayton to Susan Cayton Woodson, March 21, 1972, September 17, 1970, May 21, 1974, Cayton Papers, VGHRC.

37. Lillie Cayton to Woodson, October 29, 1974; Woodson to Lillie Cayton, n.d. [ca. February-May 1970], Cayton Papers, VGHRC.

38. Lillie Cayton to Woodson, April 29, June 3, 1971, Cayton Papers, VGHRC; Lillie Cayton, tape recorded speech at Balboa Park, San Diego, 1972, loaned to the author by Sue Martin.

39. Lillie Cayton to Revels Cayton, March 24, 1974, Revels Cayton Personal Papers; Lillie Cayton to Susan Cayton Woodson, June 12, 1975, Cayton Papers, VGHRC.

40. Revels Cayton, interview; Susan Cayton Woodson, interview; Madge Terriye Thompson, interview.

41. [Lillie Cayton Fisher, profile], Cayton Papers, VGHRC.

42. Revels Cayton, interview; Susan Cayton Woodson, interview.

43. *New York Times*, May 5, 1953; Revels Cayton, interview; Sanford, "Congressional Investigation," pp. 111, 157–161.

44. Revels Cayton, interview.

45. *Dispatcher*, April 5, August 9, 1963.

46. Revels Cayton, interview.

47. *Dispatcher*, February 8, 1963. Crawford quoted in Revels Cayton, interview.

48. Revels Cayton, interview; *Dispatcher*, May 31, 1963.

49. Revels Cayton, speech, typed manuscript, Revels Cayton Personal Papers, loaned to the author; *Dispatcher*, June 10, 1966.

50. *Dispatcher*, April 5 and June 10, 1966; *San Francisco Examiner*, March 18 and April 4, 1966.

51. Revels Cayton, interview.

52. Ibid.

53. *San Francisco Examiner*, February 8, 1978; Donald Canter, "Testimonial Thursday for Mayor Alioto Aide," *San Francisco Examiner*, June 12, 1972. Alioto provided a favorable summary of the accomplishments in Cayton's office in a speech in 1971, see "Advance Remarks of Mayor Joseph L. Alioto, Hilton Hotel, San Francisco, August 10, 1971," Joseph Alioto Papers, San Francisco Public Library.

54. Revels Cayton quoted in *San Francisco Examiner*, June 12, 1972.

55. Revels Cayton to Susan Cayton Woodson, January 30, 1970, Cayton Papers, VGHRC; Revels Cayton, interview.

56. Revels Cayton, interview. In 1958 the Supreme Court reinstated Robeson's passport, and he traveled extensively in Europe, returning to the United States in 1963. Two years later he was subpoenaed and appeared before a sub-committee of the House Un-American Activities Committee. Only after the mid-1960s did it become clear to many that Robeson had played a formative and significant role in the development of the black liberation movement, and he was dubbed "the great forerunner." Duberman, *Paul Robeson*, pp. 336–559; Delacy W. Sanford, "Congressional Investigation of Black Communism, 1919–1967" (Ph.D. dissertation, State University of New York at Stony Brook, 1973), pp. 111, 157–61; Foner, *Paul Robeson Speaks*, pp. 4–24. Cayton saw Robeson occasionally after Revels and Lee moved to California. He was one of the many mourners at Robeson's memorial service on January 27, 1976, in Harlem (Duberman, *Paul Robeson*, pp. 448, 550).

57. Robeson quoted in Duberman, *Paul Robeson*, p. 380.

58. Revels Cayton, letter to the author, June 13, 1989.

Epilogue Notes

1. "Susan Cayton Is Wed to Harold W. Woodson," newspaper clipping, September 17, 1949, Cayton Papers, VGHRC, VGHRC; Embree and Waxman, *Investment in People*, p. 252; Harold Woodson, interview; Harold Woodson, "Curriculum Vita," copy loaned to the author. Woodson was a widower and from the previous marriage had a daughter, Eleanor, a resident of Chicago. Harold Jr. resides with his family in San Francisco, California.

2. Susan Cayton Woodson, interview; Harold W. Woodson, interview; Harold W. Woodson, "Curriculum Vita." After retirement in 1985, Harold Woodson remained active as a part-time faculty lecturer at the University of Illinois, School of Public Health. He died in February 1998.

3. Susan Cayton Woodson, interview.

4. Susan Woodson quoted in LaTicia D. Greggs, "A Life-long Patron of the Arts," *Chicago Defender*, March 15, 1997, pp. 13–14; Susan Cayton Woodson, interview; "South Side Community Arts Center" file in Susan Cayton Woodson Personal Papers; *Chicago Defender*, January 9, 1990; "Art Expands Life," *Labor Unity*, October 1990, p. 12; Betty Washington, "Come to Our Party," *Parade* (*Chicago Sun-Times*), November 15, 1981; "South Side Community Art Center Holds Auction," *Chicago Defender*, May 25, 1989.

BIBLIOGRAPHY

Manuscripts and Unpublished Sources

Amistad Research Center
    Julius Rosenwald Fund Archives [microfilm]
Anne Rand Research Library, San Francisco
    International Longshoremen's and Warehousemen's Union Archives
    National Negro Congress Subject Files
Bancroft Library, University of California, Berkeley
    Horace R. Cayton [Jr.] Collection
    San Francisco CIO Council Records
Beinecke Rare Book and Manuscript Library, Yale University
    Carl Van Vechten Papers
    Langston Hughes Papers
    Richard Wright Papers
Boston University, Special Collections
    Horace R. Cayton [Jr.] Collection
Revels Cayton Personal Papers, San Francisco
Chicago Historical Society
    Parkway Community House Records
    Welfare Council of Metropolitan Chicago Records
Cook County, Illinois
    Medical Examiner's Records
Federal Bureau of Investigation
    Horace R. Cayton Files
    Lillie Revels Martin File
King County Archives, Seattle, Washington
    County Auditor, Marriage Records
    County Clerk, Civil, Criminal and Juvenile Case Files
Kansas State Historical Society
    Kansas State Penitentiary Records
Library of Congress
    NAACP, Seattle Chapter Records
San Francisco City and County
    Human Rights Commission Records
San Francisco Public Library
    Joseph Alioto Papers
Schomburg Center for Research in Black Culture, New York Public Library
    Hiram Rhoades Revels Papers
    National Negro Congress Records
    Ralph Bunche Papers
    St. Clair Drake Papers
Seattle City
    Clerk's Records
Seattle School District Archives
    Student Records and Transcripts
Syracuse University Library, Special Collections
    Arna Wendell Bontemps Papers
Thurston County, Washington
    Auditor, Marriage Records
University of Chicago
    Graduate Student Records

University of Chicago Library, Special Collections
    Horace R. Cayton Papers
    Louis Wirth Papers
    Robert Ezra Park Papers
    Society for Social Research Records
University of Washington
    Registrar's Records
University of Washington Libraries
    Fred Patterson Woodson Papers
    Norman S. Hayner Papers
    Oliver K. Wilson Papers
    Wesley L. Jones Papers
Vivian G. Harsh Collection of Afro-American History and Literature, Chicago Public
    Library, Carter G. Woodson Regional Branch
    Horace R. Cayton [Jr.] Papers
    Negro in Illinois Papers
    Parkway Community House Oral History Videotape, November 21, 1997
Washington State Archives
    City of Olympia, Mayor's Records
    Emergency Relief Administration Records
    Washington State Training School Records
Washington State Library
    Washington Pioneers Project, Susie Cayton File
Susan Cayton Woodson Personal Papers, Chicago

Interviews

Richard Berner, Seattle, July 29, 1980
Brunetta Barnett Bernstein, Chicago, February 21, 1993
Harry Branch, Grapeview, Washington, June 7, 1975
Mary Branch, Grapeview, Washington, June 7, 1975; telephone interview August 16, 1978
Lee Davidson Cayton, San Francisco, July 30, 1985
Revels Cayton, San Francisco, September 21-22, 1975; May 27-29, 1978; August 19-20, 1978;
    October 23-26, 1979; September 6, 1981; July 25-30, 1985; June 16-18, 1986; August 12-13,
    1986; July 30-August 2, 1987; telephone interview September 10, 1988; Interview by British
    Broadcasting Corporation (BBC), July 1975 (transcript)
Cyrus Colter, Chicago, September 3, 1978 (with Harold and Susan Woodson, Enoch Waters, Sidney
    Williams, and Fern Gayden)
Fern Gayden, Chicago, September 3, 1978 (with Harold and Susan Woodson, Enoch Waters, Sidney
    Williams, and Cyrus Colter)
Virginia Gayton, Seattle, June 18, 1975
Donald (Donnie) Hancock, San Francisco, October 26, 1979 (with Revels Cayton)
Bonnie Branch Hansen, Grapeview, Washington, June 7, 1975; Chicago, June 24-28, 1998
Marguerite Jamison Isaac, Seattle, July 26, 1987
Sue Martin, Seattle, April 23, 1999 (with Madge Thompson)
Setsuko Nishi, Brooklyn, New York, April 15, 1981
Edward Pitter, Seattle, August 19, 1975
Paul Robeson, Jr., New York, April 12, 1981
Doris Saunders, Chicago, June 28, 1998
Lore Segal, Chicago, November 23, 1979 (with Susan Cayton Woodson)
Madge Terriye Thompson, Seattle, July 31, 1986; April 23, 1999 (with Sue Martin)
Margaret Walker, Chicago, December 11, 1983; February 21, 1993
Enoch Waters, Chicago, September 3, 1978 (with Harold and Susan Woodson, Sidney Williams,
    Cyrus Colter, and Fern Gayden)
Irma Jackson Cayton Wertz, Chicago, December 15, 1983; February 20, 1993 (with Susan Cayton
    Woodson); June 29, 1998

Ruth Williams, Chicago, November 22, 1997
Sidney Williams, Chicago, September 3, 1978 (with Harold and Susan Woodson, Enoch Waters, Cyrus Colter, and Fern Gayden)
Harold W. Woodson, Chicago, September 3-5, 1978; November 21-25, 1979; December 10-16, 1983
Susan Cayton Woodson, Chicago, September 2-5, 1978; November 21-25, 1979; August 7, 1980; December 10-16, 1983; (December 11, with Irma Cayton Wertz; December 15 with Margaret Walker); July 28-30, 1987; December 13-15, 1988; February 18-23,1993; November 19-21, 1997; June 20, 1998

Selected Works

"An American Family." *Headlines and Pictures*, July 1945, pp. 29–32.
Aptheker, Herbert. *Afro-American History: The Modern Era*. Seacaucus, N.J.: Citadel, 1971.
Athearn, Robert G. *In Search of Canaan: Black Migration to Kansas, 1879–80*. Lawrence: Regents Press of Kansas, 1978.
Ayer, N.W., and Son. *American Newspaper Annual and Directory*. Philadelphia: N.W. Ayer & Son, 1901–1920.
Baker, Webster B. *History of Rust College*. Greensboro: University of North Carolina Press, 1924.
Bendich, Albert Morris. "The History of the Marine Cooks and Stewards." Master's thesis, University of California, Berkeley, 1953.
Berry, Mary F., and John W. Blassingame. *Long Memory: The Black Experience in America*. New York: Oxford University Press, 1982.
_____. *Climbing Jacob's Ladder: The Enduring Legacy of African-American Families*. New York: Simon & Shuster, 1992.
Bone, Robert. "Richard Wright and the Chicago Renaissance." *Calloo*, v. 9 (1986), pp. 446–68.
Bontemps, Arna W. *We Have Tomorrow*. Boston: Houghton, Mifflin, 1945.
_____, and Jack Conroy. *Anyplace But Here*. New York: Hill and Wang, 1966.
Borome, Joseph H. "The Autobiography of Hiram Rhoades Revels, Together with Some Letters by and about Him." *Midwest Journal*, v. 5, no. 1 (Winter 1952–53), pp. 79–92.
Brier, Warren J. "A History of Newspapers in the Pacific Northwest." Ph.D. diss., State University of Iowa, 1957.
California. Legislature. Third Report, 1947. *Un–American Activities in California*. Report of the Joint Fact-Finding Committee, Sacramento, California, 1947.
Campbell, Robert A. "Blacks and the Coal Mines of Western Washington, 1888–1896." *Pacific Northwest Quarterly*, v. 73, no. 4 (October 1982), pp. 146–55.
Canter, Donald. "Testimonial Thursday for Mayor Alioto Aide." *San Francisco Examiner*, June 12, 1972, p. 13.
Catalogue of the Officers and Students of Alcorn University, 1872–73. Jackson: Kimball, Raymond, 1873.
Catalogue of the Officers and Students of Alcorn A. & M. College, 1880–81. Jackson: L. Graham and Sons, Printers, 1881.
Cayton, Horace Roscoe [Sr.]. *Cayton's Campaign Bulletin; To the Colored Voters of the State; Primary Election*. Seattle: Horace R. Cayton, n.d.
_____. *Cayton's Legislative Manual: The Ninth Legislature of Washington, 1905*. Seattle: Horace R. Cayton, 1905.
_____. *Cayton's Campaign Compendium of Washington, 1908*. Seattle: Horace R. Cayton, 1908.
_____. *Cayton's Yearbook; Seattle's Colored Citizens,1923*. Seattle: H.R. Cayton & Son, 1923.
_____. *Lincoln Industrial Fair*. [Seattle: Horace R. Cayton, 1926, 1927, 1928]. Located in Fred Patterson Woodson Papers, University of Washington Libraries.
_____. *Cayton's Yearbook; New Year 1930*. Seattle: Horace R. Cayton and Son, 1930.
_____. *Autobiographical Writings of Horace R. Cayton, Sr.*, see Richard S. Hobbs.
Cayton, Horace Roscoe [Jr.]. "Black Bugs." *Nation*, v. 133 (September 9, 1931), pp. 255–56.
_____. "Negroes Live in Chicago." *Opportunity*, v. 15 (December 1937), pp. 366–69.
_____, and Estelle Scott. "At Least 225 Race Families Should be in Jane Addams Homes, Statistics Show." *Chicago Defender*, January 29, 1938, p. 2.

_____. "No Friendly Voice." Part two of "Negroes Live in Chicago." *Opportunity*, v. 16 (January 1938), pp. 12–14.

_____, and George S. Mitchell. *Black Workers and the New Unions*. Chapel Hill: University of North Carolina Press, 1939.

_____. "Negro Housing in Chicago." *Social Action*, v. 6, no. 4 (April 15, 1940), pp. 4–39.

_____, and Elaine O. McNeil. "Research on the Urban Negro." *American Journal of Sociology*, v. 47 (September 1941), pp. 176–83.

_____. "Negro Morale." *Opportunity*, v. 19 (December 1941), pp. 371–75.

_____. "Fighting for White Folks." *Nation*, v. 155 (September 26, 1942), pp. 267–70.

_____. "Negro's Challenge." *Nation*, v. 157 (July 3, 1943), pp. 10–11.

_____. "Negroes and Whites Take Race Friction Along on Migration from the South." *Chicago Sun*, October 14, 1943, p. 10.

_____. "Housing, 'Jim Crowism,' Police and some Unions Figure in Race Troubles." *Chicago Sun*, October 15, 1943, p. 10.

_____. "Film Colony Works with Liberals and Labor for Better Race Relations." *Chicago Sun*, October 16, 1943, p. 8.

_____. "The American Negro—A World Problem." *Social Education*, v. 8, no. 5 (May 1944), pp. 205–8.

_____. "Roundtable: Should Negroes in the South Migrate North?—Yes." *Negro Digest*, v. 2, no. 8 (June 1944), pp. 39–45.

_____. "Roundtable: Have Communists Quit Fighting for Negro Rights?—Yes." *Negro Digest*, v. 3, no. 2 (December 1944), pp. 66–68.

_____. "Frightened Children of Frightened Parents." *Twice A Year*, no. 12–13 (1945), pp. 262–69.

_____. "Awake to What?" Review of *Reveille for Radicals*, by Saul Alinsky. *Nation*, January 21, 1946.

_____. "Roundtable: Is 'Uncle Tom's Cabin' Anti-Negro?—Yes." *Negro Digest*, v. 4, no. 3 (January 1946), pp. 71–72.

_____. "Whose Dilemma?" *New Masses*, v. 59, June 23, 1946, pp. 8–10.

_____. "A Psychological Approach to Race Relations." *Reed College Bulletin*, v. 25, no. 1 (November 1946), pp. 5–27.

_____. "The Known City." Review of *Knock On Any Door*, by Willard Motley. *New Republic*, May 12, 1947, pp. 30–31.

_____, and St. Clair Drake. "Bronzeville." *Holiday*, v. 2 (May 1947), pp. 34–38, 130, 132–33.

_____. "America's 10 Best Cities for Negroes." *Negro Digest*, v. 5, no. 2 (October 1947), pp. 4–10.

_____. "Carey the Republican." *New Republic*, v. 119 (October 18, 1948), pp. 10–12.

_____. "The Bitter Crop." *Northwest Harvest: A Regional Stocktaking*. Edited by V.L.O. Chittick. New York: Macmillan, 1948.

_____. Review of *Bettlecreek*, by William Demby. *New York Times*, February 26, 1950, p. 4.

_____. "The Psychology of the Negro Under Discrimination." [Excerpt from "A Psychological Approach. . ."] *Race, Prejudice and Discrimination*. Edited by Arnold Rose. New York: Knopf, 1951.

_____, and Anne O. Lively. *The Chinese in the United States and the Chinese Christian Churches*. New York: National Council of the Churches of Christ in the United States, Bureau of Research and Survey, 1955.

_____, and Setsuko M. Nishi. *Churches and Social Welfare: The Changing Scene, Current Trends and Issues*. Vol. 2. New York: National Council of Churches of Christ in the United States, 1955.

_____. "A Picnic with Sinclair Lewis." *Soon One Morning: New Writings by American Negroes, 1940–1962*. Edited by Herbert Hill. New York: Knopf, 1962.

_____. "E. Franklin Frazier: A Tribute and a Review." *Review of Religious Research*, v. 5, no. 3 (Spring 1964), pp. 137–42.

_____. *Long Old Road*. New York: Trident, 1965.

_____. "Ideological Forces in the Work of Negro Writers." *Anger and Beyond*. Edited by Herber Hill. New York: Harper and Row, 1966.

_____. "Reflection on Richard Wright: A Symposium on an Exiled Native Son." [Panelist in discussion]. *Anger and Beyond*. Edited by Herbert Hill. New York: Harper and Row, 1966.

_____. "No Rent Money." *In Their Own Words: A History of the American Negro, 1961–1966*. Edited by Milton Meltzer. New York: Thomas Y. Crowell, 1967.

_____. "The Curtain: A Sojourn to the South with Richard Wright." *Negro Digest*, v. 18, no. 2 (December 1968), pp. 11–15.

_____. "Reminiscences." *Richard Wright: Impressions and Perspectives*. Edited by D. Ray and R.M. Farnsworth. Ann Arbor: University of Michigan Press, 1973.

_____, comp. "American History (Negro History): Common Historical Facts and Additional Little Known Facts." Bancroft Library, University of California, Berkeley.

For *Black Metropolis* (1962), see St. Clair Drake.

For *Report on the Negro's Share in Industrial Rehabilitation* (1935), see George S. Mitchell.

Cayton, Revels. "ILD Head Tells of Visit to Roslyn Strike Field." *Voice of Action* [Seattle], April 17, 1934, p. 3.

_____. "Herndon Called Fearless Leader." *Voice of Action* [Seattle], December 21, 1934, pp. 1, 4.

_____. "Anti Intermarriage Bill is Attempt to Smash Unity." *Voice of Action* [Seattle], February 15, 1935, p. 3.

_____. "Defeat of Todd Bill Victory of Unity between White Workers, Negro People." *Voice of Action* [Seattle], March 29, 1935, pp. 1, 4.

_____. "Challenge to Labor." *March of Labor*, March 1951, pp. 14–15, 28.

Cayton, Susie. "Sallie the Egg–Woman." *Seattle Post-Intelligencer*, June 3, 1900, p. 33.

Christopher, Maurine. *America's Black Congressmen*. New York: Thomas Y. Crowell, 1971.

Dalfiume, Richard M. "The Forgotten Years of the Negro Revolution." *Journal of American History*, v. 55 (June 1968), pp. 90–106.

Davis, Benjamin, Jr. *Communist Councilman from Harlem*. New York: International Publishers, 1969.

Davis, Charles A. "Black Greatness from the Past." *Chicago Defender*, December 22, 1983, p. 17.

Davis, W. Milan. *Pushing Forward, A History of Alcorn A. & M. College and Portraits of Some of Its Successful Graduates*. Okolona: Okolona Industrial School, 1938.

Dial, Adolph L., and David K. Eliades. *The Only Land I Know: A History of the Lumbee Indians*. San Francisco: Indian Historian Press, 1975.

Drake, St. Clair, and Horace R. Cayton [Jr.]. *Black Metropolis: A Study of Negro Life in a Northern City*. 2 vols. Rev. ed. New York: Harper & Row, 1962.

Duberman, Martin Bauml. *Paul Robeson*. New York: Knopf, 1988.

Du Bois, W.E.B., ed. *Efforts for Social Betterment among Negro Americans*. Atlanta University Publications, No. 14. Atlanta: Atlanta University Press, 1909.

_____. *The Correspondence of W. E. B. Du Bois*. 3 vols. Edited by Herbert Aptheker. Amherst: University of Massachusetts Press, 1973–1978.

Dunham, Melerson Guy. *Centennial History of Alcorn A. & M. College*. Hattiesburg: University and College Press of Mississippi, 1971.

Dunne, William F. *The Great San Francisco General Strike*. New York: Workers Library, 1934.

Ellefson, James Edward. "The Works Progress Administration and the Negro in Chicago, 1935 to 1943." Master's thesis, Western Illinois University, 1973.

Ellison, Ralph. *Shadow and Act*. New York: Random House, 1964.

Fabre, Michel. "*Mort du sociologue noir* Horace Cayton." *Le Monde*, January 29, 1970.

_____. "Report from Paris: The Last Quest of Horace Cayton." *Black World*, v. 19 (May 1970), pp. 41–45, 95–97.

_____. *The Unfinished Quest of Richard Wright*. New York: William Morrow, 1973.

Fast, Howard. *Peekskill, U.S.A.; A Personal Experience*. New York: Civil Rights Congress, 1951.

Foner, Philip S., ed. *The Voice of Black America: Major Speeches by Negroes in the United States*. New York: Simon and Schuster, 1972.

_____, ed. *Paul Robeson Speaks: Writings, Speeches, Interviews, 1918–1974*. Larchmont, N.Y.: Brunner/Mazel, 1978.

_____, and Ronald L., eds. *The Black Worker: A Documentary History from Colonial Times to the Present*. 6 vols. Philadelphia: Temple University Press, 1978, 1980, 1981.

_____. *Organized Labor and the Black Worker, 1619–1981*. New York: International Publishers, 1982.

"Former Nomad Heads Largest Negro Center." *Chicago Tribune*, April 5, 1942.

Franklin, John Hope. *From Slavery to Freedom*. New York: Knopf, 1967.

Gibbs, Warmoth T. "Hiram R. Revels and His Times." *Quarterly Review of Higher Education among Negroes*, v. 8 (January 1940), pp. 25–37; (April 1940), pp. 64–91.

Gilliam, Dorothy Butler. *Paul Robeson, All-American*. Washington, D.C.: New Republic, 1976.

Glazer, Nathan. *The Social Basis of American Communism*. New York: Harcourt Brace, and World, 1961.

Greggs, LaTicia D. "A Life-Long Patron of the Arts." *Chicago Defender*, March 15, 1997, pp. 13–14.

Hawkins, H.G. "History of Port Gibson, Mississippi." *Publications of the Mississippi Historical Society*, v. 10 (1909), pp. 279–99.

Hobbs, Richard S., ed. *Autobiographical Writings of Horace R. Cayton, Sr. Published in Cayton's Weekly, 1917–1920*. Manama: Delmon, 1987.

Hughes, Langston. "A Character." *Pittsburgh Courier*, June 12, 1948.

Kirby, John B. *Black Americans in the Roosevelt Era: Liberalism and Race*. Knoxville: University of Tennessee Press, 1980.

Lawson, Elizabeth. *The Gentleman from Mississippi: Our First Negro Senator*. New York: Privately Printed, 1960.

"The Leary Family." *Negro History Bulletin*, v. 10, no. 2 (November 1946), pp. 27–34, 47.

Libby, Jean, Hannah Geffert, and Jimica Kenyatta. "Hiram Revels Related to Men in John Brown's Army." *www.alliesforfreedom.org*.

McLean, Helen V. "Racial Prejudice." *American Journal of Orthopsychiatry*, v. 14, no. 4 (October 1944), pp. 706–13.

_____. "Psychodynamic Factors in Racial Relations." *Annals of the American Academy of Political and Social Science*, March 1946, pp. 159–66.

_____. "Why Negroes Don't Commit Suicide." *Negro Digest*, v. 5, no. 4 (February 1947), pp. 4–6.

_____. "The Emotional Health of Negroes." *Journal of Negro Education*, v. 17, no. 3 (1949), pp. 283–90.

Matthews, Fred H. *Quest for an American Sociology: Robert E. Park and the Chicago School*. Montreal: McGill-Queen's University Press, 1977.

McGinley, James J. *Labor Relations in the New York Rapid Transit System, 1901–1944*. New York: King's Crown Press, 1949.

Mitchell, George S., and Horace R. Cayton [Jr.]. *Report on the Negro's Share in Industrial Rehabilitation. . .* [No publisher], May 1935.

Morgan, Murray. *Skid Road: An Informal Portrait of Seattle*. Rev. ed. Seattle: University of Washington Press, 1982.

Mumford, Esther Hall. *Seattle's Black Victorians, 1852–1901*. Seattle: Ananse Press, 1980.

_____. "Seattle's Black Victorians—Revising a City's History." *Portage*, v. 2. no. 1 (Fall/Winter 1980–81), pp. 14–17.

Myrdal, Gunnar. *An American Dilemma*. 2 vols. New York: Harper & Row, 1944.

Nichols, Charles H., ed. *Arna Bontemps–Langston Hughes Letters, 1925–1967*. New York: Dodd, Mead, 1980.

Nishi, Setsuko. "Negro-Nisei Identifications: Some Observations from Wartime and Postwar Chicago." Paper for "Chicago Symposium in Memory of Horace R. Cayton," Chicago, February 14, 1970.

Noble, Jean. *Beautiful also Are the Souls of My Black Sisters*. Englewood Cliffs, N. J.: Prentice-Hall, 1978.

Ogden, Mary Elaine. *The Chicago Negro Community: A Statistical Description*. Works Progress Administration, mimeograph, December 1939.

Painter, Nell Irvin. *Exodusters: Black Migration to Kansas after Reconstruction*. New York: Knopf, 1977.

Ramdin, Ron. *Paul Robeson: The Man and His Mission*. London: Peter Owen, 1987.

Rampersad, Arnold. *The Life of Langston Hughes*. 2 vols. New York: Oxford University Press, 1986.

Record, Jane C. "The Rise and Fall of a Maritime Union." *Industrial and Labor Relations Review*, v. 10, no. 1 (October 1956), pp. 81–92.

Robeson, Paul. *Here I Stand*. Boston: Beacon, 1958.

Rowley, Hazel. *Richard Wright: The Life and Times*. New York: Henry Holt, 2000.

Rothe, Anna, ed. *Current Biography: Who's News and Why, 1946*. New York: H.W. Wilson, 1946.

Sanford, Delacy W. "Congressional Investigation of Black Communism, 1919–1967." Ph.D. diss., State University of New York at Stony Brook, 1973.

Schmid, Calvin F., and Wayne McVey Jr. *Growth and Distribution of Minority Races in Seattle, Washington*. Seattle: Seattle Public Schools, 1964.

Segal, Lore. *Other People's Houses.* New York: Harcourt Brace, 1964.
_____. *Her First American.* New York: Knopf, 1985.
Sewell, George A. *Mississippi Black History Makers.* Jackson: University Press of Mississippi, 1977.
Streater, John Baxter. "The National Negro Congress, 1936–1947." Ph.D. diss., University of Cincinnati, 1981.
Taylor, Quintard. *The Forging of a Black Community: Seattle's Central District from 1870 through the Civil Rights Era.* Seattle: University of Washington Press, 1994.
_____. *In Search of the Racial Frontier: African Americans in the American West, 1528–1990.* New York: Norton, 1998.
Terkel, Studs. *Hard Times: An Oral History of the Great Depression.* New York: Pantheon, 1970.
Thompson, Julius Eric. "Hiram R. Revels, 1827–1901: A Biography." Ph.D. diss., Princeton University, 1973.
_____. "The Size and Composition of Alcorn A & M College Alumni, 1871–1930." *Journal of Mississippi History,* v. 51, no. 3 (1989), pp. 219–31.
Ward, Clell G. "An Investigation of the Founding and Development of Alcorn A. & M. College, 1871–1900." Master's thesis, Tennessee A. & I. University, 1962.
Ward, Jean M., and Elaine A. Maveety, eds. *Pacific Northwest Women, 1815–1925: Lives, Memories and Writings.* Corvallis: Oregon State University Press, 1995.
Warner, W. Lloyd. *Color and Human Nature.* Washington, D.C.: American Council on Education, 1941.
Washburn, Patrick S. "The *Pittsburgh Courier* and Black Workers in 1942." *Western Journal of Black Studies,* v. 10, no. 3 (1986), pp. 109–18.
Wells, Ida B. *Crusade for Justice: The Autobiography of Ida B. Wells.* Edited by Alfreda M. Duster. Chicago: University of Chicago Press, 1970.
Wertz, Irma [Jackson] Cayton. "First Black WACS Overseas." *Dawn Magazine,* July 1979, pp. 20, 27.
_____. "A First WAC." Personal reminiscence.
Wheeler, Gerald R. "Hiram R. Revels: Negro Educator and Statesman." Master's thesis, University of California, Berkeley, 1949.
Wright, Richard. *12 Million Black Voices.* New York: Viking, 1941.

Newspapers

Argonaut (San Francisco), 1968
Argus (Seattle), 1896, 1899, 1901
Cayton's Monthly (Kent, Washington), 1921
Cayton's Weekly (Seattle), 1917–1921
Chicago Defender, 1937–1949, 1989, 1990
Crisis (NAACP), 1913–1920
Dispatcher (San Francisco), 1945, 1960–1967
Forum (Tacoma), 1913
Helena Colored Citizen, 1894
New York Times, 1946, 1949–1950, 1953
Northwest Enterprise (Seattle), 1940
Patriarch (Seattle), 1910, 1914
Pittsburgh Courier, 1940–1948
Rooks County Record (Stockton, Kansas), 1887
San Francisco Examiner, 1966–1967, 1978
Seattle Post-Intelligencer, 1894–1901, 1920, 1940
Seattle Republican, 1896–1913
Seattle Star, 1901, 1906
Seattle Times, 1901, 1909–1910, 1918
Spokesman-Review (Spokane), 1894
Voice of Action (Seattle), 1933–1936
Voice of the Federation (San Francisco), 1935–1938
Western Cyclone (Nicodemus, Kansas), 1887

INDEX